Positive Herding 201

Advanced dog training

Barbara Buchmayer

with foreword by Sally Adam

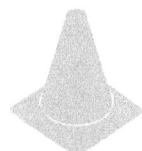

The information in this book is meant to supplement, not replace, in-person herding training. Like any sport involving speed, equipment, balance, livestock, and environmental factors, herding poses some inherent risk. This work is sold with the understanding that neither the author nor the publisher are held responsible for injuries or damage incurred while engaged in this training.

Note: This is a companion book to *Positive Herding 101*. There are explanations and training plans referred to in this book that are found only in the previous book. If you are not familiar with how to positively train basic foundation, obedience, and herding skills, you should obtain a copy of *Positive Herding 101* before attempting the training in this book.

Above all be safe, have fun, and spread the herd! If you found the *Positive Herding* handbooks informative and useful, entertaining and enjoyable, do let us know. Post your book reviews on www.amazon.com and www.cleanrun.com.

Copyright © 2021 Barbara Buchmayer
Library of Congress Control Number: 2021906481

First published in 2022 by Positive Herding 101, LLC
14649 Hwy M, Purdin, MO 64674

Go to www.positiveherdingdog.com to purchase a copy of this book or to sign up for news from Barb at Positive Herding Dog.

PHOTOGRAPHS
Barb Buchmayer: Front cover background, pp 10, 194, 326, and all photos not listed below
Laurie Burbank: Front cover author with sheep and dog, back cover author photo, all full-page photos
Pam Eloff: pp 320, 323
Loretta Jakubiec: pp 4, 150, 186, 254, 318
Tania Quarmby: pp 108, 252, 253, 254
Diane Spisak: p 294

Typography by User Friendly, Cape Town, South Africa
Set in Zapf Humanist 10.5 on 15pt

ISBN (print black & white softcover): 978-1-7368443-4-2
ISBN (print color hardback): 978-1-7368443-9-7
ISBN (epub): 978-1-7368443-2-8

All rights reserved
No part of this book may be reproduced or transmitted in any form or by any electronic or mechanical means, including photocopying and recording, or by any other information storage or retrieval system, without written permission from the publisher.

Contents

Foreword by Sally Adam   5
Mind map   7

SECTION 1   Page 8
Transitioning Herding Skills to Stock
1   Get SET for success   11
2   Penned stock 1 – Flanks   19
3   Penned stock 2 – Walk in and stop   33
4   Penned stock 3 – Modifier cues   47
5   Loose stock in small area   61
6   Loose stock in large area 1   79
7   Loose stock in large area 2   95
8   Loose stock in large area 3   111
9   Putting it all together 1   127
10   Putting it all together 2   139

SECTION 2 –   Page 148
Advanced Herding Skills
11   Outrun and look for stock   151
12   Look back, lift, and fetch   161
13   In, driving and cross-driving   175
14   Whistles   187
15   Shedding without stock   195
16   Shedding 1   205
17   Shedding 2   215

SECTION 3 – Page   229
Stockmanship
18   Stockmanship 101   231

SECTION 4 – Page 252
Trials and On-farm Skills
19   Getting ready to trial   255
20   Trial elements and obstacles   271
21   Farm and ranch skills   295

SECTION 5 – Page 307
Final Thoughts
22   Crossover dogs and handlers   309
23   Positive trainers new to herding   319
24   Where to from here?   327

Acknowledgments   331
Glossary   332
Resources   336
About the author   339

Foreword

If you're reading this book, you are probably quite serious about having a go at training a sheepdog using positive methods. Trust the process. This will be hard at times. I thought it would be impossible when I realized how driven my border collie Renn was to get to the sheep. Barb's dog Sir was even more over-the-top, yet both dogs have managed to learn self-control and to respond to cues without losing one iota of their drive and without our having to knock their confidence. Neither dog has ever quit a training session or shown any stressed displacement activity. They never ever lose that sparkle in their eye, even when we're ready to scream with frustration because we're not quite getting the performance we want.

It breaks my heart to go to clinics where dog after dog simply can no longer stand having items thrown at it and being yelled at and leaves the training arena. Trust us, you can create a biddable herding dog without breaking the dog down.

Training a sheepdog has been one of the hardest things I've ever done. I almost gave up on many occasions – it just seemed too overwhelming. There were so many things to learn and to remember and I felt deeply useless. So, we'd take a break, I'd lie awake at night thinking about sheep and dogs and whistles and trials and eventually I'd feel a renewed enthusiasm for the process.

I must confess to a wee twinge of envy towards you, dear reader, because you have this series of books to guide you, whereas I look back on a ton of things I screwed up. It wasn't so much poor training (although I shan't pretend there was none), more an astonishing lack of understanding of stock, sheepdogs, and herding principles. Annoyingly, some knowledge only comes with experience. It's hard to even read a dog when you lack that experience, and kind of nutty to attempt to train a dog before you gain it. If you're attempting this same trajectory, all I can say is, be kind to yourself and your dog for you will stumble along the way.

Two standout moments made the agony worthwhile. The first was when Renn was almost ready for trials, I asked a sheep farmer and triallist if I could come over to his place, about one-and-a-half hours away, and play with his sheep. Despite not knowing me at all, he agreed. When Renn and I arrived, he watched us work his training flock for about a minute and said, "Mmm. Okay, I have a job for you." He drove us to the other end of the farm, pointed at what seemed like a vast flock of his stud ewes, consisting of over 100 head, and said "I need this group brought into the yard" (which was about one kilometre away), pointed, and drove off.

Striding down the road behind those sheep with my dog picking up the truants like a pro was one of my proudest moments ever. We did a reasonable job, for a pair who had never previously handled more than 25 sheep, and got them all in safely.

Another 6 minutes I will never forget was our first Junior run after a couple of years of struggling to get out of Beginners. Unlike the other competitors, I opted to stay at the post and not walk with my dog. Being able to whistle Renn through an entire run gave me an enormous feeling of achievement and satisfaction.

Whatever your intentions and goals for your sheepdog, I wish you similar moments of delight.

Sally Adam
August 2022

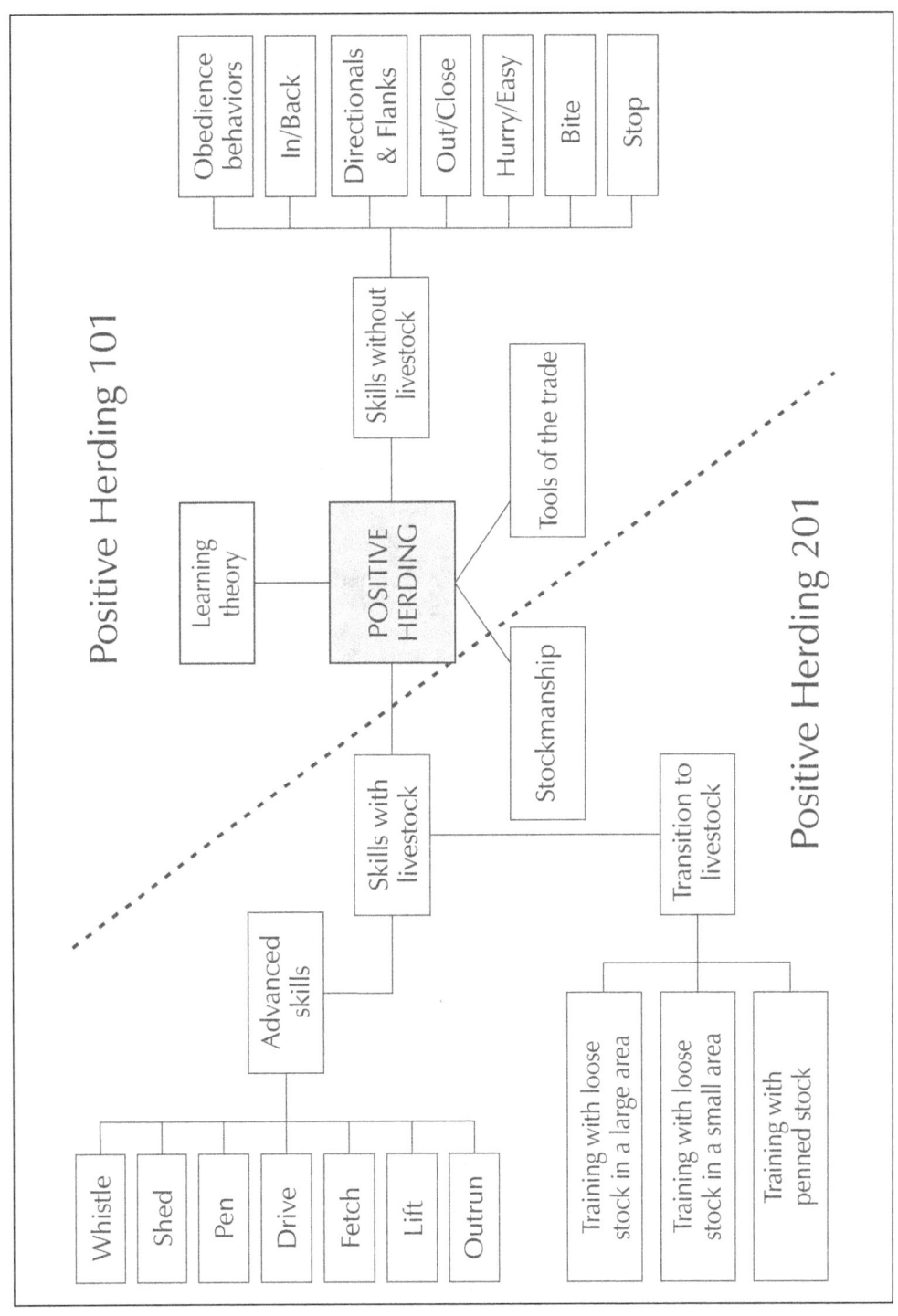

Positive herding mind map: Positive Herding 101 *covers the basics of herding through building skills, strengthening behavior, and adding penned livestock.* Positive Herding 201 *covers the transition from basic to advanced skills, stockmanship and on-farm skills. Read diagram clockwise from 'Learning Theory' (top center).*

Section 1
Transitioning Herding Skills to Stock

Chapter 1 Get SET for success   11
The Get SET mindset   12
Welcome to *Positive Herding 201*   13
Skills covered in *Positive Herding 101*   13
How this book is organized   14
Meet Shandler, Dawg, Kat, and the flock   15
Sally speaks   15
Speaking of sheep   16
Suggestions for using this book   16
Welcome to a brand new world!   16

Chapter 2 Penned stock 1 – Flanks   19
The pen and paddock   20
Video for mental health!   22
Transitioning to using livestock and cues as reinforcers   22
Flanking around livestock   23
Transition flanks to livestock – Step by step   24
Transition off-balance flanks to livestock – Step by step   25

Chapter 3 Penned stock 2 – Walk in and stop   33
Walking in to a target   33
Walk in picture series   34
Transition walk in – Step by step   36
Before you start – Flirt pole training   40
Transition the stop step by step   41
Mini-fetch sneak peek   43
Your dog is almost ready to herd   44

Chapter 4 Penned stock 3 – Modifier cues   47
Easy and hurry   48
Speed changes – Step by step   48
Hurry – Step by step   49
Easy – Step by step   51
Easy and hurry – Step by step   54
Out and close   56
Close – Step by step   56
Out – Step by step   58
Your dog is ready to herd!   59

Chapter 5 Loose stock in small area 61
Got sheep? 61
Reading your dog on loose stock 62
Sheep on the loose! 64
Paddock setup 65
Set up a time-out station 65
Paddock approach and entry 66
Ending the session 67
Heel paddock perimeter 68
Round robin recalls revisited 68
Call it a day 69
Add stops 69
Start flanks 70
Cutting corners 71
Extend flanks 72
Drop long line 72
Add the walk in and call off 73
Start mini-fetches 74
Easy/hurry and out/close 76
Remove long line 76
Success! 76

Chapter 6 Loose stock in large area 1 79
Educate yourself about pull 80
Heeling and recalls 82
Drag long line 82
Work close 82
Corner flanking 83
Fence line flanking 84
Adapting exercises 85
Short fetch setup 85
Shaping going into a corner 87
Fence line fetches 88
Corners are your friend 90
Shaping corner fetches 90
Corner fetches 92

Chapter 7 Loose stock in large area 2 95
Patterns 97
Balance 99
Steps for a basic outrun, lift, and fetch 100
Fetch cue 102
Wearing 103
Steps for wearing 104
Push past handler 106
Finishing touches 107

Chapter 8 Loose stock in large area 3 111
Squaring flanks 111
Fetches first 114
Out/close versus off-balance flanks 114
Out or close? 114
Out – Step by step 115
Close 118
Off-balance flanks 119
Before you start – Off-balance flanks 121
Off-balance flanks – Step by step 121
Beyond basics 124

Chapter 9 Putting it all together 1 127
Criteria, criteria, criteria 128
Transitions 128
In to flank – Step by step 130
Flank to in – Step by step 132
Flank to flank – Step by step 134
Circling stock away from handler 135

Chapter 10 Putting it all together 2 139
Bump flanks – Step by step 141
Hold 142
Hold – Step by step 142
Phase 1 – Holding sheep to you 142
Phase 2 – Holding using two groups of sheep 144
On leash to off leash 147

CHAPTER 1

Get SET for success

Have you ever felt that you have let your dog down? That you just aren't the trainer that your dog deserves? You are not alone. My first positive herding student faced those same nagging questions and doubts. In *Positive Herding 101,* the companion book to this book, I began with a long-distance positive herding success story. I want to briefly revisit that amazing story.

Sally and her border collie Renn, from South Africa, became very special students of mine in 2011. Sally was a wonderful positive trainer of agility and tricks but had never handled nor trained a herding dog. With over 9000 miles separating us and only Skype, YouTube, and email to work with, I was able to coach her and Renn to become the 2016 South African Sheepdog Association's National Reserve Junior Champions. Their herding success was truly amazing and their story was shared in detail in *Positive Herding 101* but she was not without her doubters and naysayers.

While Sally was training Renn she was told that her red dog would never make a good herding dog because she was red and red border collies are considered inferior by some herding trainers. She was also advised that playing tug with Renn would ruin her for herding. So what was Sally's secret to overcoming her detractors and achieving success? It was the same essential element that I had discovered many years ago as I struggled to overcome my own major training obstacle. Let me explain by sharing a short horse tale.

Growing up I always loved horses. I begged my folks for a horse for years until they finally gave in and bought me Rusty. I was 11 at the time and learned some basic horse care and riding skills from books. After a few years, my parents convinced me that I needed a horse with more potential and Destry became my dream horse.

Of course, it was not all smooth sailing and Destry and I were soon having problems. My main problem was that he would only take one lead, the leading front leg during a canter, and to show him in horse shows, which I desperately wanted to do, he needed to take both leads when cued. I needed help.

Fortunately, I found a local horse 4-H club and, after my folks bought a used horse trailer, I was able to attend "riding meetings" with my new club, the 4-H of Cherry Lane. At the riding meetings, we newbies were coached by the older more experienced club members. Over time, with direction and encouragement, Destry and I began to win ribbons and a few trophies at shows. We were on our way!

Although I found the knowledge shared by the older kids key to my advancement, what I found essential was their encouragement. It was their support and confidence in me that kept me moving forward, even when I was feeling discouraged.

So what does my horse journey from decades ago have to do with you and your dog's herding success? Get set to find out.

The Get SET mindset

Positive Herding 101 focused on the importance of your dog engaging with you, especially near livestock, and lots and lots of training of herding skills without livestock. What I have come to realize, since that book was published, is that I can give you the tools to be successful on your herding journey but you need more than training plans and Learning Laws. You need support and encouragement.

You need to hear that training herding using positive reinforcement will work. That you won't ruin your dog or make them mechanical. That you are not alone on this journey. Enter the "Get SET for success" model which includes the elements of **S**upport, **E**ngagement, and **T**raining.

It is the blending of these three elements that produces confidence, motivation, advancement, and ultimately success. Although engagement and training light your path ahead, it is knowing that you are supported by me and a community of like-minded trainers that will keep you moving along your path to successfully reach your personal positive herding goals, no matter how lofty or modest they may be.

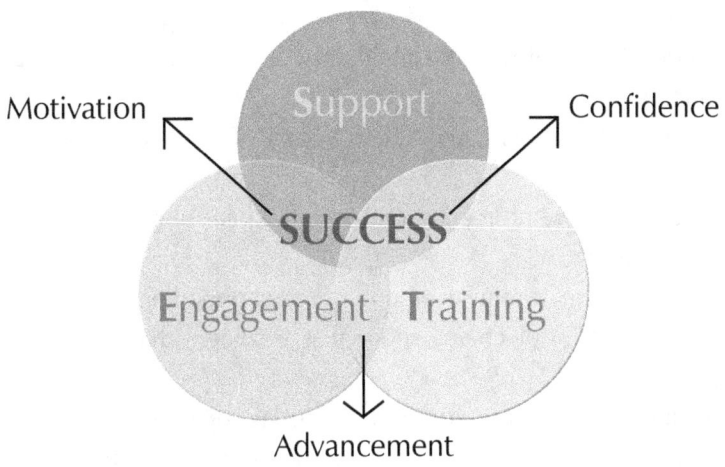

Get SET for positive herding SUCCESS!

As you go through this book, remember that I have worked through the exercises presented here with my dogs so that you don't have to start from scratch to reinvent the positive herding wheel. More importantly, you are not alone on this journey but rather part of the first small swell that is destined to become a gigantic positive herding wave. Let's get dog paddling.

Welcome to *Positive Herding 201*

You are about to continue your exciting journey into positive herding! If you have done all of the training from the previous book, *Positive Herding 101,* your dog has the foundation skills in place that will enable them to be brilliant at herding. You are now ready to transition herding behaviors, taught previously in your house or yard, into a paddock with livestock.

This is the second book in the **Positive Herding Dog** series and continues the training of herding using positive methods that was begun in *Positive Herding 101*. Your dog will need to have mastered all of the training from the first book to successfully start the training in this book. I am going to assume that you have a copy of *Positive Herding 101* but below is a very brief list of what is covered in that book.

Skills covered in *Positive Herding 101*
- Basic obedience behaviors – sit, down, stand, heel, etc.
- Basic herding behaviors – directionals, flanks, stop, walk in, back up, bite, and modifier cues
- Fluency training – performing obedience behaviors near penned livestock

Other topics include:
- Introduction of the authors and their story of how positive herding was taught long distance.
- Learning theory – including operant and classical conditioning and much, much more.
- Getting behavior – reinforcers, Premack principle, marker training, capturing, luring, and shaping.
- Timing, criteria, rate of reinforcement, no reward markers, and time-outs.
- Cueing, stimulus control, chains, sequences, dealing with mistakes, and problem-solving.
- Step-by-step training plans with troubleshooting suggestions.
- Tools of the trade – crooks, long lines, flirt poles, whistles, etc.
- Flirt pole training instructions.
- Instinct and arousal.
- Record keeping and videoing.
- Stockmanship – flight/fight zone, pull, balance, etc.
- Forward- versus sideways-moving dogs.

These topics represent just the tip of the iceberg concerning subjects covered in the first book. If you have any doubt that you and your dog are fully prepared to jump into this book, then you will do you and your dog a BIG favor by taking the time to gain the knowledge and skills presented in *Positive Herding 101* before moving on to the training in this book.

How this book is organized

If you have read the first book in this series, then most of the following information will be familiar. First, let's look at the icons that indicate important information:

TNT indicates Tips 'N Tricks which are helpful hints or important points.

These will apply to the topic being discussed. Included will be inspiring quotes, lessons Sally or I have learned, or important or interesting information.

This icon alerts you to video clips that illustrate training plans and exercises featured in this book.

Extra important information will be highlighted with this icon.

Notes usually cover safety concerns and are very important. Safety for you, your dog, and your stock, must be your top priority while training.

Before you start *will outline specific pointers for the training session that follows.*

Meet Shandler, Dawg, Kat, and the flock

In place of drawn diagrams, I use photo dioramas, which are pictures of props.

Shandler the handler is pictured to the right with her crew (and cones) and close-ups of Kat and Dawg are below.

Sally speaks

As you remember, Sally Adam and her border collie Renn are my herding students from South Africa. In the brief story above I related how they started from scratch and went on to have tremendous success by becoming the South African Sheepdog Associations National Reserve Junior Champions.

Throughout the book, Sally will occasionally chime in. At these times her comments will be found in a italicized serif font between dotted lines, next to a 'Sally says' icon.

Sally will be adding her unique insights, relating experiences, giving encouragement, or chipping in whatever else strikes her fancy.

Speaking of sheep

I train herding on sheep and use my dogs almost exclusively on the sheep on our farm, although we also have dairy and beef cattle. In this book, I will use the terms *livestock*, *stock*, and *sheep* interchangeably, unless noted. Throughout the book, all three terms represent cattle, sheep, goats, or ducks. Many dogs work all types of livestock, but some prefer one type over others. I like to start training my dogs on sheep because they flock together well and usually move freely away from even tentative dogs.

Suggestions for using this book

- Skim or read through each section completely before starting the training in that section. This will help you to see where your training is going and inform some of your decisions along the way.
- Read Section 3 – Stockmanship, early and often. Herding is based on stockmanship and every time you interact with livestock you are learning.
- Complete the exercises in *Positive Herding 101* before starting the training outlined in this book. Jumping into this book without working through the previous book is a recipe for failure.

Welcome to a brand new world!

Things are much different here than in the traditional herding world. We are going to tell our dogs when they are correct and reinforce their behavior, rather than punishing unwanted behavior. In this world, dogs are primarily reinforced, handlers use markers and clickers as well as crooks, and sheep are just another distraction.

Positive Herding 201 will transition your herding skills from working with stock in a small pen, with you and your dog on the outside of that pen, all the way to loose livestock in a field. You will then learn advanced herding skills such as driving, shedding, and whistling. We will dive into stockmanship and put your dog to work on the trial and ranch or farm field. But before we get to trials and practical work, we have a lot of training to do.

As I said in Positive Herding 101, *the most difficult part of dog training is ... starting!*

So, let's get started.

CHAPTER 2

Penned stock 1 – Flanks

Is your dog ready to herd? The time has come to find out! You will soon see how your dog instinctively reacts to livestock when in herding mode. Do they naturally want to flank, tend to clap to the ground, or want to push, push, push? Do they want to chase, control livestock, or are they happy to just observe?

You should have some ideas about your dog's instincts and herding abilities from working obedience behaviors around stock. I'll bet your dog will still have a few surprises in store for you as you transition their trained herding skills to livestock!

Can your dog perform behaviors when cued near livestock? Watch Sally and Renn show you how it is done: Renn recalling and tugging near sheep. https://www.youtube.com/watch?v=vpv7bsV21FQ&ab_channel=PositiveHerdingDog

To start transitioning your herding skills to livestock your dog must be able to sit, down, pop into a stand, or do tricks proficiently when they are within 3 feet of penned livestock. They also must be able to recall off of stock and should be able to heel around livestock.

It is best to wait until your dog is at least one year old before transitioning herding skills to livestock. Your dog needs to have the physical and mental maturity to deal with reading and controlling livestock.

Remember when it comes to training with livestock, your first job is to be the gatekeeper. All reinforcement from interacting with stock comes through you. Your dog is not allowed to interact with stock unless you permit and monitor the interaction.

If your first job is the gatekeeper, then your second job is the game master. As the game master, your job is to keep herding training fun! Training that is done in a paddock with 5 head of sheep still follows the laws of behavior and is based on learning theory. It is all science-based positive reinforcement training! Solving problems still depend on you keeping on **TRaC**, which means monitoring your **T**iming, **R**ate of reinforcement, **a**nd **C**riteria. The only thing that has changed is that you have started including livestock in your training.

If you are a crossover herding trainer, it is easy to fall back into the habit of considering herding as a "serious" endeavor. If you find yourself getting frustrated or angry, then stop and take a break. Old habits die hard, but they do die!

The pen and paddock

You will start training with your livestock in a small pen within a small paddock or fenced area. I like to start in a paddock about 50×50 feet square or a similar rectangular size. You can use a round pen with a very small pen in the center of it for your stock if you have one at hand. If you start in a small paddock, you will eventually move out of it after you get your dog stopping, walking in, backing, and flanking in both directions. You will also be able to work on out and close as well as hurry and easy in the small paddock, but most likely you will need to move into a larger area for other training.

This is the small paddock that I start in when I bring herding behaviors to livestock. In this picture, the trees are on the corners of the almost square paddock, which is approximately 45 × 55 feet.

You will always be working with your dog on a long line in these transitional exercises. The long line is an emergency brake that is used to interrupt unwanted behavior around livestock, such as lunging at the stock.

Before you put livestock in the inner pen you will need to work flanking with the entire setup, cones included, without any stock present. (See image below.) This helps your dog to generalize the cone setup to the livestock paddock, with the addition of the small pen in the center. You want to set up the cones in a circle around the small pen as close to the fence as possible while still allowing a clear 3-foot path for your dog to travel between the cones and the fence. This is just one more step toward setting up your dog for success, another slice closer to the final flanking behavior goal.

This is a setup that I use initially, pen and cones, but no sheep. For most training, the cones would be much farther away from the small pen, depending on which exercise is being trained.

Once you start working with livestock in the small central pen, you may find your excitement builds and you start skipping breaks. Breaks are important for both you and your dog. They allow you time to think, process, relax, and take notes if you desire. They also allow your dog to think, process, and relax a bit. It seems to be human nature to want to move from one trial to the next and one session to another seamlessly. The problem is that there are going to be times you need your dog to hold a stationary position while herding. *Herding is not all action!* Plus, if you jump from one trial and session to the next, your dog will tend to become more aroused over time. Give your dog time off to relax so that they can give you their best performance!

Training herding using stock is a big accomplishment and far sexier than training foundation behaviors in your backyard. It will take as much self-control for you to take breaks as it will for your dog to control themselves around stock.

You may also find yourself skipping the 10-second pause associated with the use of your no reward marker after a mistake. The pause is the response cost, the price your dog pays for a mistake. The pause also helps to break up your session and keep your dog in the game while maintaining an appropriate level of arousal. If you eliminate breaks and pauses from your training, you may find yourself depending more on the long line as a crutch. See *Positive Herding 101* for more about no reward markers.

If you find yourself giving repeated tugs on the long line, you need to backtrack and break your training down. Remember that the long line is an emergency brake and not a steering wheel or a replacement for a stop or recall.

Video for mental health!

If there is any way you can video your training around livestock, I strongly encourage you to do it for record-keeping and documenting of your progress. Training herding is a long process and it is easy to become frustrated or depressed when you hit a wall and your training seems to stall. We tend to get so caught up in figuring out how to get past problems that we lose sight of how far we have come. Looking back at previous video not only gives you perspective on your dog's progress but may also hold the key to solving the problem you are currently facing.

Remember to set up your video camera or phone so that you, your dog, and the stock are in the frame at all times. At least, make that your goal.

Transitioning to using livestock and cues as reinforcers

As soon as you are working your dog on livestock, you should start the transition from food and toys to using the working of livestock and cues as your major reinforcers. You may still want to use treats to throw in the grass to lower arousal or as occasional reinforcers for exceptional performance of stationary behaviors such as stops. Feel free to reinforce exceptionally good performance with treats, tugs, or excited praise, in addition to relying on working stock and cues as reinforcers.

If your dog has a lot of herding instinct, then herding is a very inherently reinforcing behavior. Working livestock is the highest value reinforcement you can provide to your dog. Herding cues also become very valuable because they allow your dog to continue to herd. As your dog starts working livestock, you should quickly transition from treats and toys as reinforcers to herding and herding cues as your main reinforcers. You will still be able to use your clicks and verbal markers to mark correct behaviors, but now the reinforcement will come primarily from allowing your dog to continue herding.

Once you start working your dog around livestock, it will be natural to wean your dog off of the reinforcers you used in your initial training. If your dog does not have herding instinct, you will continue to use the reinforcers, treats and/or toys, that were most effective for your initial herding skills training in *Positive Herding 101*. You will also continue to use your no reward marker while training around livestock, if you used it during previous training.

If you find yourself using a substantial number of no reward markers, you are heading down a slippery slope. Reinforcement grows behavior, so aim to keep your rate of reinforcement high and your use of no reward markers very low.

Flanking around livestock

Flanking is the first behavior you will transition to livestock. Use your dog's highest value reinforcer, treats or toys, for transitioning flanks to stock. Soon you will move from using physical reinforcers, treats/toys, to using cues and the inherent reinforcement value of flanking as your reinforcers. If your dog does not find flanking inherently reinforcing, you may have to continue providing external sources of reinforcement such as toys or treats until you build a strong reinforcement history for flanking. Since flanking was taught with positive reinforcement, the flank cues should be reinforcers you can use, even for dogs with limited herding instinct.

After you have worked flanking your dog around a small, empty pen surrounded by cones in the paddock where you will work with livestock, you are ready to move on to adding stock to the exercise. If this paddock has previously held stock, just the smell of the livestock may be more distraction than your dog can handle in this new location. Allow your dog to check out the paddock and then work flanking in this situation until they are fluently performing their flanking cues before adding stock.

There are a lot of small steps involved in transitioning flanks to livestock. Take as much time and as many sessions as necessary to shape the flanks. Be sure you understand the mechanics of what both you and your dog will do at each step before starting that step. If you have trouble, stop and go back a step until you and your dog are achieving a 90% Rate of Reinforcement (ROR) or success. Then move on to the next step.

The setup for transitioning flanks to livestock includes stock in a small pen that is within a small paddock with a cone circle around the small pen.
Be sure to have at least 3 feet between the cone circle and the fence.

Transition flanks to livestock – Step by step

1. With stock in a small pen, cones in a circle 10 to 12 feet away from and around the pen, and your dog on a long line, you are ready to begin.
2. Stand with your back to the pen holding the long line.
3. Your dog will be on the outside of the cone circle facing you.
4. Tell your dog *there* (stop cue).

---

5. If your dog has shown a preference for flanking in one direction, ask for the preferred flank. Otherwise, randomly pick a flank and cue your dog. (Initially, don't use body language to prompt your dog, such as turning or walking in the direction you want your dog to go. If your dog struggles, start by prompting them by turning your body toward the direction you want them to go but fade the prompt as soon as possible.)
6. If your dog looks, shifts their weight, takes a step, or moves off in the correct direction, mark immediately and reinforce by delivering a treat to your dog or by throwing a toy or tug to them. Repeat in both directions 3 to 5 times.

---

7. Next, as your dog starts in the correct direction, turn and walk with them. You walk on the inside of the cone circle with your dog on the outside of the cones. (Keep the long line raised so that it clears the cones as you walk.)
8. Start using your stop cue before your mark. You will cue: flank, stop, *yes*, and reinforce. Cueing the stop reinforces the flank and adds stops to the exercise. **Note:** If your dog will not stop, go on to *transitioning the stop – step by step* below.

---

9. Once your dog is taking their flanks and flanking freely along the cone circle, start to fade your movement such that your dog flanks while you remain standing still.

10. Grow the distance flanked by ping-ponging it until your dog will flank halfway around the circle, from where they started, in each direction. (You may have to walk around next to the small pen to keep the long line loose as your dog flanks.)

11. Cue random flanks and stop your dog at different places around the circle.
12. Move your dog's starting point around the circle to further generalize the flanks.

13. If your dog is walking the entire time, encourage them to trot or run by giving your cues faster, a quicker delivery. You can encourage your dog to slow down by drawing out your cues, slowing down your delivery. (Refrain from using your hurry and easy cues at this point.)
14. Over the next few sessions, work your way to the outside of the cone circle and turn to face the livestock; both you and your dog are now facing the stock. Have your dog drag the long line. Start with your dog at your side and send them away from you. (Your dog will move away from you without going in front of or behind you.) Randomly stop your dog around the circle between you and balance, which at this point most likely will be directly opposite you on the cone circle.
15. Work both directions.

You want your dog to stay outside of the cone circle, so reinforcement should be delivered to your dog outside of the cone circle. For herding breeds, flanking itself is inherently reinforcing, so you don't have to give treats or have them tug. If your dog is not a herding breed, you will have to reinforce using treats or toys. If you do use treats or toys, do *not* have your dog come inside the cone circle to you to get their reinforcer. Instead, move out to your dog or throw the food or toy outside of the cone circle.

After a few successful sessions of training flanks, you will start working on off-balance flanks. In the following training plan, you will start by asking your dog to flank toward you a few steps and grow that behavior until you can ask your dog to flank any direction around the circle.

Transition off-balance flanks to livestock – Step by step

1. Start with both you and your dog outside of the cone circle, facing the stock. Your dog should be standing next to you and will be dragging a long line.
2. Flank your dog away from you and around the cone circle.
3. As soon as your dog gets past balance, which is usually at 12 o'clock when using penned stock, stop your dog and reinforce them. The distance your dog goes past balance will be only about a foot. Your reinforcer may be the stop cue or a thrown toy or treat.

4. Call your dog back to you and send them in the same direction. This time, allow them to go several feet past balance before stopping, reinforcing, and recalling them.
5. Work this until your dog can flank from your feet, around the circle, and back to you.
6. Take a long break and celebrate!

7. Now work on the other flank direction. Grow this off-balance flank just as you did the opposite off-balance flank by repeating steps 1 through 6.

8. When your dog can perform off-balance flanks in both directions, ask them to flank, starting at different places around the cone circle. Sometimes stop your dog at balance; other times have your dog go past balance and do an off-balance flank.
9. Do several sessions generalizing starting points, flanks, and off-balance flanks.

10. Finally, mix things up! When you stop your dog, ask for another flank, either the direction they were flanking or the opposite direction. Now your dog will really have to listen.
11. The last step is to have your dog change flanks on the fly. Changing flanks on the fly means that you cue the opposite flank while your dog is flanking, without stopping your dog between flanks. Start by including the stop: *come bye – stop – away to me* and then transition to *come bye – away to me*.
12. Practice changing flanks on the fly in both directions.

After these two exercises, your dog is a flanking pro! Although we usually want our dogs to flank behind us when they pass by us, we sometimes will need them to flank between us and the stock. Passing between us and the livestock is common when we are driving stock away from us.

Thus, your dog eventually should be able to flank behind and in front of you when doing off-balance flanks. To get your dog to flank behind you, move forward so you are in the cone circle. To get your dog to flank in front of you move to where the paddock fence is only about 3 feet from the cone circle. Step back against the fence so your dog cannot go behind you, between you and the fence.

Watch Gold begin flanking around sheep in a pen: https://www.youtube.com/watch?v=PgwKVFPpXKs&ab_channel=PurpleBorderCollie

These flanking exercises are basically what you did when you started working flanks around cone circles, so your dog should catch on quite quickly. The big change is that now livestock is in the picture, so although your dog is familiar with the behavior these steps of generalization will most likely be BIG steps for them. Have patience with your dog because the sight and smell of livestock are tremendously distracting!

Take your time and help your dog successfully flank around livestock. This is a big first step! For your dog to be successful, you may need to move to a larger paddock. In a larger area, you can set up a bigger cone circle and have your dog initially flank farther away from the stock. Move back to the smaller paddock when your dog has gained more self-control. (See Troubleshooting tips below.)

Here I have cued away to me and am walking along with Sir on a long line around the cone circle. I am on the inside with Sir on the outside of the cone circle.

Over time, I stop walking with Sir, move farther from the penned sheep, and position myself to the outside of the cone circle, facing the sheep. I then send Sir from my side.

Troubleshooting

- ***Dog moves out of position before cued*** – If your dog starts to come in to you or flank before you give a flank cue, give your no reward marker, pause for 10 seconds, and reset your dog. If your dog moves early two more times, cue *there* and reinforce them for holding the stop. Then call your dog a few feet to another place on the perimeter of the cone circle, cue *there*, and reinforce again. Repeat until your dog will hold their position for 10 seconds and then start *transitioning flanks – step by step* again.
- ***Dog flanks but comes inside cone circle (1)*** – Use your no reward marker, pause for 10 seconds, and reset your dog. If your dog comes inside the cone circle three times, even if they continue flanking in the correct direction, stop the session and follow this training plan:
  1. Reset your dog, pick up the long line, and walk around the perimeter of the cone circle with your dog. Keep your dog outside of the cone circle while you walk just inside the cone circle. Walk along with your dog by turning and facing forward as you walk such that your shoulders turn away from your dog and face the direction you are walking. Start with your arm holding the long line extended toward your dog, but quickly drop your arm back to your side. (Keep the long line raised so that it does not catch on the cones.)
  2. As you walk around the circle, feed out line so you are walking farther from your dog and closer to your penned stock in the center.
  3. Your dog should not come inside the cones at any time.
  4. Work this until your dog can walk one complete circle in each direction.
  5. Now stand with your back to the pen holding the stock, face your dog, and cue a flank.
  6. If your dog indicates or starts flanking in the correct direction, stop your dog and reinforce.
  7. Build the number of steps your dog flanks by ping-ponging when you stop and reinforce your dog. If your dog comes inside the cone circle, ask for fewer steps.
  8. If your dog indicates or starts flanking in the wrong direction give your no reward marker, pause for 10 seconds, and reset.
  9. When your dog completes half a circle without coming inside the cone circle mark, reinforce, and throw a party!
  10. Repeat 10 times and take a break!

11. Work on your dog flanking the other direction while staying outside of the cone circle as you did in the first direction. Repeat steps 1 through 10 in the new direction.
12. Now, return to the step-by-step directions for transitioning flanks to livestock above.

- **Dog flanks but comes inside cone circle (2)** – Use your no reward marker, pause for 10 seconds, and reset your dog. If your dog comes inside the cone circle three times, even if they continue flanking in the correct direction take a break.
    1. If your dog knows the out cue, you can try using it just as your dog begins to come inside the circle. If your dog always comes inside the circle at a certain place, be ready and cue *out* just before they get to that point.
    2. If they stay out, mark and reinforce! Repeat twice more.
    3. On the next trial wait, don't cue out, and let your dog decide if they will stay outside the circle or come in.
    4. If they stay out, mark and reinforce. Always reinforce outside the cone circle.
    5. If they come in, go back to cueing the *out*.
    6. After 5 trials using the out cue, go back to step 3 and eliminate the out cue.
    7. Work this until your dog will flank in the correct direction while staying outside the cone circle at least halfway around the circle. Then move on to the step-by-step directions for transitioning flanks above.
- **Dog flanks but comes inside cone circle (3)** – Use your no reward marker, pause for 10 seconds, and reset your dog. If your dog comes inside the cone circle three times, even if they continue flanking in the correct direction stop the session. Change your setup from a cone circle to a *quarter* cone circle to cut down your dog's access to livestock by setting up a small pen in the corner of your paddock. (Remove your original small stock pen for this exercise.) The two fences that form the corner of the paddock are now barriers that decrease the area available for your dog to approach the stock. Make the corner pen as small as possible to limit the movement of the livestock.
    1. Move your livestock pen to a corner of your paddock.
    2. Place your quarter cone circle about 20 feet or more from the corner.
    3. Have your dog on a long line.
    4. Cue a flank and walk along with your dog as they flank, turn and face forward as you walk so your shoulders turn away from your dog and face the direction you are walking. You will be inside the cone circle and your dog will stay outside of the circle.

5. Fade your movement until you are standing still and then move away from your dog and toward the stock in the corner pen.

6. Follow the directions above for transitioning flanks step by step and substitute quarter circle for the full circle in the directions.
7. Transition to a half cone circle around a pen on the fence line.
8. Transition to a full cone circle and follow the step-by-step directions above.

This is the setup for a quarter cone circle with a pen in the corner and the cone circle about 20 feet away from the pen. This setup limits your dog's access to the stock and greatly reduces how much the livestock distracts your dog.

At this point, we are at an advanced stage of working the quarter circle flanks. I no longer have Sir on a long line but can easily block him if he attempts to come inside the cone circle or lunge at the penned sheep.

- **Dog wants to lunge, bark, or charge the stock** – Try making your cone circle larger so your dog is farther from the livestock or switch to a quarter cone circle to reduce the distraction of the livestock. If these changes do not help, you need to go back to obedience behaviors, tricks, recalls, and heeling around stock. When your dog can confidently do round-robin recalls around penned stock (see *Positive Herding 101*) revisit transitioning your flanks to stock.
- **Dog is no longer interested in your physical reinforcers** – If your dog is no longer interested in food or play around stock, you will need to use cues as reinforcers *and* transition to the working of stock as the main reinforcers for your dog. Allow your dog to continue working when correct or, when incorrect, give a no reward marker and pause. Thus, you will be allowing your dog to continue working stock when correct. At this time, you can use a stop cue as a reinforcer for flanking and then reinforce the stop with a flank cue.

In general, what your dog finds reinforcing determines what cue you would use as a reinforcer as you progress with your training. If your dog is forward-moving, they most likely will find being allowed to walk in very reinforcing, so you would reinforce with the in cue when possible. If they are a sideways-moving dog, they may find being allowed to flank highly reinforcing, so you would reinforce with a flank when possible.

If your dog is a sideways-moving dog, they will particularly like flanking and you probably will have little trouble with them trying to come in toward the stock. If your dog is forward-moving, it may take a bit more time and effort to get your dog to stay out on their flanks. Adjust your training to your dog, as one type of dog will struggle with flanking and the other with walking in. Once your dog is flanking well around the cone circle, you can move on to walking in toward the stock in the next chapter.

All aspects of herding need to be kept in balance. Feel free to ask your dog to walk toward the stock at any time during the flank training to get a feel for their response. If your dog is comfortable and confident flanking but less so walking in, you should work the in more often during future training. If your dog is pushy and wants to walk into their stock rather than stay out and continue flanking, you will need to work flanks more than ins.

CHAPTER 3

Penned stock 2 – Walk in and stop

Your dog now can flank around livestock in a pen. That is a HUGE accomplishment! Even when confined in a small pen, livestock is extremely distracting for your dog. If your dog can listen to cues and respond correctly, both while stationary (start flanking in the correct direction) and while on the move (stop flanking when cued), near livestock, they have taken a big leap from performing obedience behaviors near livestock and on to herding.

When your dog is proficient at flanking around penned stock, they will have mastered an important building block of herding. Before you are ready to let the livestock out of their pen, your dog needs to be able to confidently flank, stop, and walk in. You may have introduced stops while training flanks, but if not, you now need to transition your walk in and stop to penned livestock. Let's start with walk in.

Walking in to a target

The goal of your walk in cue is for your dog to target the stock, apply pressure, and move the livestock in a straight line. How you set the line is determined by where your dog is relative to the stock and the pull in the situation. If the pull is off to the side, your dog will have to apply more pressure on that side of the flock, not directly behind them, to move them in the desired direction. Your dog should keep the line straight on their own, without you needing to flank them.

Because the walk in is a target behavior, you were able to use a flirt pole to build this behavior away from livestock in Chapter 15 of *Positive Herding 101*. For sideways-moving or sticky dogs, make sure your dog is moving in at a steady pace without stopping, pausing, or clapping. **Clapping** is excessive downing that occurs whenever your dog is asked to stop or decides to stop. Often a dog that claps is difficult to get back up on their feet and moving again. Try to avoid stopping your dog if they are sticky or tend to clap.

Walk in picture series

The next series of 10 pictures illustrate the steps of transitioning walk in to livestock. Normally, I train this outside with sheep in a pen but it is easier to see my mechanics in the training room. Sir is a very forward-moving dog and will freely walk in on stock, but he was reticent to walk in on the flirt pole rat in my training room.

 If I were working livestock, the cone circle would be around the prey, opposite of what is shown in these pictures. Here the cones just serve as landmarks so that Sir's forward movement is noticeable in the pictures. I could have used a line of cones or, better yet, set the cone circle around the prey (tug).

This series of four pictures show steps 1 to 7 in the step-by-step instructions for walk in below.

These two pictures show step 8, Sir moving farther forward and reinforcing without turning toward him.

In these two images, I have worked past step 9 and am now on step 13, Sir between me and the prey when stopped and then fed in place ahead of me.

Finally, I moved my position back to the cone circle and started generalizing my position. The final steps would be for me to move around in a circle and then have Sir change his position around the perimeter of the circle.

Transition walk in – Step by step

1. The setup is a small pen with stock inside in the center of a small paddock surrounded by a cone circle. Have a small tug or treats in hand and a leash or long line on your dog.
2. Stand facing the stock, midway between them and your dog, a few feet to the side of a direct line from your dog to the stock, while holding the long line or leash.
3. Your dog will start on the perimeter of the cone circle, also facing the stock.
4. Look at your dog over your shoulder closest to them and cue *walk in*.

5. If your dog takes a step directly forward, mark, and reinforce by turning toward your dog, stepping directly in front of them, and offering your dog a treat or toy. Your dog should walk a few steps directly toward you and the stock to get their reinforcement.
6. To reset your dog step away from the sheep, past your dog, and call your dog back to you as you move away from the stock. Reinforce with treats or tugging as calling off of stock can be very difficult for your dog!
7. Repeat three times per side, with you on both your dog's right and left sides.

8. Now cue the in and wait for your dog to walk three steps forward when cued. To deliver the reinforcement you will no longer turn to face your dog but instead will hold out the treat or toy in the hand closest to your dog and far enough ahead of them that they need to take a few steps forward to get the reinforcer.
9. Introduce the stop cue in place of the mark
   Note: If your dog will not stop, go to *transitioning the stop – step by step* below.
10. Next cue the in, facing forward without turning your head to look at your dog and wait until your dog walks up even with you to stop and reinforce your dog.
11. Work standing on both sides of your dog.

12. Increase the distance your dog walks in by withholding your stop cue until your dog will walk past you and to within 3 feet of the penned stock.
13. Stop and then reinforce by presenting the reinforcer between your dog and the stock in the pen.

14. When your dog will walk steadily to the pen (within 3 feet) when cued, start moving your position farther out to the side of your dog's path to the stock. Now face your dog when you recall them. Also, reinforce after calling your dog back out to you.
15. Generalize your position until your starting point is on the circle perimeter with your dog. *You will be moving your position farther from the penned stock.*

16. Over several sessions move your and your dog's starting positions randomly around the perimeter of the cone circle. You want your dog to walk in no matter where you are standing relative to them on the cone circle.
17. Add random stops to the walk in, then have your dog continue walking in. Do this infrequently, about once every 15 walk ins, as you want your dog's default behavior to be walking in until their pressure generates a response in the livestock, by turning or moving away from your dog.

Does your dog walk straight in to stock without hesitation until you cue a stop? If so your dog is probably a forward-moving dog. Forward-moving dogs usually take to walking in to stock like a duck to water.

If your dog is forward-moving they will quickly learn to walk in without regard to your position. They will usually continue right up to the livestock in the pen, if allowed. Shape approaching the pen by first stopping your dog and calling them back from several feet away from the pen. As your dog shows they can cope with being close to stock without lunging or barking, they are then allowed to approach closer.

Once your dog has walked in and stopped on cue, they have earned a treat. I use food in this situation to keep Sir's level of arousal low. Then I turn away from the sheep, keeping the long line loose, and call Sir back off of the sheep to me. Coming off of the sheep earns Sir even more treats!

 *If you have a sideways-moving or sticky dog, it is probably better to not add a stop to this exercise, step 9 above. Instead, wait until* stop *is introduced later in this chapter to begin stopping your dog around livestock. Just mark and reinforce when your dog has reached the correct distance or spot.*

If your dog is hesitant to start in, shown by pausing, stopping, or just not starting in, you probably have a sideways-moving dog and will have to shape the walk in. With this type of dog, don't worry about having them get closer than about 5 or 6 feet from the pen to begin. If they can get close enough to affect the livestock; the stock turns away, moves, or bobs their heads, that is close enough! Your job is to build your dog's confidence for walking in, so you don't want the stock to feel your dog is too close or applying too much pressure. If they feel threatened, the stock may stomp their feet or butt the pen, actions that may frighten your dog.

Troubleshooting

- **Dog remains standing after cued walk in** – Give your no reward marker, pause 10 seconds, and start again. If after two more trials your dog has not stepped toward the stock when cued, take a break.
    1. Change your position by standing next to your dog on the circle perimeter.
    2. Cue *walk in* and step forward toward the stock while encouraging your dog to walk with you by patting your thigh.
    3. Walk three steps forward with your dog, mark, and reinforce. Always deliver your reinforcement out in front of your dog so that they have to walk a few steps beyond you to get it.
    4. Repeat this a total of 6 times, 3 times with you standing to the right of your dog and 3 times with you on their left.

    5. Then reset, give the *walk in* cue, and walk forward, but no longer prompt your dog with the thigh slap.
    6. When your dog will immediately walk forward with you, change your starting position to 3 steps in front of and to the side of your dog.
    7. Cue *walk in* but remain stationary.
    8. If your dog walks up next to you, mark and reinforce ahead of you.
    9. If necessary, step forward 1 step to get your dog to start walking in but fade the step after three trials.
    10. Work this exercise with you on both sides of your dog. Sometimes your dog will walk past you on the right and other times on the left.

11. Keep adjusting your starting point until you are off to the side and halfway between your dog and the stock.
12. Jump back to transitioning the walk in at step 4.

- **Dog charges the stock** – If your dog lunges at the livestock:
    1. Use your long line to interrupt the charge, give your no reward marker, and calmly move your dog back to the perimeter of the cone circle and pause for 10 seconds. (The 10-second pause is the most important part of the no reward marker process.)
    2. Stand 3 feet ahead of and to the side of your dog facing the stock and ask your dog in.
    3. As soon as your dog takes 1 step inward, cue a stop.
    4. If your dog stops, mark and reinforce.
    5. If your dog doesn't stop, turn to face them while quickly stepping between them and the stock. Give your no reward marker and pause for 10 seconds. If your dog again lunges at the stock, give them a time-out. The time-out should last for a few minutes and be out of the pen, where your dog cannot see the livestock. (See *Positive Herding 101* for time-out instructions.)
    6. Reset your dog and start again.
    7. After a few times of blocking your dog's access to the stock, your dog should start to take your stop. Once they are stopping on cue, no longer turn to block them.
    8. If your dog starts to trot instead of walking, give your no reward marker while interrupting the trot using the long line. Then pause and reset.
    9. Shape the walk in by withholding your stop cue until your dog can walk steadily to within 3 feet of the pen, stop when cued, and hold their position.

If your dog lunges at the stock, interrupt the lunge with the long line and give your no reward marker.

Next, move your dog as far from the stock as possible in the small paddock and pause for 10 seconds. If your dog lunges again, give them a time-out, outside of the pen where they cannot see the stock. I only use time-outs for major crimes such as flagrant biting or lunging at livestock. Time-outs are a type of negative punishment in which I remove the dog from the scene of the crime for a few minutes.

Now your dog can flank and walk in to penned livestock! If your dog immediately took their stop cue and performs the flanking and walk in exercises fluently, you are almost ready to move on to loose livestock! If your dog blew through your stop cue, see the step-by-step directions for stop below before turning your stock loose.

Before you start – Flirt pole training

Before you work on the step-by-step directions for the stop, go back and work the stop using your flirt pole rat away from stock. If you need instructions on using a flirt pole, see Flirt pole training in Chapter 14 of the first book in this series, *Positive Herding 101*.

Really ramp up the arousal by having the rat skitter and hop along the ground. Can your dog stop when the rat is rampaging? Grow mass on the stop until your dog's response even impresses you! Then take your stop to penned stock and see if your dog can take their stop cue. Upping the game with the rat should help lead to a smooth transition of the stop behavior from your backyard to near livestock.

If you have a forward-moving or pushy dog, you may want to use a down as your stop behavior. Using a down instead of a stand makes it easier for you to see and hold criteria on the stop. If you have a sideways-moving or sticky dog, a stand is a better choice of stop behavior because your dog may tend to get stuck when downed and be difficult to get up and moving again.

When doing the stop step-by-step exercise, be sure and use super high-value reinforcers (read steak!) to make it worth your dog's while to stop when cued.

Transition the stop – Step by step

1. The setup is a pen with stock inside surrounded by a cone circle in a small paddock.
2. Have your dog on a 6-foot leash attached to a flat collar or harness.
3. You will be just to the inside of the cone circle facing your dog and holding the leash so that it extends to only 3 feet between you and your dog. (You may be able to attach the leash handle to the clip that attaches to your dog's collar or harness, and thus turn a 6-foot leash into a 3-foot leash with a big loop for a handle.)
4. Your dog will be on the outside of the cone circle facing you.
5. Cue either flank.
6. As your dog starts in the correct direction turn and walk with them.
7. As you complete *one* step be ready, cue a stop, and then stop walking.
8. If your dog stops, mark and reinforce.
9. If your dog does not stop, allow the tightening of the leash to bring your dog to a stop. Your dog should barely have started flanking when you ask for the stop so they should not be moving faster than a trot and more likely are at a walk. Getting to the end of the leash should generate a tug on your dog's collar or harness and *not* a pop! Repeat.
10. Your dog should quickly, after 3 to 5 trials, stop when you become stationary after cueing a stop. Mark, reinforce, and have a party!

---

11. Now cue the opposite flank and repeat the same procedure.
12. Once your dog is taking your stop cue, increase the distance you walk with your dog by a step or two before asking for a stop. Ping pong the distances and work both directions.

---

13. Now lengthen your leash out to the full 6 feet.
14. Cue a flank and walk with your dog. As soon as your dog takes a step in the correct direction cue the stop but you keep walking.
15. If your dog stops, mark, reinforce with a jackpot, and have a party!
16. If your dog does not stop, you stop walking, give your no reward marker, get your dog stopped, pause for 10 seconds, and re-cue a flank.
17. Work this until your dog will stop while you continue walking to the end of the leash, in both directions. *Be sure not to pull on the leash during this exercise.*

---

18. Now go back to using your long line and cue a flank. You will remain stationary. After your dog flanks one step, cue a stop. If your dog stops, then mark and reinforce.

19. Next, drop the long line and have your dog drag it as you build the number of steps your dog takes before being cued to stop. Ping pong the distance you walk each time.
20. Grow the distance your dog flanks before stopping until your dog can go halfway around the cone circle before being asked to stop. Work both directions until your dog will stop anytime they are cued to stop.

You should now be ready to go to step 10 of the transitioning flanks step-by-step exercise, if need be.

These pictures show the beginning steps of transitioning the stop to livestock. First I cue a flank. After Sir has flanked a step, I would cue a stop and I would stop walking. If Sir stopped, I would reinforce him in place. If he continued walking, he would be stopped when he reached the end of the leash.

To begin, I would cue Sir to stop after just one flanking step.

Wait to start using your no reward marker until step 14, once you have lengthened out your leash to 6 feet. If you use your no reward marker at the start of this exercise, your dog may associate the no reward marker with the flank direction, which was correct, rather than with the incorrect behavior of not stopping when cued.

Remember to give your verbal stop cue before you stop walking. If you cue the stop and stop walking at the same time, your dog will respond to your physical movement instead of your verbal cue.

If your dog will take their stop while flanking, they will usually take it when walking in. If not, use the same procedure as you did for the flank, using a leash while walking into the stock. Allow your dog to self-correct when they do not take your stop cue.

Again, remember to ask for the stop just as your dog starts walking in so that they are moving slowly. You want the leash to give them a tug and not a pop. Since you start with only 3 feet of leash between you and your dog they cannot travel very far before they get to the end of the leash. Add the stop into the transition *walk in – step by step exercise*, step 9 and complete the exercise.

Mini-fetch sneak peek

In Chapter 5 you will start doing mini-fetches with your dog. At this point, you can do the same exercise but keep your stock in the pen. Set up a small pen along a fence, such that you have a fair amount of space at each side of the pen, and put some livestock in the pen. Set up a half cone circle around the pen using as many cones as you think will be necessary for your dog to be successful flanking from fence to fence around the stock. For this exercise, your dog will again drag a long line.

Initially, stand by the pen and flank your dog back and forth around the half cone circle, using stops and a few walk ins. Work your way out to the cone circle and continue working until your dog can flank both directions, stop, walk in, and recall back to you away from the livestock.

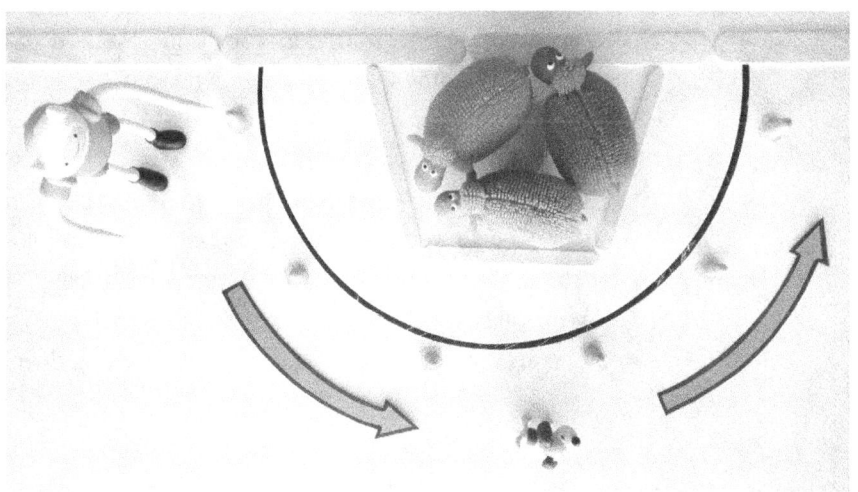

This is the final stage of the mini-fetch setup. You start standing between your dog and the penned stock to make sure your dog will flank outside of the half cone circle. Then slowly move to the outside of the half cone circle. Finally, move to one end of the half cone circle and send your dog from your feet to the opposite side of the stock, the point of balance.

Now work your way to one end of the half cone circle such that you are standing next to the fence and your dog is standing next to you. You stand between your dog and the fence. Flank your dog around the stock to the fence on the other side and cue a stop. Mark, reinforce, and reset by walking to the other end of the half cone circle. Set up and send your dog back around the livestock to the fence on the opposite side. Your dog will be flanking back to where you both originally started. When your dog will flank in both directions from your feet, around the half cone circle to the other fence, and stop, they are ready to do a mini-outrun.

To perform a mini-fetch (outrun, lift, and fetch) all you have to add to this exercise is an *in* following the stop next to the fence. You will set up your dog at your feet, while standing next to the fence, flank your dog around the half cone circle to the opposite fence, stop your dog, and then ask them in to the stock. As soon as you see a reaction from the stock you should again stop your dog, mark, and reinforce! The stock's reaction could be to turn their heads or step away from your dog, or even stomp their feet. The stock do not need to turn their backs on your dog since they are confined by the small pen.

One mini-outrun performed! I usually use just happy verbal praise as the reinforcer for this exercise. My dogs find the mini-fetch inherently reinforcing, so the most difficult part of the exercise is calling them off to reset. Use high-value treats or toys for reinforcing the recall! Repeat the mini-fetch from the other side, your dog will be flanking the opposite direction. You now have the foundation of your fetch in place!

Your dog is almost ready to herd

With the foundation herding behaviors transitioned to penned livestock your dog is almost ready to move on to loose stock. Before you release the livestock from the small pen, you still need to transition your out/close and easy/hurry behaviors to penned livestock. In Chapter 4 we will do exactly that.

You could move forward with loose livestock at this point, but if your dog struggles to adjust the distance they flank from the livestock or the speed of their flanks or ins, you will need to go through the exercises in Chapter 4 to help them read and control their stock. Since most dogs new to herding struggle with flanking too close and too fast, you will save yourself major headaches by transitioning the cues that modify the distance and speed of their flanks before your dog develops bad flanking habits.

CHAPTER 4

Penned stock 3 – Modifier cues

Before we let the livestock out of the small pen, there are two more pairs of behaviors that your dog needs to transition to stock, easy/hurry and out/close. These behaviors are modifiers or concept cues. Easy and hurry tell your dog to change speed while moving, either while flanking or walking in. Out and close modify the arc of the flank, either farther from or closer to the stock. The importance of these cues is that by having the ability to modify your dog's behavior you also tap into the connection between physically performing a behavior and mentally adopting a compatible mindset.

Slowing down from a gallop to a trot seems to naturally shift your dog down a mental gear or two. A dog that moves farther away from livestock as they flank usually starts to relax and be less frantic, while a dog that flanks closer seems to increase both their engagement with the stock and their energy level.

Often, dogs do not realize that they can slow down, speed up, move away from, or move closer to livestock. Although they may have tons of herding instinct, they may need to learn how to adjust their behavior to be more relaxed and comfortable handling livestock rather than just reacting to the stock. Putting your dog in the right place, at the right speed, helps them to learn new behaviors that they can generalize and incorporate into their herding repertoire.

Two behaviors that are not natural to your dog are backing up and moving their rear feet sideways. Not all behaviors that are useful in herding come naturally to your dog, some have to be taught.

Easy and hurry

Easy and hurry are very valuable cues for your dog to know, so let's transition them to livestock. Eventually, the sheep will be in a small pen in a little paddock and your dog will be on a long line, but you will start the transition without livestock present.

Although easy and hurry are initially taught with a target stick, I don't usually use one once I start transitioning these cues to livestock. Once livestock is in the picture, your dog probably will no longer focus on the target stick target anyway. You can use your extended arm as a prompt for your dog, but your dog should be looking at the livestock instead of you. You will need to use large yummy treats or a toy that you can toss as the reinforcer.

A long line is used from the start of this training, even though no livestock is present. This gets you used to handling the long line for when you have livestock in the pen. The long line will be your emergency brake, for use if your dog lunges toward the stock.

You may need to have livestock in the small pen to get your dog to flank around consistently. If you need to use stock from the start, it will be much more difficult for your dog to be successful, due to the high level of distraction the stock will provide. Try using an empty pen in the center of your paddock to begin!

Speed changes – Step by step

1. Set up a small pen in the center of a little paddock *without* livestock in the pen. Place a cone circle 6 feet out from and around the small pen or 3 feet in from the paddock fence.
2. You will stand near the pen facing your dog while holding the long line.
3. Your dog will be outside the cone circle facing you.
4. Cue a flank and walk or trot around the pen with your dog as they flank, for one complete circle. Your dog should stay on the outside of the cone circle.
5. Stop your dog, mark, and reinforce with a treat or toy.
6. Now repeat steps 4 and 5 in the other direction.
7. If your dog walks or trots while flanking, you will first work on hurry, but if they insist on cantering, you will begin to work on easy.

This is the setup for the first few speed change exercises. Note that there is no livestock present.

Hurry – Step by step

1. Each training session you will work only one direction, clockwise or counter-clockwise, for the entire set of these step-by-step instructions.
2. You stand near the pen facing your dog while holding the long line.
3. Your dog will be outside of the cone circle facing you.
4. Cue a flank and as your dog starts to flank, turn and walk along with them while holding the long line. The arm with your hand holding the long line will be extended toward your dog.
5. Now cue the hurry with *chit-chit* and immediately prompt your dog to speed up by speeding up your movement. Because you are circling the small pen and your dog is flanking around the much larger cone circle, you should be able to trot even when your dog is cantering.
6. When your dog increases their speed one gait, mark, and reinforce by throwing a large treat or toy ahead of them. The first few times you cue the hurry, prompt your dog by *increasing your speed until they move up one gait, walk to trot or trot to canter*.

---

7. After 3 trials repeat the first 6 steps but reduce the amount of prompting you do in terms of speeding up. Only speed up for 5 steps and if your dog does not break into a higher gait, give your no reward marker, pause for 10 seconds, and start again.
8. If your dog moves up to the next gait when you prompt them with your 5 faster steps, then mark and reinforce by throwing a treat or toy out ahead of them.
9. Continue to decrease the number of prompting steps until your dog is gearing up to the *next gait as soon as you cue the hurry*.

---

10. Now drop the prompt of your speeding up, instead continue to walk at the same pace before and after you cue the hurry.
11. When your dog immediately breaks into the higher gait on only the verbal cue, *chit-chit*, stop, repeat several times, and take a long break.

12. Later resume the session, start from the beginning, and work the hurry in the other direction.
13. When your dog immediately takes hurry in both directions stop for the day!
14. In the following sessions, work hurry until your dog is comfortable responding to the cue while flanking in either direction. Then work on easy or your slow down cue.

In these three pictures I am working Sir on hurry. I start with him facing me, he is outside of the cone circle and I am next to the pen. I cue away to me and have him trot almost one complete circle. I then cue hurry and he increases his speed from a trot to a canter while I run along inside the cone circle.

Once Sir broke into a canter I marked with yes and threw a tug out in front of him. The tug is in the center of the picture just above a cone and in front of the pen. The tug landed outside the cone circle.

If you started with hurry, you are ready to work on easy. If you needed to start with easy, begin here and work hurry after you complete the instructions for easy below.

The delivery of the reinforcer, thrown ahead versus dropped directly in front of the dog, is the key to effective reinforcement. Throwing tends to increase arousal and dropping to decrease arousal.

Easy – Step by step
1. Each training session you will work only one direction, clockwise or counter-clockwise, for the entire set of these step-by-step instructions.
2. You stand near the pen facing your dog while holding the long line.
3. Your dog will be outside the cone circle facing you.
4. Cue a flank. As your dog starts to flank you should quickly trot or run along with them while holding the long line. Your arm will be extended out toward your dog.
5. Give your hurry cue so that your dog goes into a canter while you trot or run. If your dog does not canter, work the hurry until they are comfortable cantering around the outside of the cone circle.

6. Now cue *easy* and immediately prompt your dog to slow to a lower gait by slowing down your movement, from a run to a trot or from a jog to a walk.
7. When your dog decreases their speed one gait, mark, and reinforce by feeding a treat or dropping a toy or treat slightly ahead of your dog. The first few times you cue *easy*, prompt your dog by decreasing your speed until they drop down one gait, from canter to trot.

8. After 3 trials repeat the first 7 steps but reduce the amount of prompting of the slow down. Only slow down for 5 steps. If your dog does not drop down into a lower gait, give your no reward marker, pause for 10 seconds, and start again.
9. If your dog drops down to the next gait while you prompt them with your 5 slower steps, then mark and reinforce by dropping a treat or toy slightly ahead of them.
10. Continue to decrease the steps of prompting until your dog is gearing down as soon as you cue *easy*.
11. Now eliminate the prompt of you slowing down, instead continue to trot or run at the same pace before and after you cue *easy*.
12. When your dog immediately breaks into the lower gait on only the verbal cue *easy*, stop and take a break.

13. At a later session, work *easy* in the other direction.
14. When your dog immediately takes *easy* in both directions stop for the day!
15. In following sessions, work *easy* until your dog is comfortable responding to the cue while flanking in either direction.

In this sequence, I am working Sir on easy. *He starts out facing me.*

I cue come bye *and he starts to canter.*

I then cue easy *and he starts to trot.*

The last step is for me to mark Sir's change in gait and drop a treat or tug slightly in front of him.

Troubleshooting

- **Dog does not slow down when cued or prompted (1)** – If your dog is fast and finds flanking at speed inherently reinforcing, you may have to allow your dog to circle a few times before you ask them to slow down to set them up for success.
    1. Once your dog is flanking at the canter, cue *easy* and slow down your movement as a prompt. If after 3 repetitions your dog continues to canter without dropping down to a trot, reset your dog.
    2. This time encourage your dog to complete 2 or 3 circles, depending on the temperature and how big of a circle they are running, and wait for your dog to tire a bit before cueing *easy*.
    3. Now give your cue and then prompt your dog by slowing down your movement. Because your dog is a bit tired of running, they are more likely to slow down when cued. When your dog slows to a trot, mark and drop a treat or toy slightly ahead of them and allow them to stop.
    4. Repeat until your dog is immediately taking the easy cue.
    5. In this situation do not ask your dog to hurry up after they have slowed down. You have tired your dog out so slowing down and stopping are

reinforcing. If you ask your dog to speed up at this point, when they are tired, you are setting them up for failure. Hold off on going back and forth between slow down and hurry, as directed below, until your dog is reliably taking their slow down cue.

This is one of the few times I encourage my dog to orbit, circling without looking for balance, but I fade orbiting as soon as possible! If you can work this exercise without stock in the paddock, as I can with Sir, the multiple circles are less troubling since there is no stock for him to read or try to balance.

- **Dog does not slow down when cued or prompted (2)** – If having your dog circle several times doesn't help, try giving a light tug on the long line after you cue the easy to prompt your dog to slow down. Drop the tug of the long line after 3 trials.

If you worked easy first, go back and work hurry. If you have worked both hurry and easy, go on to the instructions 'Easy and hurry – Step by step' below.

Dogs tend to find the *chit-chit* cue naturally energizing and usually do not struggle to learn it. Conversely, many dogs find it difficult to learn to slow down on cue. It would be nice to be able to have your dog flank and just wait for them to offer to slow down, but since many herding dogs are high energy and find flanking at speed inherently reinforcing, you might have to wait a long time for them to offer to slow down.

Once your dog knows both *easy* and *hurry*, it is time to put the behaviors together and later you will add livestock to your training sessions.

Easy and hurry – Step by step
1. Set up as usual for speed modifier training with your dog on a long line and cue a flank. You will still be walking around the small pen as your dog flanks around the cone circle. No livestock are in the small pen.
2. Depending on how fast your dog takes off on the flank, cue *easy* to slow them down or *hurry* to speed them up.
3. If your dog immediately takes your cue, reinforce by giving the opposite speed modifier cue. Thus if your dog starts out at a canter, cue *easy*, and if they drop down to a trot, cue *chit-chit* to put them back into a canter.

4. If your dog does not immediately take either of your cues, use your no reward marker, pause for 10 seconds, and reset.
5. Once your dog is immediately responding to your speed up and slow down cues, such that you can change their gait up and down 2 or 3 times during one complete revolution around the cone circle in both directions, you are ready to put livestock in the small pen!

---

6. Repeat steps 1 through 5 with livestock in the small pen.
7. Repeat steps 1 through 5 with livestock in the small pen with no long line on your dog.
8. Repeat steps 1 through 5 and fade cones out of the setup until you are using no cones.

Now I am working easy and hurry with stock in my small pen. Since I start with Sir on a long line, I will be moving around the stock with him. I stay fairly close to the pen so that I don't have far to go to keep up with Sir.

The closer I stay to Sir, the farther I have to go as I circle the stock. As his behavior becomes more fluent I can move away from him and toward the penned livestock.

Eventually, you will work this exercise with loose livestock and your dog on a long line. Finally, you will be working with loose livestock and no long line on your dog. These exercises may seem to have a lot of steps, but the training usually goes quite quickly, especially since you can go through all the early training in your yard, without livestock present.

Out and close

For transitioning out and close, you will work the same setup that you did for easy and hurry, except you will now stand in the pen. You also don't need your dog on a long line to start. You will be using a large flirt pole rat, instead of a toy or large treats, as a reinforcer. I like to start working on close first since my dog has just had a lot of practice staying outside of the cone circle during the training of hurry and easy.

This exercise is similar to how you taught close and out, except now you are using only one set of cones and are standing in the pen No livestock are needed.

Close – Step by step

1. You will start in the center of the pen facing your dog, holding your long flirt pole. No long line or livestock present!
2. Your dog will start on the outside of a cone circle, 6 feet from the pen, and facing you.
3. Flank your dog and after they take a few steps, cue *close*, followed immediately by *get it*, as you drop the rat in front of your dog and to the inside of the cone circle as a lure. Repeat 3 to 5 times.

---

4. Now flank your dog the same direction, cue *close*, and wait for your dog to move to the inside of the cone circle and continue flanking .
5. If your dog immediately moves inside the cone circle, mark with yes, give your release cue: *get it*, and drop the rat in front of your dog to reinforce.
6. If your dog stays flanking on the outside of the cone circle use your no reward marker, pause 10 seconds, and reset.

---

7. Repeat steps 1 through 6 until your dog is immediately moving inside the cone circle and continuing to flank when cued close.
8. Work close several sessions to generalize your dog moving toward the pen and continuing to flank, when cued.
9. Now work on close in the opposite direction until fluent.

---

10. Repeat steps 1 through 9 with livestock in the small pen, using a long line, and you outside of the pen. You may have to switch to a different reinforcer such as allowing your dog to continue flanking halfway around the stock if they have herding instinct.
11. Repeat steps 1 through 9 with livestock in the small pen with no long line on your dog.
12. Repeat steps 1 through 9 and fade cones.

To help your dog get the idea you can also use here, *your recall cue, to prompt your dog to come toward you and inside of the cone circle. Drop the prompt of cuing* here *after three uses.*

Sir starts flanking outside the cone circle and comes inside when cued close. He is then marked with yes, released with get it, and reinforced by tugging with the flirt pole rat!

For the out, you will be looking for your dog to move from flanking inside of the cone circle to moving to the outside of the cone circle. These instructions are just the opposite of the instructions for close. See Out – Step by step below.

Getting to this point in your training is a huge accomplishment! You are fine-tuning behaviors that will help your dog to be successful throughout their herding career.

Out – Step by step

1. You will start in the center of the pen facing your dog, holding your long flirt pole. No long line or livestock present!
2. Your dog will start on the inside of a cone circle, 6 feet from the pen, and facing you.
3. Flank your dog and after a few steps cue *out*, followed immediately by *get it*, as you drop the rat in front of your dog and to the outside of the cone circle as a lure. Repeat 3 times.

4. Now flank your dog the same direction, cue *out*, and wait for your dog to move outside of the cone circle.
5. If your dog immediately moves outside the cone circle, mark with *yes*, give your release cue: *get it*, and drop the rat in front of your dog to reinforce.
6. If your dog stays flanking on the inside of the cone circle use your no reward marker, pause 10 seconds, and reset.

7. Repeat steps 1 through 6 until your dog is immediately moving outside the cone circle and continuing to flank when cued *out*.
8. Work out several sessions until your dog can immediately move away from the pen and keep flanking when cued.

9. Repeat steps 1 through 8 with livestock in the small pen, using a long line, and you outside of the pen. You may have to switch to a different reinforcer such as allowing your dog to continue flanking halfway around the stock, if they have herding instinct.
10. Repeat steps 1 through 8 with livestock in the small pen with no long line on your dog.
11. Repeat steps 1 through 8 and fade cones out of the setup until you are using no cones.

Once your dog has mastered out and close, without any livestock present, you will add stock to the pen in the center of your paddock and work a session or two. Of course, you will no longer be standing in the pen. Instead, you will stay near the pen but may move around it as needed.

Be sure your dog is on a long line once livestock is present. Then work the exercises with your dog off of the long line with stock present. Eventually, the next step is to work loose stock with your dog on a long line and finally work both your dog and the stock loose.

Sir starts inside the cone circle and flanks out when cued. He is then marked, released, and reinforced.

Hurry and easy in action (followed by a mini- fetch): https://www.youtube.com/watch?v=uDryaIv7Jy0&ab_channel=PurpleBorderCollie

Your dog is ready to herd!
The time has come! Now that your dog can flank both directions, walk in, and stop, as well as move closer/farther and quicker/slower around stock, it is time to turn the sheep loose. Of course, your dog will remain on the long line until they demonstrate that they can perform all of their herding skills to criteria while herding loose stock.

It takes courage to make the leap from livestock in a pen to loose stock and this step is not for the faint of heart! Your dog will tell you when they are ready for the next step by demonstrating stunning self-control. It's time to take down the pen, release the stock, and buckle your seat belt!

CHAPTER 5

Loose stock in small area

At last, your dog will be working loose stock! This is an exciting and challenging transition for you and your dog. Suddenly you have a third element to keep track of – the livestock! Until now you have primarily concerned yourself with what you and your dog were doing. Now you will also have to pay attention to your stock because, believe me, your dog will be paying close attention to them!

The distraction level of moving livestock is infinitely higher than penned stock. When stock is penned, your dog does not have to control them because the pen does. Once the stock is loose, your dog's herding instincts will kick in big time and their instincts will tell them to chase, stalk, grab, or gather the stock.

Got sheep?

Although you can use almost any type of stock in a pen, once you move on to loose stock it is important to use livestock that flock or stay together. In the small paddock, this is not as critical as it becomes once you move to the larger area, but it is still a big concern. I suggest you use 4 or 5 hair sheep ewes, wethers, or half-grown lambs. Hair sheep tend to be lighter and will move more easily off your dog than wool sheep. Goats generally tend to flock more loosely and ducks' desire to stay together varies depending on the breed. I have herded primarily sheep and cattle so am not an expert on herding other types of livestock such as goats, ducks, chickens, geese, etc.

Wethers are castrated male sheep, while rams are intact or uncastrated male sheep. Wethers are suitable for herding training, most rams are not!

Most docile sheep will flock and move as one unit. You can think of the group of sheep as one animal since they will usually move as a cohesive group. If one sheep goes in a certain direction, the rest will usually follow. If you do have one free spirit who wants to go their own way or fight your dog, sort them off until your dog has worked through the basic herding exercises. When you and your dog have some experience and are ready for more of a challenge, then add the wayward ewe back to the group and give your dog experience keeping the group together while dealing with a contrary soul.

When you start doing fetches in the larger area, you will have enough to keep track of without your stock heading in different directions. Do yourself a favor and beg, borrow, buy, or steal some calm sheep that flock well to train on at this point. You don't need high-priced sheep to work. Many farmers will sell you some **cull ewes** for a reasonable price, these are females that usually have bad udders and thus are not suitable for raising lambs. These cull ewes can provide you with nice sheep to work for years. Just be sure to buy culls that can see and move well.

Warning!
If the stock you intend to herd is guarded by a livestock guardian, be aware that the guardian may view your dog as a threat. Never send your dog after a flock that is guarded without being close at hand to protect your dog.

Reading your dog on loose stock
When your dog is exposed to moving livestock, a whole new set of instinctual responses may appear. Many of the traits you looked for when your dog initially went to stock will still be apparent, but other instinctive traits may appear or traits that surfaced earlier may become more pronounced.

Enhanced behaviors your dog may show around *moving* livestock:
- *Hook up* – A stronger hook up or focus
- *Interest* – More interest (laser focus)
- Confidence – More or less confidence (Although your dog's level of confidence will initially be determined by instinct and other innate characteristics, you can

boost or erode your dog's confidence by how you set your dog up to interact with livestock. Helping your dog win against tough stock = more confidence, allowing your dog to lose against tough stock or get hurt = less confidence.)
- *Stickiness/Pushiness* – More or less freedom of movement
- Attention to handler – Usually less
- *Tail position* – More likely to see tail rising as anxiety increases
- *Barking* – More likely to bark
- Pace – A dog that normally walks into livestock with a steady, workmanlike pace may rush or get sticky
- Cover – Dog shows an increased desire to control livestock or not allow it to move

The italicized behaviors above are instinctual. You have no control over their appearance and you cannot train your dog to do them.

Cover is the desire to control stock by instinctively flanking around them to prevent their escape. If one animal tries to take off or break away from the group, your dog should immediately flank out to prevent the wayward animal from getting away. Dogs with a lot of herding instinct may naturally cover stock and should be encouraged to do so. If your dog does not immediately move to get around the escaping animal, then you need to flank your dog.

If a single animal manages to break away and travel a good distance from the flock you will have more success taking the flock to the single than trying to bring the single back to the flock. Single animals are notorious for behaving erratically.

Here a lamb has broken away from the small flock and Liz, the border collie, is flanking out and around to cover it. At this point, the lamb is just starting to turn away from Liz.

After covering the lamb, Liz flanks back the other direction to encourage the lamb to rejoin the flock. **Notice** *how far off of the lamb that Liz is working. Liz naturally stayed off of or away from the lamb as she covered and controlled it.*

Keep instinctual behaviors in mind as you take your dog to loose stock and watch to see if and how your dog displays them. When working loose stock, there may be too much going on for you to notice if your dog covers or walks in with nice pace, so having video to review really comes in handy. You will be amazed at how much you missed of what you, your dog, and the livestock did, during even a very short session!

You can compensate somewhat for a lack of instinctual behaviors in your dog but the more instinct your dog naturally possesses, the more aptitude they have for herding. The less instinct your dog naturally possesses, the more you will have to read the stock and direct your dog to keep them in the correct position relative to the livestock.

Sheep on the loose!

The most difficult part of working your dog on loose sheep or other stock is trusting yourself and your dog to be up to the challenge. Fortunately, you will start with your dog on a short leash so that you can maintain control of the situation. Keep your sessions short, 5 to 15 minutes to start, and include breaks even during these short sessions. It takes a tremendous amount of self-control for your dog to correctly respond to cues in this situation, so celebrate small successes and take baby steps forward.

One great indicator of your dog's self-control is the reaction of the loose sheep when you bring your dog into the small paddock. If the sheep mill, move quickly around in a confused mass, or try to climb the fence to get away from your dog, you still have a lot of work to do before you move forward! A self-controlled dog usually translates to calm livestock.

Paddock setup

Setting the paddock up is the first order of business. Leave your dog at home or keep them out of sight of the paddock while you set the stage for training. Remove the pen you have been using to hold the stock and store it out of the paddock or move to a different small paddock without a pen in the center. Move your stock into the paddock and allow them to settle.

The sheep are loose in the small paddock and have been allowed to settle. The next step is for the handler to enter the paddock, without their dog, and move the sheep to get a feel for them.

Without your dog, enter the paddock and move the stock around. Are they calm and relaxed or do they blindly run from one end of the paddock to the other? If you have docile livestock, they should settle and only move when you approach them. If they are running or milling excessively, they may not be appropriate stock to use for starting your dog. If your livestock will not settle when you are alone in the paddock with them, they will be even more unsettled when your dog shows up. It would be rare for your stock to be so high strung that they are not suitable for further training, but if they won't settle while you are in the paddock with them, then you need to change to some stock that will remain calm.

Now that you have stock in your paddock that move when you approach but quickly settle and stand looking at you when you stop moving, you are almost ready to get your dog.

Set up a time-out station

Before you start training on loose livestock decide where you will take your dog if they attempt to chase or lunge at the stock, thereby earning a time-out. The time-out area should be close to, but outside of the paddock and your dog should not be able to see the stock when in time-out. Time-outs should be handled calmly and unemotionally, even if you are upset or frustrated. Your dog should remain in time-out for 3 to 5 minutes per infraction.

This time-out station is inside the paddock because I was training with the stock in a pen in the corner of the paddock. It is best to have your time-out station outside of the paddock in which you are working your dog. Your dog should not be able to see the stock when in time-out.

If you find yourself putting your dog into time-out several times in one training session, you probably need to backtrack and move farther from your stock to make things easier for your dog to be successful.

Paddock approach and entry

Put your dog on a 3-foot leash or make one by hooking the handle of your 6-foot leash into the clip that connects your leash to your dog's flat collar or harness. Now instead of a 6-foot leash you have a 3-foot loop hooked to your dog's collar. Have your dog heel on leash while approaching the paddock, as usual.

When your dog sees the loose stock, they will know immediately, even before entering the paddock, that the game has changed. If your dog starts to pull on the leash or stops dead in their tracks, stop, move farther from the paddock, and work on heeling. Your dog must be able to heel with you up to the gate, sit before you open the gate, wait while you enter, recall to you, and then sit again inside the paddock beside you. This chain of behaviors should be solid since you have been repeating it from the time you started bringing your dog to penned stock.

You may be surprised that your dog struggles with the paddock entry because the stock is now loose. Be ready for this degradation of behavior! Loose stock can sharply increase the levels of arousal and distraction for your dog. Work the gate approach and entry until your dog demonstrates that they can control themselves and you feel confident you are in control of the situation.

At this point, the stock should be calmly standing in a group watching your dog. If the stock is milling, running around, or trying to climb the fence, *but* your dog is sitting quietly, watching them, then relax and wait for your stock to calm down and settle. After your stock settle, start by working some stationary behaviors such as sit, down, and stand. Then move to very, very short recalls. Your dog is still on the 3-foot leash at this point. When the stock is calmly standing and watching your dog, you are ready for the next step, which is heeling around the paddock.

If your livestock jam themselves in the corners of your paddock you may have to put panels across the corners to slightly round them off. If you do add panels, remove them, one at a time, as soon as possible. When you are ready, remove one panel and see if the livestock still hides in that corner or if they now move freely around the paddock. If they move freely, then remove the other panels over time. Conversely, you may find there is no need to block off the corners. Initially, work in the paddock without blocking the corners and only put up barriers if necessary.

Ending the session

Before you take your dog into a paddock with loose stock you need to have a plan in place for ending the session and getting your dog out of the paddock when you are done training. The first few times you train on stock that is loose in a paddock, stay near the gate through which you and your dog entered. Then when you are done training you can heel your dog only a short distance to get to the gate. Make sure to hold on to the leash or long line as you exit the paddock so that your dog does not get the opportunity to get away from you and rehearse unwanted behavior. As soon as you get out of the gate, reinforce your dog with very high-value reinforcers.

Later, as you move on to flanking your dog around the stock, end your session by stopping your dog near the gate. If you decide to end your session while you and your dog are opposite the gate, such as for a time-out, calmly walk with your dog around the perimeter of the paddock until you reach the gate. Your dog will not be entering the interior of the paddock until later in your training when you start working on walk in and recall around loose stock.

Ending your training session near the gate makes it easier for your dog to be successful when beginning to work loose livestock. Many dogs won't want to stop interacting with livestock, so reinforce them heavily for leaving the paddock.

Heel paddock perimeter

Work on a few steps of heeling and grow the number of steps until your path around the perimeter of the paddock causes the stock to move away as you approach. Your dog should be between you and the paddock fence. Can your dog maintain the heel once the sheep start moving? Work the heel until your dog can heel around the perimeter of the paddock. This may take several training sessions.

After successfully asking your dog for stationary behaviors and short recalls, start heeling around the paddock. You, your dog, and the stock should remain calm at all times. You are to the inside of the circle with your dog to the outside near the fence and your dog is always on-leash.

When heeling or walking with your dog around livestock you want your dog to be on the outside, away from the stock, with you closest to the stock. There will be times you want your dog to go between you and the stock, but the default position is you next to the stock and your dog next to the fence.

When your dog can heel and stop with you while on a loose leash, anywhere around the perimeter of the paddock and in both directions, they are ready to move on to doing some longer recalls.

Peek ahead: Watch Gold flank, in, and recall while on a long line and near loose sheep(Note I repeated several cues, bad trainer!): https://www.youtube.com/watch?v=MB-BwLsKnjY&ab_channel=PurpleBorderCollie

Round robin recalls revisited

Change from your leash to a long line and practice short recalls around the perimeter of the paddock. Extend the length of the recalls as your dog shows proficiency. Both heeling and recalling around loose livestock are very difficult for your dog, so be patient. It takes as long as it takes for your dog to be successful. If your dog struggles, shorten up the length of the recall.

Use very high-value reinforcers once you start working around loose livestock.

Be sure to take breaks while you are in the paddock with the stock. If you or your dog cannot relax while in the paddock, move out the gate and take your breaks there. Breaks give you and your dog time to relax and process all of the new stimuli you are experiencing, so don't skip them! I suggest you have a chair outside of the paddock to use while taking breaks.

Call it a day

When you have worked for 10 to 15 minutes or have progressed to this point, it is time to call it a day. Don't be concerned if getting to this point takes more than one session or several sessions over several days. This is your dog's first exposure to loose stock, and you are establishing the criteria of their behavior around moving livestock. This is a critical time, so allow yourself and your dog enough time and correct repetitions to gain fluency at this stage of training.

You and your dog have made a huge leap forward and you should take time to savor your success! Just getting your dog into a paddock with loose stock is a big step! To start the next training session, again follow your procedure for getting your dog into the paddock. Pick up where you left off in the last session and continue to work your heel and recalls until your dog is recalling a quarter of the way around the perimeter of the paddock in either direction and from any starting point. Your dog will always be on a leash or long line until they demonstrate they will take cues, call off of loose livestock, and refrain from lunging.

Add stops

Now add some stops to your recall. Start close to your dog and as soon as they start toward you, cue a stop. If they stop, then call them the rest of the way to you. Reinforce using treats if your dog is keyed up or play if your dog is apprehensive or sluggish. When you are confident that your dog will heel, recall, and stop around loose livestock you are ready to move on to flanking.

Stopping your dog is easiest and most natural for them when they have control of the livestock. Plan to give your stop cue when the stock is stationary and not when the livestock are moving around the paddock.

Start flanks

You will start working short flanks just as you did when the stock was penned, except you will start directly in front of your dog and use a 6-foot leash. Set up your cone circle around the perimeter of the paddock. The cones will indicate to you and your dog when they are flanking correctly. You will be inside of the cone circle and your dog on the outside.

The stock may knock over your cones, but if they are moving calmly, they most likely will walk around them. Don't sweat it if some cones get knocked over.

Work both flanks until you can stand still and your dog flanks the length of the leash. Always cue a stop before your dog gets to the end of the leash. As you work your flanks keep an eye on the stock so you know when they are likely to move, due to your dog flanking closer to them.

When your dog is flanking the length of your leash in both directions and stopping, start walking along with your dog so that they may flank farther but will still be quite close to you. Be ready for when your dog's flanking motion prompts the stock to move, as this is the time your dog is most likely to have their instincts kick in and speed up, chase after, or lunge at the stock.

Sir is staying behind the cones as he flanks while dragging a long line. If he were on a 6-foot leash this is about as far away from me as he could be and I would have asked him for a stop before he got to the end of the leash. Be sure to use a leash the first few times you work on flanks around loose livestock in case your dog lunges at them.

When your dog's flanking motion causes the stock to move, your dog will either keep flanking, keep flanking but speed up, stop, or dive toward the stock. If your dog keeps flanking, cue a stop, mark, reinforce, and have a party! If your dog stops, re-cue the flank and continue walking with your dog. If your dog tries to chase the stock, stop your dog with the leash, give your no reward marker, and calmly give your dog a time-out away from stock by leaving the paddock and moving to your time-out station. Wait 3 to 5 minutes and return to training. Your dog will quickly learn that their decision to chase stock ends the fun.

Remember if you find yourself using several time-outs in a training session, you need to go back a step or two in your training and add mass to your dog's trained behaviors. This may mean putting the stock back into a small pen or working completely away from stock for a while.

When your dog is flanking the length of the leash in each direction and stopping when cued, end the session for the day. Short successful sessions are better than one long session that ends in a train wreck. Be kind to your dog and yourself by celebrating small successes along the way. Once your dog is consistently flanking on the perimeter of the paddock, you can begin to fade out the cone circle.

Cutting corners

If you find your dog is cutting corners in your small paddock, once you have faded the cone circle, you may need to add back 4 or 5 cones per corner to delineate how deep you want your dog to go into the corner. (See picture below.) Shape this behavior until your dog is going into the corners readily and then start fading the cones. In a very small paddock, you need your dog to go quite deep into the corners, within a foot or two of the fence, to gain distance off of the stock. In a larger area, there will not be the need for your dog to go so deeply into the corners unless the stock is actually in the corner. Fade the corner cones as soon as possible.

Going calmly into and stopping in the corners takes a lot of self-control. If you find your dog rushing into corners, start stopping them in the corner and heavily reinforce them for staying there. Soon you should see your dog calm down. Your dog may be concerned that being stopped in a corner opposite the paddock gate will allow the stock to escape from the paddock through the gate. Once your dog learns that the livestock will not escape while they are in the opposite corner of the paddock, they will start to relax.

If the sheep stick in the corners, then walk with your dog into the corner and help them push the sheep out. You may need to be slightly ahead of your dog to encourage the sheep to move out of the corner, especially if your dog is uncomfortable in this tight situation. You should be between the sheep and your dog as you enter the corner. Use a crook or stock stick, if necessary, to encourage the sheep to move by tapping them lightly on the head or rump. It should not take much encouragement for your light sheep to be persuaded to move. After a few repetitions, your dog will gain confidence and the sheep will start to exit the corner as you and your dog approach.

If your dog is reticent to go into the corner with you, then you should push the sheep completely out of the corner before asking your dog to walk into the corner. Never pull or drag your dog into a corner or other area!

Extend flanks

Now your dog is ready to be on a long line so that they can flank farther. Work flanks all around the paddock perimeter and randomly add stops. Always cue a stop before your dog gets to the end of the long line. Because you are stopping your dog before they get to the end of the long line, they probably can only get an eighth to a quarter of the way around the stock.

Once you drop the long line you will extend the length of flanks until your dog can go all the way around the stock in both directions. Focus on stopping your dog primarily at balance, the point where they are in control of the livestock and where, if you asked your dog to walk in, they would bring the sheep to you.

Drop long line

This is a very scary step in the training but is the last major hurdle to overcome. Once you drop the long line, you no longer have complete control of your dog. Now you will find out if you have a solid foundation in place or need to go back and shore it up. Until now you have been holding the end of the leash or long line. For your dog to flank to the other side of the stock, you will now have to drop the long line and allow your dog to drag it. Slowly extend the distance your dog flanks until they are going all the way around the stock. Don't have your dog go more than one revolution. Usually stop your dog directly behind the stock at the point of balance. Balance is the key to herding, so have your dog go to balance often at this stage. It is also easiest to stop your dog at balance because this is the place where they have control of the livestock.

Balance will often not be directly across from you, even in a very small paddock. The gate into the paddock always creates a strong pull and affects the point of balance. Other factors such as nearby livestock may also affect balance.

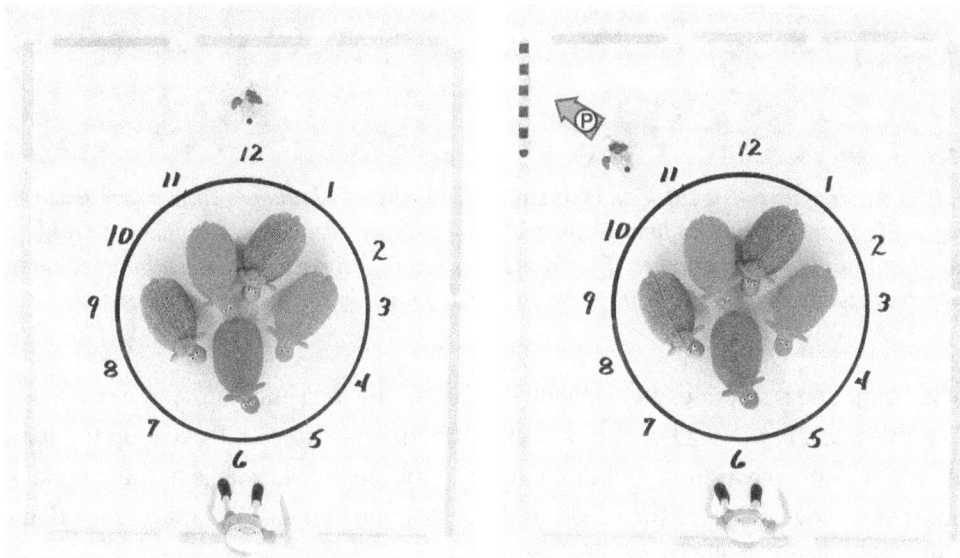

With no pull (LEFT) the point of balance is at 12 o'clock but when there is pull (P) to a gate or other livestock, then balance shifts around to offset the pull 10:30 (RIGHT).

Ping pong the length of flanks so that your dog has some easy, short flanks as well as longer flanks. When your dog is flanking freely in each direction, no matter the length of the flanks, end the session for the day!

Add the walk in and call off

At this point, you are ready to start working on the walk in to stock. Start just as you did when the stock was penned but make sure you always allow your dog to walk in until they get a reaction from the stock, such as moving away from your dog, turning their heads, backing up, or bunching together. You don't want your dog to get into the habit of stopping before they make contact with the livestock.

Sometimes you will want to stop your dog before they make contact with the stock. Ask your dog to walk in and then stop them. Once your dog takes the stop cue, give your *walk in* cue to reinforce the stop. Now let your dog continue in until they make contact with the stock. You know your dog has made contact with the stock when the stock shows some reaction to your dog. You will start out holding the long line but can drop it once your dog demonstrates that they will stop when cued and won't charge the livestock.

Gold is walking up to the stock and has stopped. Just by continuing to stare at the sheep, they begin to turn or give to him. In the picture (LEFT) the near ewe is stomping at Gold, but he continues to focus on her. If Gold kept his head stationary but flicked his eyes away from that ewe she would not have turned away as shown in the picture on the right.

When your dog is stopped after walking in, pick up the long line, turn and move away from the stock. Now recall your dog back off of the stock to you. Picking up the long line is just insurance against your dog lunging at the stock. You will keep the line slack unless your dog goes after the stock. In that case, you can easily manage your dog's unwanted behavior calmly and efficiently.

Start mini-fetches

You now have all of the major pieces in place to perform a mini-fetch. Set up a cone circle around the perimeter of your paddock, within about 3 to 6 feet of the fence. Flank your dog, who is dragging a long line, around to the other side of the stock using a flank cue, stop them at balance (which at this point is often but not always directly opposite you) and ask them in. If you have stopped your dog at the right place they will bring the stock toward you. You may need to adjust where you ask your dog to stop due to the pull in the paddock.

Sir starts his fetch opposite the sheep (his head is barely visible in the lower right corner of the picture.) I am standing just to the right of Sir and out of the frame.

Sir flanks around clockwise, staying outside the cone circle.

Sir turns in at balance and starts to bring the sheep to me. The pull is to the left because the gate into the paddock is there. Sir will have to flank a bit to his right, away to me, to bring the sheep straight to me.

If your dog is bringing the sheep to you and you are not against the fence, then walk backward and allow your dog to bring the stock to you as you back away. At this point, you will be using flank, stop, and walk in cues. Later, you will add a fetch cue that tells your dog to bring the stock back to you and at that point, you will allow your dog to decide where to turn in to bring the stock to you.

If you have taught your dog cues to set up for heeling, you may use those cues for setting up your dog at your feet for a fetch. You may also want to point your dog outward to encourage them to open up as they begin their fetch.

If you started the small fetches by standing between your dog and the stock, work your way to the perimeter, outside of the cone circle, turn to face the stock, and start your dog flanking from your feet. You and your dog will be side by side facing the livestock. Put your dog on your right side to flank *away to me* and on your left to go *come bye*. You will not be working off-balance flanks until you move into a larger area. **Off-balance flanks** are flanks where your dog goes past the point of balance and flanks back toward you. At this point, you want to concentrate on your dog finding balance. Too much off-balance flanking early in training around stock, especially loose stock, can interfere with your dog going to balance.

Easy/hurry and out/close

Now you are ready to transition your flank modifier cues to loose stock. Refer back to the step-by-step directions in Chapter 4. This exercise is exactly like the training from the previous chapter, except now your dog is dragging the long line and the livestock is loose. Concentrate on the behavior from each pair of modifier cues that your dog finds more difficult. If your dog struggles with speeding, up concentrate on hurry. If they struggle with moving away from livestock, concentrate on the out.

Work on only one set of modifiers per day to begin, either easy/hurry or out/close. Mixing up too many modifiers too quickly can be very confusing for your dog.

Remove long line

At this point your dog is flanking both directions, walking in, and recalling off of loose livestock, as well as stopping. Your dog has also done some mini-fetches. When you are confident your dog will not charge or chase the stock, you are ready to remove the long line! Since your dog has been dragging the long line, this should not be a huge step for them.

Success!

You now have your dog herding! Congratulations!

Getting to this point will take many training sessions over weeks or even months. Take as much time as needed for your dog to gain fluency and confidence. You are building your and your dog's foundation for herding success.

Continue to work in the smaller area many times to gain fluency. Once your dog is working loose stock confidently in the small paddock, you are ready to move to a bigger area. In a larger paddock, you will graduate to working on off-balance flanks. The livestock will remain loose when you transition to the larger area, but your dog will be back to dragging a long line as an emergency brake. Do you have enough confidence in yourself and your dog to take the next step?

Confidence is an important part of herding. Letting go of the long line, moving to a larger paddock, training move advanced herding skills, running your dog at a trial, or using them for chores on a farm or ranch, all require that you have confidence in yourself and your dog. Confidence is only achieved by thinking, planning, training, and assessing each step of your training along the way.

CHAPTER 6

Loose stock in large area 1

Moving into a larger paddock opens up the world of herding to you and your dog! You are going to see your dog do some amazing things and be enthralled as your dog shows you just how well they can control stock by combining their instinct and athleticism. Watching a good herding dog work livestock can be addictive.

Along with amazing possibilities, comes the potential for epic failure. As you move into the larger area you will no longer have the control over your dog that you have had up to this point. So far, you have been working fairly close to your dog and could immediately step in to interrupt any chasing or unnecessary biting. Soon your dog will be working at a fair distance from you and although they will still be dragging a light long line, they will have much more latitude to behave erratically.

My larger paddock is about 60 feet wide by 150 feet long. Use an area roughly that size for the exercises in this chapter, but not too much bigger. If necessary, set up panels to reduce the dimensions of an area that is too large. You don't want your dog working too far away from you at this point in their training.

The careful and solid foundation you have laid over the past months will be tested as your dog works faster and farther away from you. Fortunately, you have learned a lot about how your dog reacts to stock. You should now have a good feel for when to give your dog more freedom and when to reel them in a bit. When in doubt, always break things down and ask for close, slow behaviors you are confident your dog can perform, rather than taking a flyer just to see what happens.

Educate yourself about pull

The first exercise in the larger area is designed to show you how the livestock is going to pull in this paddock, by having you move the livestock *without* your dog. Where the livestock wants to go, depends on the pull in the paddock. Although you may have noted the pull toward the gate in the small area, the stock did not have much room to move toward that pull. In the larger area, the pull will probably be much stronger and more evident. Your dog, if they have herding instinct, will read the pull naturally, but to set your dog up for success, you need to know where the stock will pull and how hard the pull is.

Usually, the pull is toward the gate the stock used to enter the paddock. There may also be a strong pull toward any similar livestock that your stock can see, hear, or smell. Plus, your stock may pull away from or avoid any objects, animals, or areas that they find threatening.

The sheep in the foreground are pulled toward the flock of sheep in the adjoining pasture, just as the sheep in the far pasture are pulled toward those in the foreground.

 *The pull is toward safety and away from danger. There is safety in numbers so animals are strongly pulled toward other animals.*

To ascertain pull in the new paddock, leave your dog at home. Move your livestock into the paddock; they will show you where they are comfortable in the paddock. Walk to the far end of the paddock, away from the gate through which the stock entered. Watch where the stock settles or comes to rest. The stock will probably keep an eye on you since you are the only predator in sight. Depending on how familiar and comfortable your stock is with you, they may choose to ignore you. If your stock has been dry lotted, kept in a small area, and fed hay, and they now have access to grass in the paddock, they may pay little attention to you as they begin to graze.

Note where the stock settles and then begin to step toward them to move them around. Do they pull or move toward a gate, fence, corner, or certain area of the paddock? When you try to drive them from one end of the paddock to the other, do they rush in some directions and resist moving in others? When you drive the livestock, do they stay together or tend to drift apart? When driving them are you always directly behind them or do you have to stay off to one side to keep them moving in the desired direction?

To drive the sheep into the corner near the road I had to stay well off to the left of them because the pull is toward the gate into the paddock, which is on the left side of the picture. If I had moved to my right, directly behind the sheep, they would have run across in front of me to get to the gateway.

While moving the stock without your dog, you are collecting important information that tells you where your dog will need to be to control the livestock, where the pull is, and how much pressure your dog will have to apply to move the stock. How quickly the stock return to their preferred area of the paddock also tells you how strong the pull in the paddock is.

Pull is an intriguing concept and understanding it is vital to herding success!

Let's look at how pull might change the behavior of stock. When you flank your dog *come bye* at one place in the paddock, the stock may remain stationary, but when you flank them *away to me* at that same place, the stock may run off because your dog has moved from blocking the stock's escape to enabling it.

The key is knowing which direction the pull is drawing your livestock and using that information to your advantage. Figuring out the pull will probably take some trial and error. If you can determine where your stock wants to settle, without pressure from you or your dog, that area is most likely where your stock will want to pull toward.

Experience will be your best teacher as to how to use pull to your advantage. If your dog has little herding instinct, you will want to learn all you can about pull. When your dog does not read and react to the pull, you will have to take on the responsibility of positioning your dog to counteract the effect of the pull.

Heeling and recalls

Get your dog and start doing some on-leash heeling around the livestock in this larger area. If your dog has herding instinct, you may see it displayed as reluctance to maintain the heel when you and your dog walk from where you are blocking the stock's escape to where you are allowing their escape. Most dogs are reluctant to allow the livestock to escape and will want to stay between the stock and the pull or the escape route. This reluctance is a double-edged sword. On one hand, it means your dog is reading the stock and has lots of instinct, while on the other hand, it means you will have to have a lot of mass on your taught behaviors to overcome your dog's instinctive behavior to control stock.

Another test of your dog's instinct is for you, with your dog heeling beside you, to push the stock to the opposite side of the paddock from where they naturally settle. Then both you and your dog will heel off to the side and allow the stock to trot or run back to where they feel safe. If your dog stands calmly and watches the stock leave, they are demonstrating either very little herding instinct, since they are losing control of the stock and allowing it to escape, or great self-control. If your dog tries to shift over to block the stock's escape, whines, drops into a down, or bounces, they are likely demonstrating strong herding instinct to control stock and prevent its escape.

Drag long line

When moving from the smaller to the larger paddock, your dog should drag a light long line as they begin working on flanks and short fetches, especially when your stock is not penned. The long line serves two purposes, to remind your dog that you are nearby and to make it easy and efficient for you to interrupt any unwanted behavior your dog displays. Although the long line is just an emergency brake, its presence when your dog is at the far end of the field will bolster your confidence by giving you the feeling of having some control of the situation.

Work close

As you start working in the large area, set things up so that your dog is working the same distance or less from their stock as they did in the small area. Don't start out asking your dog to flank 50 feet from the stock when the farthest they have been from the livestock in the small paddock is 20 feet. You will soon stretch out your flanks and work on small fetches, but initially, you want the setup to be the same as in the smaller area, except now you are working in the larger paddock.

To begin, you will set up in the section of the paddock where the livestock wants to settle. This may be near a fence, gate, or in a corner. All of these directions are formulated with one goal in mind, to set your dog up for success! The more you know about how your dog and livestock will respond in this new paddock, the more likely you are to have a smooth and uneventful transition.

Corner flanking

In the larger area, you will start by working on flanking. Be sure to have your crook or stock stick available as you transition to the larger paddock. If your livestock settles in a corner, that is a good place to start. If your stock doesn't settle in a corner or you feel you need an intermediate step between the small paddock and having your dog drag a long line on loose sheep in the larger area, then you will want to initially set up a small pen in a corner.

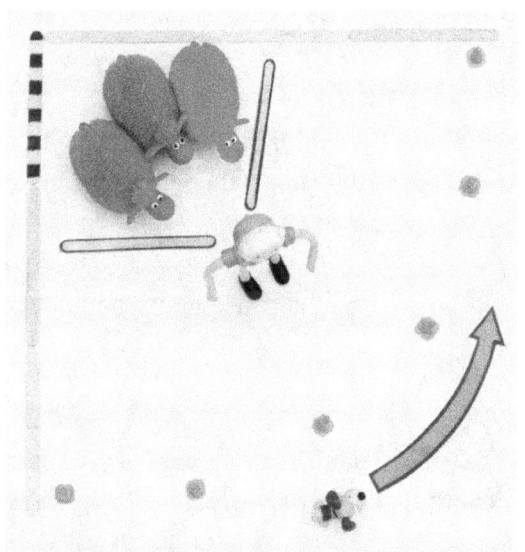

The advantage of working in a corner is that it is relatively easy for you to keep the stock stationary and control your dog's access to it while your dog generalizes the lessons they learned in the small paddock to this paddock. Set up your quarter cone circle so that your dog will be flanking the same distance they were flanking off of the stock when in the small paddock.

The sheep are penned in a corner of the large paddock. This image shows the pen next to the gate, which is indicated by the dashed line, but any corner will work. The setup is the same as in the small paddock, the quarter cone circle is the same distance from the penned sheep as in the small paddock.

Move close to the stock, face your dog, and flank them back and forth along the quarter cone circle. Throw in random stops and then have your dog continue flanking in the same direction. At other times have them flank back the way they came after the stop. If your dog is doing well, step out along the cone circle, turn to face the stock, and flank your dog back and forth behind you. This should be easy for your dog. Once they are taking your cues reliably, you can move on to fence line flanking.

Fence line flanking

If your stock wants to settle along a fence, you can set up a half cone circle around them. Otherwise, you need to set up a pen along the fence and then add your cone circle. Do random flanks, stops, and changes of flank direction. Again, you will start near the stock, facing your dog but will quickly move out and stand along the cone circle facing the livestock, so that your dog is flanking behind you and then from your side.

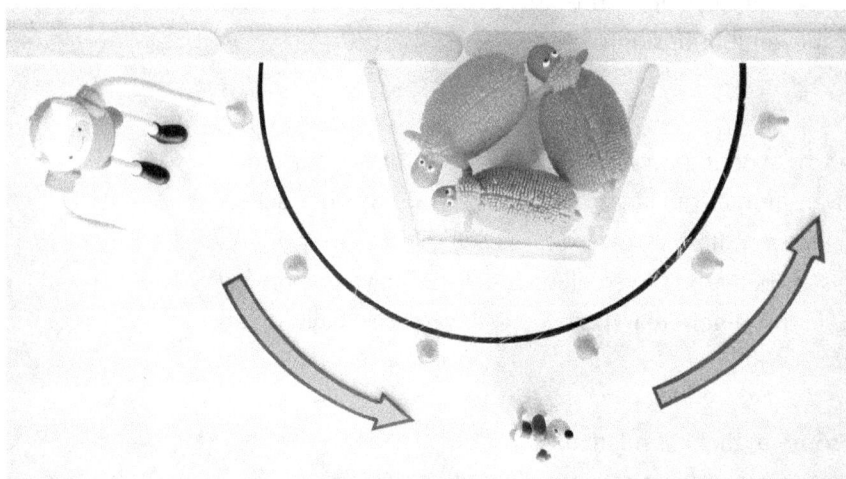

It is very difficult to get stock to settle and stay at one place along a fence line so plan to use a small pen to keep your sheep where you want them to stay.

For the last step, move to one end of the cone circle, next to the fence, and send your dog from beside you, on a flank to the fence on the other side, a half-circle flank. Stop your dog at the opposite fence. This will soon become a mini-fetch, once you allow your dog to walk into the stock and bring them to you after stopping. See below, for growing this exercise into a fetch.

The setup for the mini-fetch is you standing next to the fence with your dog standing next to you. Your dog will flank out away from you and around to the opposite side of the stock, staying outside of the half cone circle.

The fetch is built starting very close to the livestock. Once your dog understands the basics of fetching, flanking, and driving to you, you can easily grow the length of your outrun. The main advantage of short half circle flanks is that you can quickly do a lot of repetitions which, because these behaviors are very inherently reinforcing for your dog, should greatly increase mass on the behaviors.

Adapting exercises

At this point, you no longer need to use a pen for your stock. Later in your training, if you feel it would be helpful, you can *always* set up a pen, move back to your smaller paddock, or move away from livestock and back to your yard or front room. From here on, you should adjust the training exercises to suit you, your dog, and your livestock.

Every paddock, set of stock, weather condition, time of day, handler, dog, and scenario brings different and unique influences to the exercise. Herding is fluid, not static, and it is impossible to exactly replicate a trial. Each time your dog interacts with the livestock, you, your dog, and the stock learn and change subtly, so that your next interaction is altered in some way.

Thus, there is no way I can tell you every step to take or every move to make from this point onward. If your training is not progressing as outlined, you need to stop, think, plan, and move forward. Work with your dog as an individual and adjust as necessary.

The questions you will have to wrestle with may include:
- What is the point of the exercise?
- Why is it working or not working?
- How can I adapt it to suit my situation?
- How can I make it easier for my dog?
- Where is the pull?
- Where do I need to position my dog?
- Do I need to get help?

Be sure to review your video, especially when your training is not going well. You may be able to pinpoint what needs to change when you watch your training as an observer, instead of while you are involved as a participant.

The previous step-by-step training plans were to help you get started and offer guidance along the way. You will now employ the positive reinforcement principles and scientific laws of learning from the first sections of *Positive Herding 101* to complete your dog's training. Exercises will still be provided, but you should change or adapt them as much and as often as necessary. Remember, putting safety first, maintaining confidence second, and keeping training fun, are fundamental to positive herding success.

Short fetch setup

Once your dog can flank to the other side of the livestock from your feet, starting next to you, you are ready to start short fetches. At this point, your stock can no longer be penned, since you will be asking your dog to walk in and bring them to you. Now is when the time you spent exploring the pull in your paddock will pay off.

If your stock is happy settling along the fence, you are golden. Set up a half cone circle as you did for the last exercise, but without a pen, flank your dog to the other side of the stock from your feet, stop your dog, and then ask them in. When the stock gets close to you, within 3 to 10 feet, stop your dog, mark, and go around the stock to your dog, and reinforce. If your dog has a lot of herding instinct, the fetch will be reinforcement enough, no other reinforcement will be necessary. Then call your dog off away from the stock and have a party! Your dog has just completed their first fetch!

If your dog is a sideways-moving dog, feel free to omit the stop on top and instead allow or ask your dog in as soon as they flank behind the stock. If any dog starts acting sticky on top, not wanting to immediately walk in, temporarily eliminate the stop on top before the lift.

Once your dog is consistently staying outside of the half cone circle when fetching, you can start to fade the cones until they are completely gone. Be sure to pick out a clump of grass, a bare spot, or some other point of reference that you can use to make sure your dog is maintaining their distance from the stock as they flank around behind them. Many dogs will start to slice their flanks, move closer to the stock as they flank, once the cones are removed.

If the stock wants to settle in a corner, you have several ways to set up this exercise.
- If your dog is *confident* around the stock, you can set up the half cone circle along one fence such that it extends almost to the corner fence. Leave just enough room, about 3 feet, between the cone circle and the fence for your dog to flank into the corner behind the stock.
- If your dog is *not confident* around the stock, you can take your dog with you into the corner and see where the stock settle. Remember that although the stock readily moved out of the corner when you and your dog arrived, the pull will most likely be back into that corner. Leave your dog in the corner and set up your half cone circle from 3 feet away from the fence at your back and around to the other side of the stock. Go back to and send your dog around the stock.
- Alternately, if your dog is *not confident* around the stock you can have a helper stand, or tie another dog, in the corner to push the stock out of that corner. This will change the pull in the paddock because you have added another dynamic to

the situation. (If you do use a dog you need to use one that your dog is familiar with, gets along with, and that will remain calm, quiet, and stationary.) In this case, determine where to position your helper or second dog to get the stock to settle along a fence. Once you have determined where the stock settle you can set up your half cone circle from the closest point you can stand with your dog and not have the stock move.

Shaping going into a corner

In the following sequence, I am shaping Sir to flank into a corner where he is reluctant to go. There is a lot of pressure in the tight corner for him to overcome. The pressure is from the nearby gate and the presence of the stock. There is a strong pull to the gate, as an escape route, and the rams are very intimidating, as they are heavy and difficult to move. Penning the rams controls them and protects my dog from them, while Sir gains enough confidence to go into the corner.

This sequence is basic shaping. I start standing close to the corner to give Sir the confidence to flank into the tight corner.

You can just see Sir behind the pen, beyond the cones, in the corner. I reinforced with treats that were fed when Sir was in this exact position.

Now I have moved about a yard away from my original starting position but Sir's starting position remained unchanged.

I have now moved to the side of the pen farthest from the corner but Sir is still starting at the same place.

LEFT: *Over time I have worked my way farther from the corner and have slowly shaped Sir's starting position back toward the fence behind me.*

BELOW LEFT: *The final stage was for me to work my position back toward Sir until we were standing side by side, my goal starting position for both of us! (Note the long line in the picture.)*

Once Sir could flank into the corner from my feet, I faded the cones and released the rams from the pen. Sir was then able to fetch the rams out of the corner. If he had struggled, I would have sent him from the same place but I would have moved closer to the corner as an intermediate step.

Fence line fetches

Once you have fetched the stock to you, reset the entire scenario and send your dog again from the same starting point. Have your dog do another fetch, which includes: flanking, while staying outside the cones, stopping, walking in, and stopping again. Repeat once more, a third time, and then move your starting point to the opposite side of the stock. If you started out sending your dog *come bye* around behind the livestock, you will now be sending them *away to me*.

Remember that if your dog gets stuck on top, does not want to walk into the stock, then skip the stop when your dog gets to the fence and just ask them in.

As you have probably realized, you may have to change your setup to get your stock to settle along a fence such that you can now send your dog in the opposite direction. You may need to switch to a different fence line or corner. Be creative! Once you have your stock settled, send your dog to the other side of the stock, stop your dog, and then ask them in. Again, when the stock gets close to you, within 3 to 10 feet, stop your dog, mark, and go around the stock to your dog, and reinforce. Your dog has now fetched in both directions! Reset the exercise and repeat twice more. *Celebrate!*

After your dog has fetched both directions is a great time to stop for the day. The next time you train, have your dog do a few fetches with cones and then start fading the cones out of the picture. Eventually, all of the cones will be removed and your dog will be doing fetches in both directions.

In this sequence, I have removed the cones and am sending Sir from my feet on a short fetch.

Sir starts next to me and begins to flank in an arc around the sheep. (Note Sir is dragging a long line.)

At this point, Sir is continuing to flank until he arrives behind the sheep.

Sir is now behind the sheep and has stopped at balance.

Sir then walks in and brings the sheep directly to me.

At this point, your dog may have only completed 6 fetches but both you and your dog have had to process a lot of new information about pull, settling stock, setting up an exercise, applying pressure to stock, and performing herding behaviors around moving livestock. It does get easier from here!

Feel free to break these exercises down and spread them out over several days. You can work on corner flanks one day, fence line fetches another, and flanking into corners yet another day.

In the next training session, you will work on fence line fetches again, but you will know where to position yourself and your dog, place the half cones circles if needed, and where the stock should settle – hopefully, the same place as previously. The next session should go more smoothly, but don't be surprised if the stock change where they want to settle. Stock have minds of their own and are not shy about showing you what they think!

Corners are your friend

It is time to have your dog learn to get stock out of a corner. Corners are great for teaching your dog to be calm, confident, and self-controlled as they learn:
- How to get stock out of a corner.
- How to get stock off of a fence.
- How to deal with stock facing them.

Be sure to initially go into the corner with your dog to help them gain skill and confidence working in tight places. You always want your dog to be successful, so your presence at your dog's side is important. These essential lessons, about how to deal with stock in corners, will transfer to all close livestock work.

Shaping corner fetches

This builds on the "Shaping going into a corner" exercise above. If your dog is confident, you may already be fetching livestock out of a corner; if not, it is time to bolster your dog's courage. Settle your stock in a corner, but do not pen them. Put your dog on a 3-foot leash and heel with your dog along one fence toward the corner, keeping your dog to the outside of the stock and next to the fence while you stay to the inside.

As you and your dog heel into the corner the stock will move out of it. Cue a stop, mark, and reinforce when you reach the corner. Use a lot of high-value reinforcement! You want your dog to think that corners are the best place in the paddock, so don't be stingy with your super high-value reinforcement. Now, heel your dog 10 to 15 feet out of the corner, go as far as it takes to get the stock to drift back into the corner but no farther. Repeat heeling your dog into the corner 10 times.

*Your dog **must** win when facing bold livestock! If the sheep are reticent to move out of the corner as you and your dog enter, then you need to push them out. If any animal challenges your dog, especially at this point, you need to step in and force the challenger to retreat by any means necessary, such as waving an arm or hat, stomping, kicking, or smacking them with a stock stick or crook.*

Now you are going to change from heeling with your dog into the corner to recalling your dog to you while you are in the corner. Put your dog on a long line and hold the line. If you had to move 10 feet out of the corner to get the stock to drift back into it, then leave your dog there, walk back into the corner with the sheep and call your dog to you. Mark and heavily reinforce!

If your dog will not come into the corner, move closer to your dog before calling them and then build distance. Slowly step closer to the corner until your dog is coming into the corner to you. Work this exercise until your dog will immediately recall to you, while you are in the corner. Repeat the recall 10 times, with your dog starting as far away as necessary to get the livestock to drift back into the corner and your dog ending next to you in the corner. Always hold on to the long line.

Reset your dog to the same starting point, but now you move halfway between your dog and the stock, while still holding the long line. Ask your dog to flank along the fence and into the corner. As your dog flanks, turn and walk in an arc in the direction your dog is flanking until your dog reaches the corner. Then stop your dog, mark, and reinforce! Repeat but fade the number of steps you walk until you can stand still and your dog will readily flank into the corner.

Shaping corner fetches is no different than any other shaping. Break the behavior down into small slices to set your dog up for success. If your dog struggles, break the exercise down even further.

At this point, you are ready for your dog to push the stock out of the corner. Flank your dog in to the corner, stop your dog, step over to them, and ask them in. Walk with your dog until the stock takes a step or two away from the corner. Stop, mark, and reinforce. Build up how far you and your dog are pushing the stock by ping-ponging the distance. If you are using a square or rectangular paddock, work this over several sessions and several days, until you and your dog are pushing the stock from one corner, along the fence, and to the far corner.

The last step is for you to flank your dog in to the corner and then ask them to *walk in* while you stay off to the side and stationary. When you are no longer going into the corner with your dog, you will be walking parallel to them. Fade your movement as soon as possible and let your dog push the stock. Once your dog can flank into the corner and drive the stock out, they are ready to start doing corner fetches.

Corner fetches
Set up a half cone circle that extends almost into the corner. Although your dog will start on the fence in this instance, you may want to position yourself partway around the circle, between your dog and the stock to start. As your dog is successful, work your way back to the fence, such that you end up sending your dog from your feet. You are repeating the above sequence, when the stock was in a pen near the corner, except now the stock is free. You are again shaping your dog to go into the pressure from the stock in the corner.

At this point, you are still sending your dog with a flank cue rather than a fetch cue. Because you are using a flank cue, you want to tell your dog where to stop behind the sheep and when to walk in. Later, you will switch to a fetch cue which tells your dog to go around the sheep and bring them to you. Your dog is then free to turn in and walk into the stock without waiting for a stop or walk in cue.

When given a flank cue, your dog should continue flanking until given another cue.

Of course, you need to work corner fetches in both directions, *come bye* and *away to me*. Most likely you will have to repeat the entire process of shaping your dog to go into the corner when you switch to sending your dog in the opposite direction.

Start as you did for the first direction and again train each step to proficiency. Training this side may go faster or it may take longer. Your dog will show you how fast you can move forward. Be patient! You want this to be a big win for your dog and to bolster their confidence. Use as much time and as many sessions as it takes to grow your dog's confidence. Always do everything in your power to grow and protect your dog's confidence. A herding dog without confidence is not a herding dog at all.

Lastly, you want to fade the cones out of the scenario and send your dog into the corner to fetch the livestock. The first few fetches, recalls, flanks, etc. at each stage of development will most likely not be perfect! See what you have, what needs to change, and develop a plan to help your dog be successful at each new step along the way. Don't move on to the next step until your dog is meeting all your criteria for the current step, and also don't expect perfection as you move forward to more difficult steps. Stay at each step as long as necessary for your dog to be competent and confident at that step.

This is Qwest's first corner fetch with no cones to guide him in the large area. It is far from perfect but a good start. https://www.youtube.com/watch?v=l9EZ8tWYPHM&ab_channel=PurpleBorderCollie

Once I get to this point, I am using very little external reinforcement, treats or tugs. Now the main reinforcers are working of stock and herding cues. I still use treats, but they are used primarily to lower my dog's level of arousal. I sometimes use a box clicker in the paddocks because the click tells my dog exactly when they are correct. It is also very salient and stands out from other noises in this environment.

In the next chapter, you will continue working in the large paddock to build your dog's skills in handling livestock. The next order of business will be learning to identify and deal with your dog slicing in as they flank. Not sure what slicing in is?

Read on!

CHAPTER 7

Loose stock in large area 2

After your dog is competently performing fence line and corner fetches, they are ready to move on to short fetches without a fence as a barrier. Your dog has already been doing short outruns and lifts. The flank around the stock was the **outrun** and the stock beginning to move away from your dog was the **lift**.

You will now be sending your dog a short distance, approximately as far as you have usually been sending them around stock to this point, but you will no longer be using a half cone circle. If you have not already faded the cones out of your fence line fetch training, you need to do that before moving forward. Fade the half cone circle by slowly removing cones from the cone circle as your dog shows continued proficiency. Eventually, the cone circle will be completely removed. Your dog will continue to flank around behind the stock, stop or pause, and then walk in and fetch the stock to you, with no cones present.

If you find your dog slicing in, coming in extremely close, as they flank around the stock once you remove the cones, you may need to jump ahead to the next chapter and work on transitioning the out to loose livestock before you move forward with fetching.

Many dogs **slice** their flanks, come in toward the stock as they flank around them. Slicing in is also called **winding in** as the dog moves closer and closer to the livestock as they flank around them, instead of maintaining the same distance as they flank.

LEFT TO RIGHT: *On this square away flank, Sir maintains his distance from the stock as he starts his flank.*

In this sequence, Sir slices his come bye flank. Instead of shifting his weight backward, he steps forward toward the stock.

Sir has taken one step toward the sheep in the pen as he starts his flank.

Note how much closer Sir is to the pen in this picture as compared to his starting point.

Slicing in can be hard to catch because it usually starts quite mildly with your dog coming in only a few feet or a yard or two over a significant distance. If not noticed, eventually your dog will slice in more and more until it becomes a major problem. Some dogs slice in when flanking one direction but not the other, or they may slice in only when over-aroused or worried that the stock is escaping.

To tell if your dog is slicing in, notice the distance from the stock when your dog starts to flank and compare it to the distance from the livestock when you ask your dog to stop flanking. If your dog is 20 feet from the stock at 3 o'clock they should not be 14 feet from the stock when they arrive at 9 o'clock.

Over time, you will notice when your dog is slicing their flanks because the stock will move off of the pressure your dog puts on them as your dog moves closer to the stock while flanking. Generally, the stock should not move away from your dog while your dog is flanking.

To correct slicing, you can give an *out* (discussed in the next chapter), or you can stop your dog, call them back to their starting point, and start again. Young, inexperienced dogs tend to want to flank tight, so your best bet may be to use an out cue. Older or more experienced dogs usually respond to having to re-run the flank a time or two.

Send the dog and as soon as you realize they are slicing in, give your no reward marker, stop your dog, pause for 10 seconds, and then recall your dog to their starting point. Repeat a few times to see if your dog will self-correct and open up as they flank. If they do not self-correct, you will have to use an out cue to get them to maintain their distance from the stock while they flank.

Patterns

Every time you set your dog up for a fetch, you should follow the same steps which sets up a pattern for your dog. Patterns are extremely helpful in herding as they provide a consistent framework for both you and your dog in different locations and situations.

The basic pattern for the fetch is:
1. Determine the direction of the pull.
2. Decide which side to send your dog. (Usually, you should send your dog *into* the pull unless there is an obstacle or other reason for not sending that direction. Sending into the pull means whichever direction the stock wants to head, right or left, you send your dog to that side of the stock. If the stock wants to move to your left toward a gate or other draw, then you send your dog to the left or *come bye*. If you send your dog away from the pull, the stock will usually head toward the draw long before your dog can get around behind them.)

3. Have your dog heel to the starting position on the side you intend to send them or call them to that side.
4. Position your dog beside you, next to your legs, facing slightly outward in the direction you will be sending them.
5. Pause so that your dog does not leave until you give your cue.
6. Cue your dog to fetch.

Call your dog to the side you want to send them from, preferably sending them into the pull.

Set your dog up next to you, facing slightly outward.

Send your dog!

The only change in this pattern will be which side your dog heels on or gets called to and thus which side they get set up on. By following the same steps every time, this pattern will become a habit for your dog. When you lengthen the outrun, go to a new paddock, work different stock, or add the excitement of competing at a trial, this pattern will indicate to your dog that they will be performing the same chain of behaviors in this new situation. This pattern helps your dog to quickly generalize the fetch to new situations and environments.

*There is a difference between teaching your dog a fetch setup pattern, a good thing, and making your dog mechanical, a bad thing. A **pattern** is a series of steps that tell your dog what to anticipate. A mechanical dog is a dog that does not think for themselves and instead waits to be told every move to make.*

Dogs love patterns because they provide comfort, like old habits. But like habits, not all patterns are good. Your dog will discern patterns that you have no idea you are teaching. Sometimes you may need to watch your video or have a friend watch you to figure out what behavior your dog is cueing on. Your dog may be cueing off of a physical signal that you don't realize you are giving. Visual cues are much more salient to dogs than verbal cues and dogs learn patterns from physical and verbal cues that we don't even realize we are using.

Balance

Up to this point, you have usually positioned your dog for the lift by stopping them behind the stock and then asking them in. Since you will no longer be using a fence as a barrier for the fetch you will need to transition from telling your dog where to stop and walk in to allowing them to find balance.

Balance is the point where your dog turns into and applies pressure to the stock so that they will move straight to you. The point of balance depends on the pull the stock feels. During the fetch exercises, you have most likely come to appreciate and understand a great deal more about pull. It should make sense to you that often the point of balance will not be directly across the stock from where you are positioned. How easy it is to stop your dog at a certain point also depends a lot on balance.

It is easiest to stop your dog if they are at balance because they have control of the livestock. If your dog struggles with stopping initially, ask for stops only when they are at balance. Dogs also call off of stock most readily when they are at balance and you are directly between your dog and the stock.

Every time you stop your dog when your dog is not on balance, your dog loses control of the stock. If the stock is moving when you stop your dog, your dog may also lose contact with or influence over the stock.

Again, you will transition through several stages to move your dog from always cueing them when and where to stop and walk in, to allowing them to find balance, turn in, and bring the stock to you at a nice pace.

Steps for a basic outrun, lift, and fetch

1. Have your dog drag a long line.
2. Settle your stock in the middle of the paddock or near a fence, but not in a corner.
3. Set your dog up to go on the side that will send them into the pull. (Remember that if you send your dog away from the pull, the stock will usually be long gone, trying to escape, before your dog gets a chance to get around behind them.)
4. Pause for a moment.
5. Send your dog with a flank cue. (If your dog crosses over, goes in between you and the stock, immediately use your no reward marker, stop them, pause for 10 seconds, call them back, and reset. **Never** let your dog finish a fetch if they cross over in front of you on the outrun, either right in front of you or out near the livestock.)
6. Just before your dog gets to where you think balance is, stop your dog. (If your dog is a sideways-moving dog you will omit the stop and just cue the *walk in*.)
7. Ask your dog to *walk in*.
8. If the stock head in any direction other than toward you, flank your dog to get them **back on line,** in position to bring the stock directly to you, and then ask your dog in again.
9. When the stock gets close to you, about 10 feet away, stop your dog.

Once your dog is stopped you can go around the stock and call your dog off the stock to you. If the stock settle in place, then walk a short distance away and do another fetch. If the stock goes back to where they started, then set up and repeat the fetch.

Practice an outrun at the end of every training session, no matter what you are working on during the session. You always want to keep your dog seeking balance and using their herding instincts.

Sir overran the point of balance on this fetch and sends the sheep running off line and toward the gate and the pull.

Now Sir is flanking back to catch the sheep and bring them back on line.

The sheep are on line and Sir is bringing them directly to me. Note that because the pull is to my left Sir seems to be in the wrong place, but as long as the sheep come directly to me, he is correct.

Do a few more fetches, spending no more than 10 to 15 minutes working, and call it a day. After the first day, you can start taking a break and then work another 10 to 15 minute session, but limit yourself to only one session the first time you work this exercise.

If your dog struggles with flanking while walking in, work on transitions; walk in to flank, flank to walk in, and flank to flank as found in Chapter 9.

As soon as your dog is comfortable fetching in one direction, you need to start changing things up. If you have not been able to fetch using both flanks in this session, figure out a setup so that you can fetch going the other direction. You will still be telling your dog where to stop.

Some people think slingshotting their dog around behind them encourages their dog to open up on the outrun. Don't do it! Instead, depend on turning your dog slightly out to the side when setting up your cones, and lastly your out cue.

When people **slingshot** an outrun they set their dog up behind them and on the opposite side from the direction they want the dog to go. They bring the dog behind them as they start the outrun. The thinking is that since the dog has to flank behind them to start the outrun, staying open or wide as it flanks, that the dog will continue this trajectory and stay wider on the outrun once it gets beyond them. This maneuver is a crutch that usually isn't effective and also sets up a bad pattern for the future. If you have trouble with your dog running too tight on their outrun, you need to address that problem rather than settling for a temporary, defective fix.

Fetch cue

As soon as your dog is fetching to both sides, *come bye* and *away*, change from sending your dog with a flank cue to your fetch cue. I use *shush* to cue fetch no matter which side my dog is set up to go. The setup at my side is the physical cue that tells my dog which way they are to run. You can use a different cue or use two cues, one for each side, but drop the use of your flank cue at this point because you now want your dog to automatically turn in on the stock at balance and bring them to you.

The fetch cue tells your dog to get around the stock, turn in at balance, and bring the stock to you. The flank cue tells them to flank and keep flanking until you give them another cue. If your dog does not take off when you give your new fetch cue, just give the new cue, pause a beat, and then add the flank cue. In no time your dog will be taking off when they hear their new fetch cue. Drop the flank cue as soon as possible.

It is normal for your dog to be a bit confused when you change to using a fetch cue. You need to remember that shush = fetch and a flank cue = keep on flanking until cued to do a different behavior. Do not allow your dog to turn into the stock on top, at balance, if you have flanked rather than shushed them, cued a fetch!

If you have to add the flank cue after the fetch cue, then tell your dog where to stop and turn in. As soon as they take off on the fetch cue, drop telling them where to stop and turn in. If your dog goes past balance, stop them immediately and ask them in. Be ready to give a stop as your dog may still think they are to continue flanking when given a fetch cue.

Once your dog is going on your fetch cue, drop the stop cue at balance on top. If your dog goes on by balance, stop them and ask them in. If they stop at balance, quickly cue walk in! Yay! If they turn in at balance without stopping and bring the stock to you, all the better! Yay, yay!

I always carry a box clicker at this point in transitioning my dog to going to balance and turning in without a stop or in cue. I watch closely and the moment my dog turns in, I click to make it clear that the turn in was the correct behavior. Allowing my dog to bring the stock to me is the reinforcement for the mark.

You are transitioning your dog from waiting for your walk in cue, to taking the initiative to bring the stock to you without a verbal cue. It will take each dog a different number of trials to figure out that they now have the freedom to make this decision for themselves. If they have a lot of herding instinct, they will figure it out quickly. If they have very little instinct you will probably always have to tell your dog when to turn in. If your dog is not pushy, you can transition from cueing a stop, to cueing walk in instead. As noted previously, if your dog is a sideways-moving dog, you will start out asking for the walk in and skip using the stop.

Wearing

If your dog doesn't seem to be getting the idea of turning in at balance after several days of using your fetch cue but shows a lot of other herding instinct, you may need to stop fetching and do some wearing to help your dog find balance.

Wearing has two meanings:
1. When your dog moves laterally or side to side behind stock to keep it moving.
2. When your dog holds stock to you. When your dog drives a large flock or herd, they have to wear back and forth behind the group to keep the stock together and moving in the same direction. By combining wearing with fetching, walking backward, and having your dog hold the sheep to you, you can stimulate your dog's instinctual balance response.

Although you want your dog to wear when handling large flocks, you don't want excessive side-to-side flanking when moving small groups of animals. Your dog should normally only be wearing, flanking side to side, if they need to tuck a corner of a large group. Usually, your dog should walk straight in to the stock. Excessive sideways movement can be a sign of inexperience, insecurity, or weakness.

If your dog has the instinct to balance, they will wear or bring the sheep to you while you walk backward. As you walk backward your dog will have to control the movement of the sheep to keep them moving toward you, especially if you walk backward in a curved or circular path. The idea is that your dog balances the stock to you while you walk backward. You need to walk backward so that you can keep an eye on the stock and the position of your dog.

Initially, you may have to help your dog find balance and stay behind the sheep by blocking them with your crook or stock stick when they come up too far on one corner or side toward you. Your crook or stick acts as a moving barrier to encourage your dog not to come so high that they turn the sheep away from following you.

If you have not been carrying a stock stick or cane, you need to grab one now. The cane is just an extension of your arm and is not used to intimidate or hit your dog! A crook is just a portable barrier.

Steps for wearing
1. Start anywhere in your large paddock.
2. Flank your dog around behind the stock.
3. When the stock is between you and your dog, start walking backward.
4. Cue your dog *walk in*.
5. Your dog should stay opposite you, be on the other side of the stock, and push the stock to you.
6. If your dog flanks too high, comes up on the side toward you and pushes the sheep off the path to you, extend your crook/stock stick to block your dog and encourage them back behind the stock.

7. When your dog has learned to bring the stock to you as you walk straight backward away from them, start adding some curves.
8. As you curve to one side your dog should flank to the opposite side to keep bringing the stock to you.
9. Again, if your dog flanks too high, comes up on the side toward you, extend your crook to block your dog and encourage them back behind the stock.
10. Eventually, you should be able to walk backward in circles, figure 8s, or random patterns and your dog should flank in the opposite direction that you move to hold the stock to you.

Sir has come up too far on my side so I am using my arm to encourage him to flank around behind the sheep and bring them to me. To practice wearing I would walk backward, possibly walking in a circle or a serpentine, while Sir brought the sheep to me. If he came off balance toward me, I would extend my arm or crook to block him.

To practice wearing, you need livestock that stick together or flock well and is fairly calm. Sheep, goats, and some ducks usually stay together well, but cattle tend to be free spirits and are not great candidates for teaching wearing.

When your dog is proficiently wearing, go back and work on fetching again. Wearing usually triggers your dog's instinct to go to balance. If your dog can wear or hold stock to you as you back up, they should quickly catch on to finding balance on their outrun.

Push past handler

As soon as your dog is proficient at bringing the stock to your feet, start asking your dog to push them past you. As the stock approach, turn your body so that the stock is approaching your side and have your dog push the stock right on past you. You don't want your dog to get into the habit of always holding the stock to you. Sheep that learn to stay with a handler are called knee knockers or Velcro sheep.

As the sheep get near you, turn your body to reduce the pressure on them, and ask your dog in to push the sheep past you.

Knee knocker or **Velcro sheep** are sheep that have learned that they are safest at the feet of the handler. These sheep will immediately run to a handler as soon as a dog is sent on an outrun or flank and will then stick close to the handler. They can be miserable to drive away from the handler or shed. Velcro sheep have been trained into a bad habit that may ruin them for herding if your dog is not powerful enough to push them off of you. To prevent your sheep from learning this habit, push the sheep past you at least as often as you bring them just to your feet.

I help Qwest push the sheep by me by turning my body: https://www.youtube.com/watch?v=xhBRg-WMd6E&ab_channel=PurpleBorderCollie

Soon your dog will be driving stock away from you, turning them around you, and pushing them into pens and chutes. Your dog needs to learn that bringing stock to you is paramount, but it is not the end of the game.

Finishing touches

Your dog has learned to set up, go around stock, turn in at balance, and walk in to bring the stock to you. Ideally, the lift is a gentle transition of the stock from standing, to moving directly toward you. How your dog approaches stationary stock will determine how you will handle your dog on top.

- If you have a forward-moving dog, you may find them pushing the stock too hard when lifting. In this case, you may either stop your dog on top about *half* of the time or slow your dog down as they finish their outrun. The idea of stopping your dog often, just before the lift is to get your dog to anticipate being stopped so that they pause or at least come in slowly instead of rushing. Another option is to cue your dog to slow down as they finish their outrun to soften the lift by decreasing their speed just before they turn in to move the stock. Try both options and see what works best for your dog.
- If you have a sideways-moving dog, you may *not* want to ask them to stop on top as they may tend to get stuck once stopped. Sticky dogs may need a quickly cued *walk in* to encourage them to come on to their stock and apply pressure.

If you have trouble getting your dog to take their slow down or speed up cues, refer back to training easy and hurry in Chapter 4.

With experience, you will learn to handle your dog so that you move them along the continuum, away from being pushy or sticky and toward being free but gentle while lifting. If your dog hesitates, you may need to encourage walking in, but if your dog jams the stock, you will need to encourage slowing down or stopping. Behavior is dynamic, ever-changing, so your dog's behavior will always be changing. Training and handling are never static!

Over time flanks may become sliced or wide while walking in becomes too fast or too slow. After stopping your dog, it may become difficult to get them moving again or you may find your stop deteriorating. Behavior is not static!

Criteria, criteria, criteria! The better you are at determining, seeing, and holding criteria the more consistent and precise your dog will be performing cues.

Often your dog will change their behavior in such small increments that you will not even realize anything has changed until one day you wonder where that extremely sliced flank came from. It was slowly changing before your eyes, but because there is so much to observe and keep track of, you didn't notice the slight changes in behavior until they became a glaring problem!

Don't beat yourself up! Everyone finds themselves in this boat at some point. Fortunately, you have used positive reinforcement to train your dog, so no real harm has been done. You will find that as you maintain desired criteria, your dog will quickly change their behavior!

Your fetches should be coming along nicely, so in the next chapter, you will begin working on out and close and then off-balance flanks. Keep working fetches until your dog is confident and capable when bringing the stock to your feet or pushing them beyond you.

You can also start working on turning the stock around you, going clockwise or counterclockwise in preparation for **turning the post**, a herding trial maneuver. To turn the post, you bring the stock to your feet and turn them almost completely around you. Eventually, you will fetch the stock to you, turn them around you and the post, and drive them off toward the first drive gates. The **post** is a fence post or other object that indicates where the handler stands to begin their run on the trial field.

In this picture of Sally and Renn, the post is the flag pole next to the white rock. Sally is shedding, but if she were turning the post, she would stay within arm's length of the post and flank Renn to maneuver the sheep around herself and the post while keeping the sheep as close to the post as possible.

At this point you should be very proud of yourself and your dog, or as Sally might say, "chuffed"! Give yourself a big pat on the back, go out for a special dinner, and give your dog a big, meaty raw bone. You both deserve some special reinforcement!

Well done!

CHAPTER 8

Loose stock in large area 3

Before working on flanking exercises, let's zero in on square flanks as they are an important aspect or criterion of flanks and off-balance flanks. Once we have squared up our dog's flanks we can reassess our fetches before moving on to the dilemma of which to train first: out/close or off-balance flanks.

Squaring flanks

Your dog should always start their flanks by turning 90° and then moving off to circle the livestock. Turning 90° to start a flank is known as a square flank. Building square flanks is why you used barriers from the beginning of teaching directionals.

If you find your dog stepping forward and then turning, they are putting pressure on the stock. To get your dog back to meeting the square flank criterion, you can do a simple exercise around stock. Use this exercise as soon as you realize your dog is not squaring their flanks. You don't want slicing or stepping forward at the start of a flank to become a habit.

Pen your stock or get them settled in the paddock. Set up a cone circle, far enough away from the stock that your dog's flanking movement will not unsettle or move them. Get a clicker and treats, or a toy, and get between your dog and the stock. Cue a flank and mark if your dog squares their flank as they head in the cued direction. Allowing your dog to continue flanking 10 to 15 feet will be the reinforcer for the square flank in the correct direction. Stop your dog and flank them back in the opposite direction or farther around in the same direction. If your dog doesn't square their flank, just stop your dog. Do not use a no reward marker if the flank was not squared off.

 *If you use a no reward marker in this situation, your dog may interpret it to mean that they have flanked in the wrong direction.*

Initially, you can help your dog be correct by setting them up directly in front of a cone. The cone becomes a barrier to block your dog from stepping forward before turning to flank. Work this off and on, randomly over days and weeks, until your dog always squares their flanks. Move the exercise around the field and bring out cones and work it in a particular area where your dog is having trouble squaring their flanks. Be vigilant in maintaining your square flank criteria every time you ask your dog to flank.

You may also notice that on the outrun your dog will open up nicely as they leave on one side, but start out moving too directly toward the stock before they open up to go around on the other. Try setting up your dog pointing a little more to the outside, their body on the arc that you want them to take. If your dog starts out heading too directly toward the stock on one side, you can use some cones to guide your dog along the path that you want them to take and then fade out the cones.

Sir struggled with staying open when starting his away fetch. I used several cones to shape the correct path. I waited too long to deal with this situation, allowing too much mass to be built on the incorrect behavior.

Fading the cones too quickly resulted in a failure. In this situation, I gave my no reward marker which caused Sir to stop. I paused for 10 seconds and then called him back.

The following day I slowly faded cones out of the arc with success! Note that the sheep are running (escaping) to the left side of the picture, so there was a lot of pressure for Sir to slice in to catch them.

The outrun, lift, and fetch, is a chain. Each link in the chain has specific criteria. If you are clear on your criteria in training, you will make it easier for your dog to learn how to be correct and gain reinforcement.

Another behavior that should be avoided is having your dog run behind the plane of your body as they start their outrun. Even though your dog does not cross behind you, they should also not swing way out behind you to start their outrun. Instead, your dog should run out to your side, both sides should have about the same arc, and they should run even with the plane of your shoulders as you face the stock. If your dog wants to run back away from the stock as they start the outrun then back up to a fence so that they must run parallel or a bit in front of you as they flank out to start their outrun.

Flaring out behind you, as your dog starts their outrun, is usually only a problem with sideways-moving dogs. Forward-moving dogs often want to slice in as they start their outrun. Addressing flaring out or slicing in is best done early in training. The longer the unwanted behavior is reinforced, by allowing your dog to complete the outrun, the more mass you build on that behavior.

Again, video can be your best friend in observing what you, your dog, and the stock are doing. When watching video, be sure to note problems, but also be aware of

Sir has flared out wide, far beyond the plane of my shoulders. If this were his default behavior I would want to modify it, but he tends to slice the start of his fetches, especially to the away to me side.

As Sir continues his outrun, he holds his distance from the sheep without going extremely wide. As a dog who usually wants to slice in, I am happy to see him opening up during this outrun. Knowing your dog helps you determine when a behavior is desirable and when it is problematic.

successes. If you feel stuck or frustrated, go back and watch some videos from the past. I guarantee you will be amazed at the progress you and your dog have made.

Fetches first

Before you move on to getting your dog more comfortable with out, close, and off-balance flanks, be sure your fetches; outrun, lift, and drive to you, are solid. Herding is based on your dog finding balance and controlling stock. You want to keep balance as the foundation of your training even as you work off-balance exercises. Balance underpins fetches and going off-balance underpins driving. Both maneuvers are important for herding since there are times you need your stock brought to you and other times you need them driven away.

Out/close versus off-balance flanks

I usually train out or close before working on off-balance flanks. If your dog runs tight on their flanks or outrun, then definitely work on *out* before you tackle off-balance flanks. There is no absolute right or wrong when it comes to the order of training off-balance flanks versus out/close. If my dog tends to flank extremely close, I will work on the out even *before* I start fetching. You have to take into account what your dog's natural tendencies are and adjust the order of training herding skills accordingly.

Out or close?

Working out/close is another time that I like to use a box clicker. Usually, your dog needs training on working closer or farther from stock, but not both. Sideways-moving dogs tend to work too far off of their stock and forward-moving dogs tend to work too close. These are general tendencies, but your dog may be the exception to the rule.

When you worked your dog in the smaller paddock, it was acceptable and preferable that your dog stayed out and followed the fence as they flanked. The paddock was so small that your dog should have been using all of the real estate available to them to get off of or away from the stock. In the bigger paddock, things have changed.

How to determine if your dog is working too close or too far from the stock:
- In the larger paddock, your dog should have enough room to get off of the stock without constantly running the fence. If your dog always flanks along the fence, you need to work on **close**, unless you are working very, very light stock.
- In the larger paddock, your dog should be able to flank around the stock without forcing them to move, unless they are close to a fence. If your dog tends to push the stock when flanking or winds in, flanks closer and closer as they flank, you need to work on **out**.

Let's first cover the training of out, since most inexperienced dogs tend to run too close to their stock. First, determine where in the paddock you have noticed that your dog is flanking too close. Often your dog will flank too close when the flank will take your dog away from the pull and the stock are then free to run to the opposite end of the paddock. Your dog cuts in because they feel they are losing control of the stock.

The act of cutting in on a flank usually increases the chances that your dog will lose control of their livestock by forcing the stock to flush out, away from your dog.

The following directions assume that you have worked out/close with your dog away from livestock using two cone circles and a flirt pole as explained in Chapter 21 of *Positive Herding 101*. If your dog has not mastered out and close away from livestock, go back and build that skill before asking for out or close around stock. You may need to pen your livestock to gain control of the situation and remove one moving element in the equation. If you can work this exercise with penned stock, it will help to set your dog up for success.

Out – Step by step
1. Put your dog on a long line. (Pen your stock if possible.)
2. Set up a partial cone circle, use about 5 cones spaced about 3 feet apart, in the part of the paddock where your dog is slicing their flank. (The cones will help remind your dog to stay out rather than slice in as they flank.)
3. Pick up the long line if your dog has been dragging it and give your dog a bit of slack.
4. Stand between the penned stock and the partial cone circle.
5. When the stock is in the position that usually prompts your dog to slice in, stop your dog. Your dog should be just behind the first cone or two of the partial cone circle and you should be facing and standing within 10 feet of your dog.

6. Cue *out*. (The out is cued first to get your dog thinking about moving away from the stock. If you cue the flank first they often will slice in before you can cue the out.)
7. Immediately cue the appropriate flank. (Out, then flank cue, with no pause in between.)
8. If your dog flanks and stays to the outside of the cones, mark with a click, drop the long line, and stop your dog. Reinforce the stop by then sending your dog on the same flank around to catch the stock or cue another flank or walk in, if your stock is penned.
9. If your dog slices the flank by moving inside of the cones, give your no reward marker, stop your dog (let your dog reach the end of the long line if they don't take your verbal stop cue), pause for 10 seconds, and reset the scenario from the beginning.
10. Work the out until your dog flanks behind the cones 5 times.

11. Now set up the scenario and reverse the order of your cues, give the flank and then *out*.
12. When your dog takes the flank plus *out* and stays behind the cones, repeat 5 times.

13. Leave the cones in place but drop the stop cue as your flanking dog approaches the trouble spot and replace the stop with an *out* cue. (Your dog is already flanking so just give the out cue to remind them to continue to flank outside of the cone circle. No flank cue is needed as your dog is already flanking.)
14. Drop the out cue as a reminder. Your dog should flank past the trouble area and remain on the outside of the cone circle.

15. Remove 2 cones and repeat the exercise 5 times.
16. Remove 2 more cones and repeat the exercise 5 times.
17. Remove the final cone and repeat the exercise 5 times.
18. Be ready to use your out cue when your dog is flanking in the part of the paddock where they typically slice in.

Use your *out* whenever you see your dog starting to slice in. If slicing in becomes a problem in another area of the paddock and your dog is not taking their *out*, set up another partial cone circle and repeat these steps.

After you work with your dog in one or two areas of the paddock, usually where they are flagrantly slicing in, your dog will generalize the learning to other areas and start taking your *out* cue. It is easy to teach the out, but often difficult to realize that your dog is slicing in. If you have trouble figuring out if your dog is starting to slice in, note the distance your dog is from the stock when starting to flank and the distance from the stock as they continue flanking. Unless your dog is forced closer to the stock by a fence or other obstruction, they should maintain the same distance from the stock as they flank around them.

Sir slices his flank. He is stopped and given a no reward marker and paused. I move between Sir and the sheep and cue the out and the flank.

Sir takes the out cue. Note that I don't move. Sir is now back flanking outside the cone circle.

Remember to work *out* on both flanks, although your dog may tend to only slice one flank. If your dog slices one flank more than the other, work out more on that side than the other.

Do not push your dog out too far as they will tend to run wider as they gain experience working stock. This is another balancing act. Your dog should run far enough off of the stock so they are not influencing them as they flank, but not so far off that they lose contact with their stock.

Close

Although you want your dog to maintain their distance as they flank, not pushing the stock as they flank, you do *not* want them flanking so far off that they lose contact with their stock.

Training the *close* on loose livestock is very similar to working the *out*. Use more cones, at least half a circle with cones spaced 3 feet apart. You should also use a box clicker as a marker but can dispense with your dog dragging a long line since they are likely to stop when cued. Substitute *close* for *out* in the step-by-step directions for training out. Of course, you will be having your dog move inside the cone circle after cueing close, rather than to the outside of it as you did for out.

Since dogs tend to consistently run too wide, you can set up your partial cone circle anywhere that your dog is not forced to flank along a fence because of the stock's proximity to it. Set the cones in an area that your dog has a lot of room to be off of the stock, without flanking along a fence. You want to pen your stock to work the close.

If your stock moves around the paddock as your dog flanks, you need to move your cone circle farther out and away from the stock. If your stock is penned, they should not be moving excessively in the pen.

To train close, follow the step-by-step instructions for training the out. Start with your dog just to the inside of the start of the cone circle. Cue *close* and the flank. Now you mark if your dog flanks *inside* of the cones. If your dog goes to the outside of the cones, give your no reward marker, stop your dog, pause for 10 seconds, and reset. Work on this until your dog is flanking the entire half cone circle while staying on the inside of it.

If your dog struggles to stay inside of the cone circle, move it a bit farther from the stock to start. When your dog is comfortable, try moving it closer again. Also, if your dog's flanking forces the stock to move excessively, they may be too close.

Work the opposite flank, the other direction, until your dog can flank, stop, continue flanking in the same direction, or go back the other direction while staying inside the half-circle. Then start removing cones by taking out every other cone. Remove cones over time until they are all faded out of the picture.

Now flank your dog again. If they start to open up too far, run too wide, cue the close and mark or use your no reward marker as appropriate. If your dog comes in just a few feet, mark and celebrate!

If your dog consistently flanks along the fence, try stopping them, ask them to walk in. Then try flanking them again to get them used to flanking closer to the stock.

Most dogs do not consistently run too wide. Some dogs run along fences because they were pushed out too soon and too far. Initially, err on the side of having your dog run a bit too tight rather than forcing them to run too wide.

When you cue out or close, your dog will usually move about a yard (3 feet) farther or closer to stock while continuing to flank. They should then hold that distance from the stock as they continue flanking. If your dog moves a yard but you need them farther or closer, just re-cue the *out* or *close*. As your dog gains experience they will learn how far they need to be away from the stock and that will become a comfortable distance for them. Over time you will find you use your out cue less, but if you have a sideways-moving dog, you still may find yourself depending on your close cue to bring your dog into contact with the livestock.

Dogs that flank too close usually learn to open up because they eventually realize they can control stock more efficiently by being farther off of them. Dogs that tend to flank too wide seem to always tend to flank well off of their stock.

Off-balance flanks

Off-balance flanks allow you to cross-drive and drive away from you. They are also necessary when penning or putting stock through a chute or loading them in a trailer. **Off-balance flanks** are flanks that bring your dog toward you, rather than away from you. As your dog flanks toward balance, they are just flanking, but as soon as they pass balance and start flanking back toward you, they are flanking off-balance.

If your dog has a lot of herding instinct, they will struggle with off-balance flanking because as they move off-balance they are losing control of the livestock. It is much easier for a dog to go off-balance when circling a cone circle with a rat as the prey. The rat never runs off to the other end of the room or yard and down a rat hole. Although your dog considers the rat prey, their experience is that the rat typically stays in the center of the cone circle no matter where they flank. The rat never runs away and escapes. Stock, on the other hand, will run to the other end of the paddock to escape if they are given half a chance.

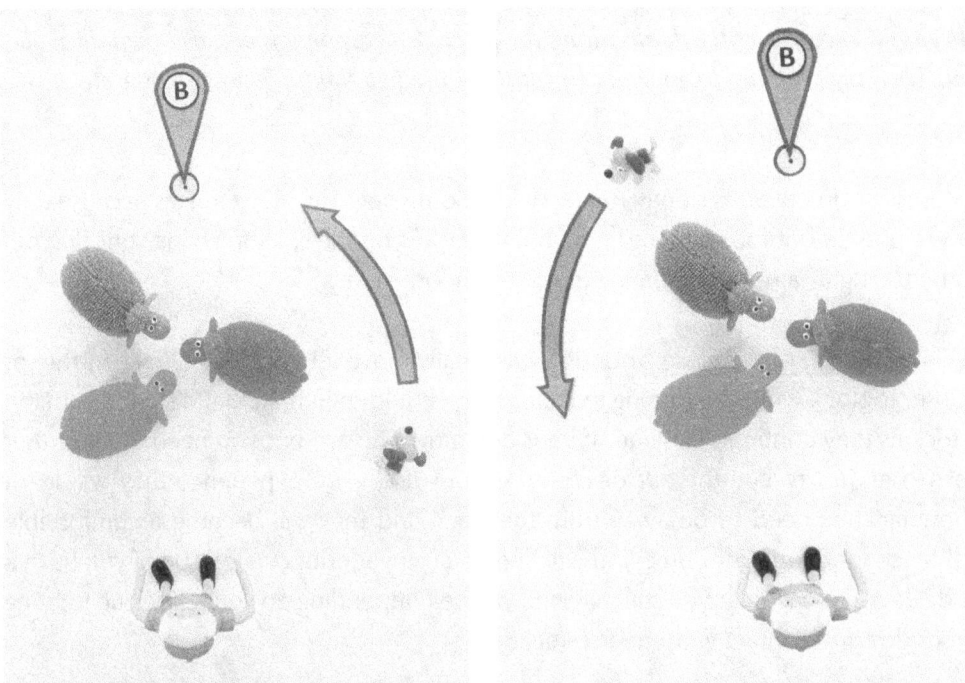

A flank (LEFT) moves your dog toward balance, while an off-balance flank (RIGHT) brings your dog away from balance and back toward you.
It is natural for a dog with herding instinct to go toward balance, as that is the point where they control the livestock. It is difficult for that same dog to move away from balance and lose control of the livestock.

You should have solid flanks on your dog by now, so you should not need to use any cones when working off-balance flanks. Settle your stock anywhere in the paddock that they will stay stationary. Start with penned stock if your dog struggles with off-balance flanking.

To settle stock in a certain area you can put some grain or hay on the ground. I have never had a lot of success with this method but some people use it quite successfully. I pen my stock when I need them to remain stationary.

I like to use a box clicker in this situation because it tells my dog they are correct at the moment that they decide to continue in the uncomfortable direction. I also initially use my recall cue *here* to encourage my dog to flank back toward me. The use of your recall to prompt your dog should be faded as soon as possible. The advantage of using it is that it gives your dog the idea that you want them to flank past balance and back toward you.

If your dog does not have much herding instinct, you may not be able to use your recall as a prompt for teaching off-balance flanks. If you use your recall and your dog comes straight to you, cutting in close to the stock instead of flanking around the stock toward you, then you may not find using your recall cue is practical.

Before you start – Off-balance flanks
To build mass and bolster reinforcement history, it would be advantageous to train a few sessions of off-balance flanking away from stock. For instructions, revisit off-balance flanks around cone circles in Chapter 20 of *Positive Herding 101*.

Your dog has recently been turned on to balancing stock, so it is good training to go back and review off-balance flanking in a less distracting situation to make it easier for your dog to be successful. When your dog is flanking off-balance around the cone circle, with no hesitation, they are ready to move on to off-balance flanking around livestock. For working off-balance flanks on stock you use a box clicker, leash, and treats or a toy.

Off-balance flanks – Step by step
1. Pen or settle your stock anywhere in your paddock.
2. Stand about 20 feet away from the stock with your dog beside you and both of you facing the stock.
3. Flank your dog around the stock, using a flank cue. Just as they reach balance, re-cue the flank and add your recall cue to prompt your dog to continue flanking toward you. (Your dog will often slow down as they approach balance: re-cue the flank just as you see them start to slow down, don't wait until they stop at balance.)
4. If your dog continues flanking toward you, mark and reinforce by allowing your dog to continue flanking toward you. Woo hoo!

5. If your dog stops at balance, give your no reward marker, keep your dog stationary, pause for 10 seconds, and then walk around the stock until you are about 3 feet to the side of your dog. You will be on the side of your dog that originally would

be off-balance or the direction you originally wanted them to continue flanking. (Because you are flanking your dog toward you, instead of to balance, you are cueing an off-balance flank.)

6. Cue the flank that will bring your dog toward you and immediately cue *here*.
7. If your dog flanks even one step in your direction, mark and heavily reinforce with treats or play!
8. If your dog stands still or attempts to flank away from you give your no reward marker, pause for 10 seconds, and attach a 6-foot leash to your dog.

9. Repeat step 6, but hold the center of the leash, so it is only 3 feet long, with just a little slack in it.
10. If your dog starts to flank away from you prevent your dog from moving away from you by them reaching the end of the 3-foot leash. Give your no reward marker, pause for 10 seconds, and try again.
11. If your dog stands still after the cue, give a light tug on the leash to prompt your dog to flank toward you. Reinforce with a treat or play. (Verbal reinforcement can also be helpful in this situation.)
12. When you get your dog flanking toward you when cued, start moving farther away from them until they will flank toward you 6 feet, or the distance of the leash.
13. Repeat 10 times.

14. Remove the leash and repeat 5 more times.
15. Rework the entire exercise with the other off-balance flank, asking our dog to go only the length of the leash, 6 feet, toward you if they struggle with off-balance flanks.
16. Stop for the day! Then build distance using a long line in a few more sessions.
17. Over the next few sessions, grow off-balance flanks until your dog can flank all the way around the stock and back to you with only one flank cue.

Sir is coming off-balance without hesitation! Next, I would work my way to the outside of the cone circle.

Off-balance flanks are VERY difficult for most dogs, so be prepared to be patient and work in small steps. Every off-balance flank step is a victory! Be generous with your reinforcement. This training takes as long as it takes. Be sure to stay upbeat and not allow frustration to creep into your voice. Your dog already is uncomfortable flanking off-balance and any slight punishment will only increase their discomfort and make the training more difficult.

Sir circling the stock and performing off-balance flanks: https://www.youtube.com/watch?v=ql-FmZ3uSWQ&ab_channel=PurpleBorderCollie

Troubleshooting
- **Dog starts coming off-balance then stops** – When you start off-balance flanking around stock, your dog may flank past balance toward you but stop before they flank all the way back to you. Just as they are slowing down to stop, re-cue the flank and add your recall cue again, to prompt them to continue flanking toward you. Repeat as needed, then fade the re-cueing. (It is important to re-cue the flank while your dog is still flanking. If you wait until your dog stops, you are reinforcing the unwanted stop with the flank cue.)
- **Dog starts coming off-balance then flanks back to balance** – Pen your stock to remove your dog's need to control the stock's movement.
- **Dog seems confused or frustrated** – If things are not progressing after a few sessions, stop working on off-balance flanks for a few days and then revisit them.
- **You are confused or frustrated** – If you get mixed up or frustrated, stop immediately and take time to think and plan your next session. Do not continue training if you are frustrated with your dog!

When you work off-balance flanks, alternate off-balance sessions with fetching. Alternating off-balance sessions with fetch sessions will remind your dog that although they can work off-balance they need to remember where balance is. From this point forward, begin and end training sessions with fetches.

From now on, always start and end training sessions with a fetch or two. As your dog learns to work off-balance, you want to preserve their instinct to go to balance. Too much focus on off-balance flanks can temporarily have your dog running past balance on outruns. If this happens, work more fetches.

Beyond basics

You and your dog now have all the basic herding skills in place! From here on the emphasis will be on combining and refining your dog's herding skills and growing your handling skills. As you and your dog move on to advanced herding skills, you will learn to trust each other and your partnership will grow stronger. You will come to admire and respect your dog and their abilities more than you ever thought possible. Maybe even of greater importance, you will come to depend on your dog's capabilities to control and move livestock and see them as an eager and amazingly capable partner.

CHAPTER 9

Putting it all together 1

You and your dog now have all of the basic herding skills in place! As you work livestock with your dog, you will no longer encounter any frustrations or difficulties – if only! As you certainly know by now, herding is a complex activity. There is always a new twist or scenario to deal with, but you also may have encountered problems along the way that have not been addressed. As helpful and convenient as step-by-step instructions are, they can never replace a solid understanding of the laws of behavior that govern science-based positive training, and having a good coach doesn't hurt either.

Mistakes are just information and frustrations just indications.

In this chapter, a few ideas are presented that may help with some problems you have encountered. Since this book can't cover every unique situation, anytime you find yourself becoming frustrated while working with your dog, stop and take some time to think about what is causing your frustration. Review any video you have for clues.

Frustration is an indication that something is wrong. Figure out the problem, decide on a plan, and train the skill your dog lacks. Don't be afraid to go back to using a flirt pole, treats, cones, a small pen for livestock, or moving back into a smaller area with no livestock. Do whatever it takes to make it easier for you and your dog to be successful!

Try not to get down on yourself as a trainer or person. We are all doing the best we can with the knowledge and skills that we possess. You are not alone but part of a growing positive herding movement!

Criteria, criteria, criteria

Behavior is dynamic, always changing. Thus, you constantly need to assess if your dog's behavior is meeting your criteria. There is so much to keep track of while herding that it is easy to allow your criteria to slip. Every cue you give your dog has multiple criteria associated with it. Often you will not realize a criterion or two has degraded until it is a glaring problem.

Everyone, no matter how experienced or advanced, will find that their criteria have slipped somewhere along the way and will have to go back and retrain skills with murky criteria. Give your dog an inch and they will often take ten miles before you ever realize what has happened!

The first hint you may have that your criteria for a certain behavior are being compromised is that you become frustrated with your dog. If you can catch the problem at that point, it should be easy to fix. The longer you wait, the worse the problem becomes, the more re-training you will have to do to address the situation.

Besides indicating a slip in criteria, frustration may also indicate that a skill or transition between skills needs to be trained or re-trained. Although your dog knows how to perform skills in isolation, that does not mean that they will automatically be able to perform the same skills in a series. Transitioning smoothly from one behavior to the next is also a skill.

Transitions

Not all dogs struggle with transitions. Your dog may switch from one behavior to the next without a hiccup, but some dogs will have trouble transitioning between behaviors. Some of the transitions you may find your dog struggling with are from walking in to flanking or from flanking to walking in.

The flank to walk in transition is particularly important for sticky dogs. If you stop these dogs, they may be reluctant to move again. These dogs need to be able to smoothly transition between flanking and walking in. You will use both of these transitions often while fetching, driving, and cross-driving. If you always have to stop your dog to change from walking in to flanking or flanking to walking in, you will find your dog is often too late responding to the situation. Being too late makes your dog play catch up with the stock. Ideally, you want your dog in the right place, at the right time, every time. With experience, your timing will get better and better.

Another transition that your dog may find difficult is changing from one flank to the other, without stopping between flanks, which is known as **changing flanks on the fly**. Most dogs have trouble with this transition because they are in motion, often moving quickly, and they have to interrupt that movement to perform the opposite cued flank.

I guarantee that if your dog has trouble with any of these transitions, you will become frustrated working your dog.

Sometimes it is difficult to pinpoint the source of your frustration, especially if it is the lack of a smooth transition. Your dog flanks well and walks in nicely, but you have to stop them each time you want to transition from one behavior to the next. Your dog walks in at a steady pace but struggles to flank when cued. How would you train these transitions? Take a few minutes to come up with a plan. Really, formulate a basic plan that you think would work for your dog.

Now that you have a plan in mind, let's see if it is the same as mine. I would (and have) taken a dog away from livestock to work on transitions. It's back to the flirt pole and cone circles. I like to go back to training away from livestock because you are eliminating the huge distraction of reading and controlling the stock. Give your dog a chance to master transitions in a low distraction environment before you take transitions back to livestock.

When going back to using cones and a flirt pole you may need to take a significant break of a week to 10 days with only limited training time. This will help get your dog enthused about working with cones again, instead of livestock.

You may find that your dog has lost interest in working with cones and a flirt pole once they have worked livestock. Also, they may look for livestock when you cue a flank, instead of circling the cones. If your dog will absolutely not work without stock, you may have to put your livestock back into a small pen to work transitions. Work transitions at a great distance from the livestock to decrease the level of distraction from the stock to a manageable level.

If your dog has no trouble transitioning, then skip these exercises or do them just for fun. If you dog has difficulty transitioning, then these exercises are super valuable.

In to flank – Step by step

1. Stand outside of a 12-foot cone circle with the flirt pole rat positioned on the ground in the center of the circle.
2. Your dog stands directly across the circle from you, 5 to 10 feet beyond the circle.
3. Ask your dog to walk in.
4. When your dog passes between two cones and into the center area of the cone circle mark, release, and tug.
5. Repeat step 4 until your dog walks steadily into the cone circle toward the rat.

6. Now ask your dog in, but cue a flank just before they get to the circle of cones.
7. If your dog takes the flank, even if they pause for a moment, mark, release, and tug. You will flip the rat to the outside of the cone circle and in front of your dog.
8. If your dog does not take the flank, use your no reward marker, pause, and reset.
9. Work this with both flanks until your dog will immediately transition from walking in to flanking without stopping in between. Often ask your dog to walk in without flanking.

10. Make your cone circle smaller and increase the distance between your dog and the circle.
11. Cue the walk in and randomly cue a flank at different distances *before* your dog gets to the cone circle to generalize the transition. (You will not always be asking your dog to flank just as they get to the cone circle. Cue the flank at various distances away from the cone circle.)
12. Fade the cones out of the picture.
13. Take the transition to livestock.

To start, you want your dog walking readily inside the circle to the rat. Your dog should wait for their release cue before grabbing the rat. No release cue means no access to the rat!

CHAPTER 9 PUTTING IT ALL TOGETHER 1 | 131

Sir starts walking in to the rat from about 6 feet beyond the cone circle.

I cue a flank as he gets to the cone circle and verbally mark the correct behavior.

As Sir flanks around me I flip the rat to the outside of the cone circle and give my release cue, get it. Sir is now free to grab the rat and have a short tug session as a reinforcer.

Fading the cones means you eliminate every other cone until they are all gone. You may need to use other props, such as conveniently located trees or some garbage cans to finish generalizing this transition. Some dogs find it difficult to flank around just a flirt pole rat without any props to use as visual markers.

This should be an easy, yet important, exercise for your dog. Some dogs will not need this training and some will. Your dog will most likely figure out how to transition from walking in to flanking, but both of you may become frustrated until they figure it out. If you see your dog struggling, take the time and effort it requires to teach your dog how to transition successfully.

Working on the out with a tree as a prop in place of a cone.

The next time Sir approaches the tree while flanking, he is cued out and then flanks around the far side of the tree.

Flank to in – Step by step

1. Stand outside of a 12-foot cone circle with the flirt pole rat positioned on the ground in the center of the circle.
2. Your dog stands directly across the circle from you on the outside of the circle.
3. Ask your dog to walk in.
4. When your dog passes between two cones and into the center area of the cone circle mark, release, and tug.
5. Repeat step 4 until your dog walks steadily into the cone circle toward the rat.

---

6. Reset your dog to the outside of the circle and ask your dog to flank around the cone circle a quarter to almost halfway around the circle each way.
7. Reset your dog across from you, cue a flank, and as soon as your dog starts to flank, cue *walk in*. The sooner you catch your dog as they start flanking the more likely they are to take their in cue.
8. If your dog stops flanking or turns and walks toward the rat then mark, release, and tug.
9. If your dog continues to flank, give your no reward marker, stop your dog, pause 10 seconds, and reset.
10. Repeat until your dog is successful transitioning when asked to in both directions.

---

11. Allow your dog to flank farther around the circle before asking them to walk in.

12. Generalize the transition to flanks at increased speed.
13. Fade the cones out of the picture.
14. Take the transition to livestock.

Troubleshooting

- **Dog struggles to transition from flank to in (1)** – If your dog struggles with this exercise, insert a stop between the flank and the in cue. Once your dog is proficiently transitioning, with the stop between the flank and the walk in, drop the stop cue.
- **Dog struggles to transition from flank to in (2)** – If your dog struggles with this exercise, remember to cue the *in* as soon as they start flanking. The farther your dog flanks, the less likely they are to transition easily to the walk in. Catch them before they start flanking fast.

It is usually easier to teach a dog to transition from a slower movement (walking in) to a faster movement (flanking) than from a faster movement (flanking) to a slower movement (walking in).

ABOVE LEFT: *Sir is flanking away to me around the cone circle with the rat in the center.*

ABOVE: *I then ask Sir to walk in and mark the turn in.*

LEFT: *I give Sir his release cue, he grabs the rat, and we have a short tug session as reinforcement.*

Flank to flank – Step by step (Changing flanks on the fly)

1. Stand outside a 12-foot cone circle with the rat positioned on the ground in the center of the circle.
2. Your dog stands anywhere along the circle.
3. Cue a flank.
4. When your dog has flanked a quarter to halfway around the circle, stop your dog.
5. Flank your dog in the opposite direction.
6. When your dog has flanked a quarter to halfway around the circle, stop your dog.
7. Flank your dog in the same direction they were heading before you stopped them.
8. Repeat 3 to 5 times using random flanks, either cue the same direction or the opposite direction.

---

9. Now cue a flank and immediately cue the opposite flank, without giving a stop cue.
10. If your dog flips to the opposite flank, immediately, mark, release, and tug!
11. If your dog continues to flank without making any effort to reverse directions, give your no reward marker, stop your dog, pause for 10 seconds, and begin again.
12. Work this until your dog is changing flanks immediately. (This is called changing flanks on the fly.)
13. Work several sessions. You want your dog changing flanks on the fly with confidence before you bring stock back into the picture.
14. Take the transition to livestock.

Troubleshooting

- ***Dog struggles to change flanks on the fly (1)*** – Work only one transition at a time. Start with come bye to away to me and work on only this transition until your dog is proficient. Work the opposite transition in a different training session.
- ***Dog struggles to change flanks on the fly (2)*** – Give the opposite flank as soon as your dog takes a step on the initial flank, before they get moving fast. The sooner you can catch your dog as they start to flank the easier it will be for them to process the new cue and perform the behavior. Once your dog is quickly moving, it becomes much more difficult for them to change directions on the fly.

Sir starts flanking come bye.

After flanking a quarter of the circle he is cued away to me.

Sir immediately flips around to flank in the opposite direction.

Circling stock away from handler

A final exercise that your dog needs to know, to be fluent in flanking in order to drive in any direction, is circling stock far enough away from you that your dog flanks around in *front* of you. You can start this exercise close to the stock such that your dog flanks behind you. The idea is for the dog to flank around the stock, thus going from a flank to an off-balance flank and then back to a flank.

To keep the stock settled, initially use your small pen to corral them. This will keep them in one place and remove some of the burden from your dog of having to read and react to the livestock. You may start using a cone circle or not, handler's choice. When your dog can circle completely around the stock, start to fade and then eliminate the cone circle.

Sir starts at my side and flanks all the way around the sheep without stopping. The next step is for me to move back against the fence and have Sir flank in front of me. Note the movement of the sheep.

Remember to start and end circling sessions with fetches! You always want to protect your dog's sense of balance and excessive circling can be detrimental to maintaining balance.

Once your dog can flank a complete circle, or 1½ circles, start backing yourself out of the picture such that your dog starts flanking in front of you. If your dog struggles with flanking in front of you move to a fence and stand with your back to it. The fence is a barrier that will force your dog to flank in front of you.

Now that Sir is used to flanking between me and the sheep, I no longer have to stand against a fence to encourage him to flank in front of me.

After your dog is comfortable flanking in front of you, start moving farther away from the stock and have your dog flank all the way around the livestock in both directions. Then move on to adding stops and changes of direction. Finally, add walking in.

At no time should your dog begin orbiting the stock, blindly circling. Your dog should always be reading the stock, so watch to see that your dog is occasionally looking in at the stock as they flank.

If your dog does start to orbit, then stop your dog and ask for shorter flanks, less than one complete circle, with stops in between. If your dog tends to orbit, work this exercise in short sessions with lots of fetches in between.

Now your dog has the skills to drive or cross-drive in any direction! Driving and cross-driving will be covered in detail in Chapter 13, later in this book.

At this point, it is often said that you have a lot of handle on your dog. Now it's time to put on the finishing touches. As you refine your handle on your dog, you will realize that, at times, you need total control, especially when asking for precise movements when penning or shedding. At those times controlling your stock may come down to your dog moving only inches or simply shifting their weight. That is when bump flanks are invaluable. How do bump flanks differ from regular flanks? You'll find out in the next chapter.

CHAPTER 10

Putting it all together 2

Bump flanks are very useful for moving your dog slightly sideways at the pen or in other close work. **Bump flanks** are mini-flanks that range from your dog taking a step or two sideways while continuing to face the stock, to just shifting their weight from one front foot to the other. Bump flanks are more of a sidestep than a real flank.

These two pictures illustrate a bump flank. On the left, Sir is standing while penning sheep. I needed a bit more pressure on the sheep to his left side, so I cued a bump come bye flank.

Sir's response (in the photo on the right) was to move his left front paw about 6 inches to the side and forward. A bump flank can vary from a weight shift, with no paw movement, to several steps sideways, while continuing to face the livestock.

 *Teaching your dog to sidestep or side pass can help them generalize that behavior to a bump flank. A bump flank is a sidestep, or three, or just a weight shift side to side, without paw movement.*

I cue bump flanks with **to me** or **bye**, said slowly and softly. Bump flank cues are just the ending of the regular cues for flanks. So *to me* cues a bump away to me flank and *bye* cues a bump come bye flank. For longer, faster flanks you will use *away to me* and *come bye* as usual.

Practice bump flanks until your dog learns what your criteria are. Bump flanks are easier to train on livestock than using cone circles because they are used in tight situations and your dog will naturally read the situation and most likely will react cautiously.

 *With bump flanks, you will allow your dog to stop flanking after only leaning or taking a step or two **without** giving them a stop cue. With regular flanks, you are asking your dog to continue flanking until cued to do another behavior.*

A bump flank is a slow, sideways move, with the dog always facing the stock.

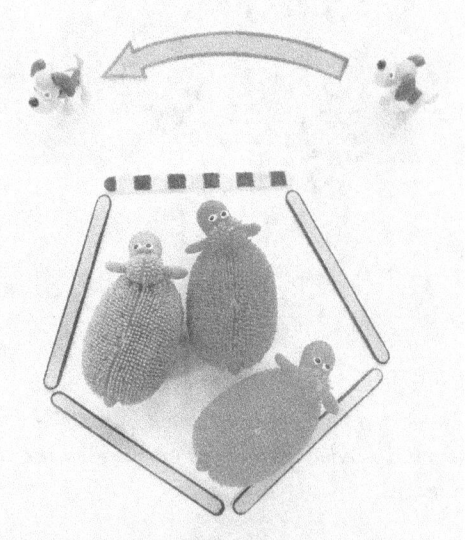

A regular flank is longer and faster, with the dog turning their body as they flank.

Some dogs may still need to be cued to stop when bump flanking. If you prefer, you may continue to use a stop cue to end bump flanks. Your dog should learn to flank slowly, not turn and take off like a rocket when calmly and quietly given a bump flank.

If you slowly cue the bump flank and immediately cue a stop, you are teaching your dog that the length of a flank may only be inches or just a weight shift. Up to now, a flank cue has indicated a fairly fast and lengthy maneuver. Flank criteria to this point have included forward movement, with your dog's body arcing around the livestock. Now we are introducing bump flanks with sideways body movement while facing the livestock. The topography of a flank and a bump flank is completely different.

Bump flanks – Step by step

1. Put stock into a small pen in the middle of a paddock.
2. Flank your dog around the pen once in each direction.
3. When your dog is stopped, walk them in toward the livestock until you get a reaction from the stock, such as a head turn or dip, ears coming forward, a stomp, backing up, bunching together, etc.
4. Once the stock reacts to your dog, stop your dog.

5. If you **can** determine which way your dog is pulled, then quietly cue the opposite flank, your dog would flank away from the direction they want to go to cover the stock. By flanking away from the pull you will tend to get a slower, more reluctant flank response.
6. If you **cannot** determine which way your dog is pulled, then quietly cue either flank.
7. Slowly and softly cue the flank and *immediately* cue a stop. If your dog only flanks a step or three, mark and reinforce.

8. Repeat this until your dog will slowly flank only a step or two.
9. Calmly cue a flank in the opposite direction and immediately cue a stop. If correct, mark and reinforce.
10. Repeat this until your dog will flank only a step or two in each direction.

11. Free your dog up by flanking them around the stock again, once in each direction.
12. Stop your dog.
13. Cue a bump flank and see if your dog will take a step or two *sideways* while they continue to face the livestock, or will just shift their weight. Mark and reinforce if correct. (If your dog will not take a step sideways you may need to work on side passing, away from livestock.)

14. Work this exercise in both directions until your dog can perform bump flanks in both directions.
15. Let the livestock out of the pen and put them in a corner of the paddock.
16. Practice bump flanks while the stock remain in the corner.
17. When your dog is confident doing bump flanks with the stock in a corner, practice bump flanks while penning or putting stock through a chute.

Hold

All dogs need to be taught to hold livestock. To perform the **hold**, your dog freely flanks, without cues, to keep stock in front of them, while not allowing the livestock to get away from or past them. A hold cue comes in handy at both trials and around the farm or ranch. At trials, the hold can be used at the pen or chute, when shedding or setting out, or any time the stock tries to break to the exhaust or toward any strong pull.

For practical use, the hold is handy for having your dog guard gates or keep livestock away from feed bunks as well as to contain stock when corralling or loading them onto trailers. The hold is most easily taught using sheep and can then be transferred to other types of livestock.

Hold – Step by step
Phase 1 – Holding sheep to you

1. In a paddock drive 5 to 10 head of sheep into a corner.
2. Move into the corner so that the sheep are between you and your dog, who is on the perimeter of an imaginary quarter circle around the corner.
3. Flank your dog back and forth a few times to group the sheep fairly tightly to you.
4. Cue your dog *out* or *back* to release some of the pressure off of the sheep.
5. Quickly move into the sheep while lifting your arms to spook them, so that they attempt to bust out of the corner. As the sheep start to bolt, cue your dog to hold. (You may need to make a whooshing noise to scare the sheep and activate your dog's instinct to come into the sheep and control them.)
6. If any sheep escape from the corner, flank your dog to cover and bring them back.
7. Repeat this until you can't push any sheep out of the corner past your dog.

This should be a fun exercise for you and your dog. This exercise depends on your dog having herding instinct. If your dog lacks instinct, you will have to flank them and tell them what to do to prevent the sheep from escaping. Modify this exercise in any way that you need to for your dog to be successful.

Above left: Sir holding sheep to me.

Above: Sheep quiet, then spooked by me.

Left: Sir covers to hold them to me.

Your dog may be reluctant to flank or cover, without being cued, so encourage them by marking any offered flanks and reinforce with tons of praise!

Troubleshooting

- **Sheep will not attempt to leave the corner (1)** – You may have to back your dog up farther for the sheep to attempt to leave. You might also want to add more sheep to the group you are using.
- **Sheep will not attempt to leave the corner (2)** – You may have to become more animated to startle the sheep.
- **Dog doesn't cover sheep** – Try splitting the group: send one group in one direction along the fence. Flank your dog to cover those sheep, meanwhile send the remaining sheep in the other direction, along the other fence. Then flank your dog to cover the second group. Repeat this until your dog either covers each group without being cued or responds immediately to cover each group when cued.

Now we are going to modify the hold from asking our dog to hold the stock to us, to having our dog hold stock away from other livestock. Our criteria for hold becomes to keep the livestock that is in front of your dog controlled and not allow them to get back past your dog to rejoin the other livestock.

Phase 2 – Holding using two groups of sheep

1. Put several sheep in a small pen in the corner of a paddock and leave a few out in the paddock. The smaller loose group will most likely move toward the larger penned group to regroup. (Situate the pen in a corner by a gate or other draw to encourage the loose sheep to be strongly drawn to the penned sheep.)
2. Help your dog push the loose sheep along the fence away from the penned group.
3. Move slightly away from the fence so that you are helping to hold the loose sheep along the fence. Your dog should be between the loose sheep and the penned sheep.
4. Walk a bit ahead of the loose sheep such that they turn back toward your dog and the penned sheep.
5. Cue your dog to hold.

---

6. If the sheep try to get past your dog, your dog should freely flank to prevent them from getting past. (Cue flanks only if necessary and drop cueing as soon as possible.)
7. If the sheep don't try to get past your dog, then you should attempt to push the sheep past your dog, as you did in the previous corner hold phase.
8. Move off to the side so that your dog is no longer holding the loose sheep to you but away from the penned sheep.
9. When your dog actively prevents any sheep from getting past them and regrouping with the penned sheep, take a short break. Celebrate!

---

10. Reset and repeat until your dog will freely move to cover sheep attempting to get back to the penned group on only the hold cue. (You should not need to give your dog flanks at this point unless they don't have herding instinct.)
11. To increase the level of difficulty put all but two sheep in the pen and eventually have only one loose sheep. (The fewer loose sheep, the greater the challenge for your dog to hold them apart will be.)

Many dogs love to hold and control stock. For them, actively holding is one of the highest value reinforcers you can provide!

Warning! A single loose sheep may do *anything* to return to the safety of the flock, including running into or jumping over you or your dog. Hold singles with care, for only a short time, and don't attempt to hold a single if your dog is not confidently holding stock. Also, a young dog can easily become over-aroused by working singles and may grip or chase. Safety first!

It takes confidence for a dog to hold stock that really wants to get by them. Work the hold over time and gradually increase the level of difficulty for your dog by either having your dog drive the held sheep farther from the penned sheep or by decreasing the number of sheep your dog is asked to hold. When your dog gets tested, by an animal actively trying to get past them, you will see if your dog has the strength, instinct, and confidence to control contrary livestock.

RIGHT: The setup is a group of sheep penned and a free group.

BELOW LEFT: Moving loose sheep away from penned sheep.

BELOW RIGHT: Sir moving into position to hold the loose sheep off of the penned sheep.

The next step is to generalize this to other situations and then other livestock. If you feed your sheep in a bunk, you can generalize the hold by placing the bunk near a gate to an adjoining paddock or lot. Have your dog drive the sheep out the gate of the paddock containing the bunk. Stop your dog in the gateway, with the gate open, and put a little feed in the bunk. As the sheep approach the gateway, cue your dog to hold. Your dog is free to move to prevent the sheep from coming through the gateway to the bunk.

If your dog does not move to cover intruding sheep, cue a flank, and then re-cue *hold*. If any sheep get by your dog, flank your dog and help them move the sheep back out the gate. Put your dog back in the gateway and again ask them to hold. After a few repetitions, your dog should start moving to hold sheep trying to come through the gateway, without any further cues from you.

Once your dog controls the sheep long enough for you to fill the bunk with feed, call them off and allow the sheep to eat at the bunk. Do this for several days, until your dog consistently prevents the sheep from coming through the gateway, when cued to hold, and only allows the sheep to enter when called off.

I use "that'll do" as the cue to release my dog from holding. It is also my call off cue for ending work for the moment or day.

Now move the bunk farther from the gate, roughly 100 feet, and put some feed in the bunk. You and your dog should be positioned between the gateway and the bunk. After the sheep have come through the gateway and are approaching the bunk, about halfway to the bunk, cue your dog to hold. Now your dog should hold the sheep in a group off of the bunk, but not necessarily at the gateway. In the beginning, don't wait until the sheep are close to the bunk. Ask your dog to hold when they are still quite a distance off to give your dog a better chance to stop and control them, especially if you have a large flock.

Again, you should help your dog if they initially need it. You always want your dog to be successful! If you are going to work and hold cattle, your dog should first be confident holding sheep and must also be willing to bite.

A bite is essential for all dogs. A dog with a bite is more confident and usually will not need to bite. Biting is the only way a dog can protect itself, so taking away their bite does a disservice to your dog. For instructions on teaching the bite see Positive Herding 101, *Chapter 23.*

The hold is an integral part of shedding. **Shedding** is separating two groups of animals and keeping them apart. Shedding is useful for practical situations and is required in upper-level trial classes. Shedding will be covered in Chapters 15 through 17.

Teaching the hold, as well as most other behaviors, is built step by step over time. Challenge your dog as they become proficient. Most dogs like to control livestock movement and find holding very reinforcing.

On leash to off leash

Another major transition that you will make is from having your dog on a leash or long line to being off leash. As your confidence grows in your dog, you will start giving your dog more and more freedom. Give your dog more freedom as you feel more comfortable. Each dog and handler team is different and grows and develops at their own rate.

Once your dog is working stock without being attached to a leash or long line, you may find that they are now able to reliably be around other livestock and highly distracting situations while off leash. If you walk your dog where there are cattle or sheep in pastures nearby, you may have to keep your dog on leash until your dog is reliable around the stock you are using in training. Transition from a leash to a long line, for extra safety, before you let your dog off leash. In herding and all dog training, safety should be your top priority.

In the next section of this book, we will revisit the outrun, lift, fetch, and in, as well as look at teaching and using whistles cues. We will also tackle advanced herding skills such as driving, cross-driving, penning, and shedding. When you have completed training the skills in the next section you and your dog will be ready to go to a trial or move stock skillfully around your farm, ranch, or acreage. How cool is that?

Section 2
Advanced Herding Skills

Chapter 11 Outrun and look for stock   151
Extending the outrun   152
Look for stock   153
Look for stock – Step by step   153
Cross overs   155
Slicing in on top   157
Set-out stock   158
Silent gathers   158
Blind gathers   159

Chapter 12 Look back, lift, and fetch   161
Before you start – Stand at home base   162
Before you start – Target stick   162
Look back – Step by step: Practice handling target stick and treats without your dog!   163
Phase 1 – The flip   163
Phase 2 – Fade target   164
Phase 3 – The look(Use large flirt pole)   165
Phase 4 – The flank   166

Phase 5 – The sheep   167
Look versus look back   169
The lift   170
The fetch   171

Chapter 13 In, driving, and cross driving   175
Anticipation   175
Adding a criterion to the in   176
Establishing the line   177
Tucking the corners   179
Flanks on the fly and flank directly to in   179
Circle stock away from handler – again!   180
Cross-driving   181
Cross-driving along a fence   182
Cross-driving without a fence   183
Cross-driving to panels   184
Driving a course   185
That's it!   185

SECTION 2 CONTENTS | 149

Chapter 14 Whistles   187
Types of whistles   188
Learning to whistle   189
When to add whistles   190
Adding whistle cues   190
Whistles versus verbal cues   191
Say what?   192

Chapter 15 Shedding without stock   195
Before you start – Necessary skills   197
The four-part shed   199
Sheep-less shedding   199
Sheep-less shed – Step by step   200
Before you start using sheep   202

Chapter 16 Shedding 1   205
Shed – Step by step   205
Phase 1 – Recall between penned sheep   205
Phase 2 – Hold   207
Phase 3 – Hold becomes shed   208
Phase 4 – Call dog next to sheep   210
Phase 5 – Make gap and call dog   211

Chapter 17 Shedding 2   215
Phase 6 – Dog makes gap   215
Phase 7 – Move away from fence   218
Shed – an alternate approach   221
Why shed?   224
General rules of shedding at trials   225
Reading the shed   226

CHAPTER 11

Outrun and look for stock

Your dog has mastered all of the foundation herding skills and is becoming more confident and capable every day. Now it is time to grow your dog's experience so that the fetch becomes usable around your acreage or at a trial. First on the agenda is extending the distance your dog can go on an outrun.

In a small paddock, and often in a larger area, your dog will run an arc from your feet to the backside of the stock. As you lengthen the outrun, behavioral economics will come into play. Instead of your dog running a huge arc, they will start to run more of a half pear-shaped outrun, with the smaller end of the pear at your feet.

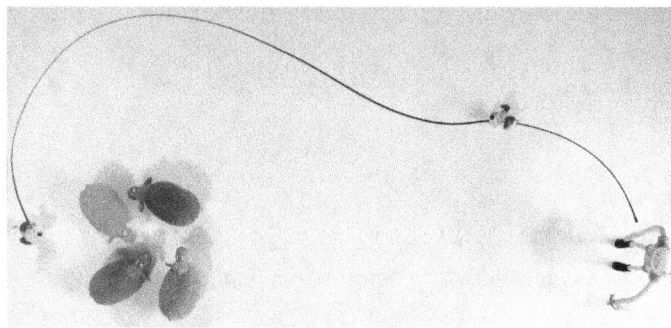

When the stock is a great distance away, dogs should run a pear-shaped path on the outrun to save time and effort. Running a half circle on a 300+ yard outrun would be a very inefficient path.

Your dog will take off from your feet, on either side of you, and flank out as they go. As your dog gets closer to the stock they will **kick out**, open up, and flank even farther from the stock to avoid disturbing the stock as they get around behind them for the lift. This is the natural and desirable shape of a long outrun. If your dog runs a huge arc from your feet on a long outrun, they will waste a lot of energy and time covering unnecessary ground and may lose contact with their stock.

Extending the outrun

Most people pick a place to stand in a new field and set their stock out at the distance their dog was fetching in the old field. Then they slowly increase the distance of the outrun by moving the **stock set-out** point, the place stock is set or standing in a paddock, farther from where the dog is sent. The dog is sent from the same place and the stock is set out farther and farther away from where the dog starts their outrun.

A better training design is to set the stock out at the distance your dog is used to outrunning in the smaller field, but instead of picking a fixed send point, start by setting the stock at the farthest point in the field, a fixed set-out point. Once your dog is comfortable doing the short fetch in this larger field, move your send point back away from the stock. The stock is set out at the same place and you and your dog move farther and farther from the stock to start the outrun. By moving your dog away from the stock, your dog always moves from a new, slightly unfamiliar place to more familiar territory.

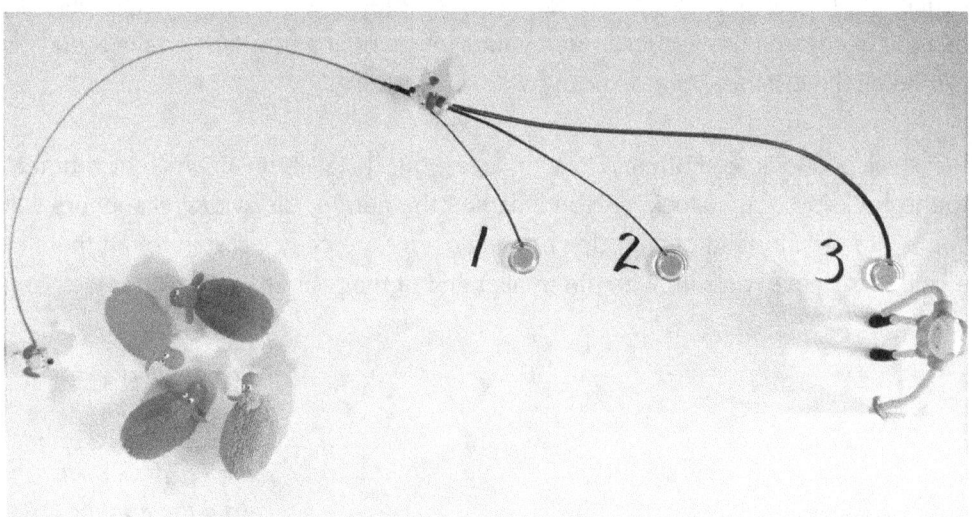

Train longer outruns by starting close and then moving farther from the stock. Dawg would first be sent from point 1, then moved back to point 2, and finally to point 3.

When your dog is used to running 100, 200, 400 yards or more, they will have generalized the outrun and will be looking for stock to be out a great distance from where they are starting their outrun. If you don't generalize the outrun distance, your dog may run out their usual distance and come in for the lift where they normally do, even though the stock is well beyond that point. If they continue flanking across in front of you and go beyond the midpoint of the line between you and the stock, they will have crossed between you and the stock, which is known as a **cross over**.

You *never* want your dog to cross over on their outrun. Your dog should cast out on the side you set them up on. There may be an important reason that you sent them in that direction, such as the pull or geography of the field. Also, if running in a trial, you will lose all of your outrun points if your dog crosses over on their outrun.

Look for stock

Once you start sending your dog on longer outruns, you need to add one more element to your fetch setup pattern. Everything will remain the same but you will add one more step before you send your dog.

> *Looking for stock is something that can be taught away from sheep. I used toys and Renn seemed to transfer naturally to sheep.*
>
> **Sally says**

This is another behavior that is handy to have on cue when you go to a trial or a new field. Once your dog knows this cue, they usually will give some indication when they have seen the stock. Common indications are a change in alertness, clapping, or staring toward the stock.

Look for stock – Step by step

1. Start with a tug or large treats, to be used as targets, in a room or fenced yard. Tugs will be better to use once you are placing the target at a distance since they are larger and easier for your dog to see.
2. Place the toy or treat directly in front of your dog on the floor, about 2 feet away from them. The tug or treat is now a target.
3. Stand next to your standing or sitting dog with both of you facing the target.
4. As soon as your dog looks at the target give your release cue. I use *get it*.
5. Your dog will go out and get the target. If it is a treat, they will eat it and if it is a tug, you will tug with your dog.
6. Repeat 3 times.

7. Now put the target 6 feet in front of your dog and tell them to *look*.
8. As soon as your dog looks at the target, give your release cue. Reinforce as before.
9. Now move the target 12 feet away from your dog and release them to it once they look at it. (Move the target farther away in smaller increments if your dog struggles to see it.)
10. Generalize this behavior by moving the target off to the side so it is no longer directly in front of your dog and release them to it once they look at it.

11. Next set your dog up as before, but make a noise or quietly call your dog's name. You want your dog to look briefly at you.
12. As soon as your dog looks at you, cue *look* and send your dog to the target as soon as they look at it, with your release cue.

13. Now withhold the release cue so that your dog has to wait between when they turn their attention away from you, see the target, and are released to the target. If your dog does not wait for your release cue, use your no reward marker procedure, and then reset your dog for the next trial.
14. Generalize the starting position to both sides of you, on your right and left sides.

15. Transfer this behavior to stock by cueing your dog to look, pause, and then start an outrun as soon as they look at or hook up to the livestock. The cue to begin the outrun has now become the reinforcer for the look behavior. Both you and your dog will be facing the livestock directly in front of you.
16. Finally, withhold the outrun cue so that your dog has to wait longer between when they see the stock and when they begin their outrun. You want your dog to leave on your verbal cue and not on the physical cue of seeing the livestock. Use your no reward marker procedure if necessary.

Training the look with a tug away from stock while going only a short distance, steps 7–9.

The tug is a little farther away and Sir is now on my left side.

After giving my look cue, Sir waited, then I released him to grab the tug.

Troubleshooting
- **Dog stares only at target** – If your dog stares only at the target, you need to get them to look at you so that you can insert the look cue before they look at the target. If making a noise or calling your dog's name prompts them to move around in front of you, try stationing your dog on a platform at your side. Reinforce your dog sitting or standing on the platform with several treats. Now try making a noise or calling their name to get them to look at you without moving their body.
- **Dog stares only at handler** – If your dog stares only at you and will not look at the target, the tug or treat, you will need to up the value of the target. Try switching to super high-value treats or having a rousing game of tug before you go back to working this exercise. You may even use your flirt pole rat as the target.
- **Dog loses track of the target** – Try pointing at the target to give your dog an idea of its location. Watch your dog closely to determine when they pinpoint the target's location.
- **Dog moves when you cue look** – Change your dog's position, from your dog standing next to you to sitting or lying down. Your dog will be less likely to move out of a sit or down than from a stand.

After working away from stock, move back into your paddock with livestock and set up your dog for a fetch. When your dog is set up on the side you want them to go, put a hand on your dog's collar so they don't take off, look out at the stock, and tell your dog to *look*. You want your dog to notice the stock before you send them on their outrun. As soon as your dog spots the stock, send them to fetch them.

For the final look behavior, you don't want your dog to leave as soon as they spot livestock. Instead, they need to wait several seconds for your verbal cue to begin their outrun. You will cue your dog to look, pause, and when ready, cue the outrun.

At a trial you want your dog to spot the livestock as soon as they walk onto the trial field. If they do not, you can use your look cue once you get to the post. Often your dog will spot the livestock while the stock is being moved to the set-out point, so there will be a delay while the stock is correctly positioned for you to start your run. If your dog has spotted the stock, you do not need to use your look cue.

Cross overs
Any time during the fetch that your dog goes over an imaginary straight line between you and the stock, your dog has **crossed over**. Your dog can cross over right in front of you, right in front of the stock, or anywhere in between. Your dog may run almost

straight up the field at the stock and then flare out just as they get to the livestock without crossing over, but this approach is not desirable as it will most likely push the stock away from you. In a trial, you will be docked significantly for your dog taking this direct path. If your dog does cross over, you will lose even more points, usually all of the points allocated for the outrun.

If your dog starts to run straight up the field toward the stock or crosses over, stop your dog immediately! Give your no reward marker, pause for 10 seconds, and call your dog back. If this is the first time your dog has not opened up correctly, reset and try the outrun again. If your dog repeats running up the field or trying to cross over, stop them, use your NRM procedure, and move closer to your stock for your next outrun.

Do NOT allow your dog to continue and fetch the livestock if they run straight up the field or cross over! By allowing your dog to complete the fetch you are giving huge reinforcement for incorrect behavior!

If you have patterned how you set up your dog for the outrun from the time you started fence line fetches, your dog should not be trying to run straight up the field or cross over. Always be aware that your dog may offer this behavior, seemingly out of the blue, and be ready to stop your dog immediately. This is one habit that you do not want your dog to start!

Some dogs will try to cross over if you send them away from the pull. They sense the stock will get away from them and they want to go to the side that keeps them in control of the stock. If this is the reason your inexperienced dog is trying to cross over, you need to send them the other way or move much closer. When your dog gains experience, you can send them away from the pull if you need to and your dog should be able to adjust to get out around the livestock. Sometimes you don't have a choice of which direction you send your dog because there is an obstacle, such as a pond or dangerous terrain, that dictates which way your dog must be sent.

Your dog must go all the way around behind the stock, staying on the side you sent them from until they get behind the stock, or they don't get to bring the livestock to you. Instead of completing an incorrect outrun, they are stopped, given a time-out, called back, and re-sent.

Slicing in on top

As you extend the outrun you may find your dog slicing in on top. Your dog **slices in on top** when they come in too close before getting behind the livestock and force the stock to move sideways, before the lift. The goal is for your dog to get all the way around to the back of the livestock without disturbing them so that the **lift**, the first movement of the livestock, is calm and straight toward the handler.

Some dogs learn to slice in because the stock they are fetching, usually sheep, have learned to head to the handler as soon as they see the dog start their outrun. If you do a lot of outruns and end the fetch with the stock at your feet, the livestock will learn that being near you is a safe zone and they may head to you when your dog has barely left your feet.

The problem is that your dog will fall in behind the stock as the stock heads to you rather than getting behind them and lifting them. Preventing your stock from developing the bad habit of running to you just as you send your dog is the reason you should often drive the stock past you on the fetch rather than having your dog always bring them to your feet or in front of you.

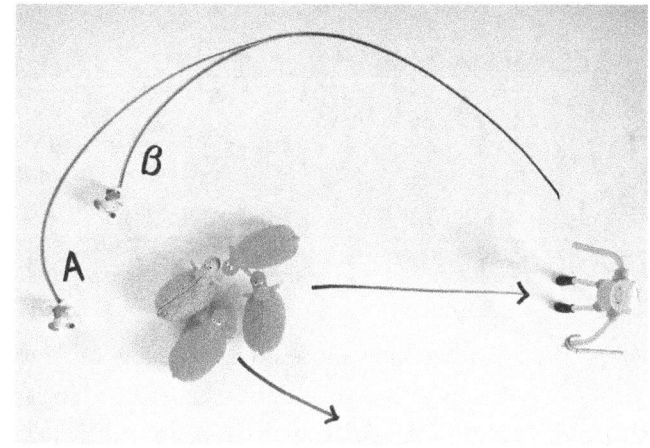

This diagram shows Dawg coming in on top correctly behind the sheep (A) and slicing in on top (B). If there is no strong pull, which direction would you expect the sheep to lift in each scenario?

If you notice your dog is pushing the livestock off to the side on top as you extend the outrun, you should cue an out just as your dog starts to slice in. If your dog takes the out and goes on around, as they should, then allow them to bring the stock. If your dog continues slicing in, use your no reward marker, stop your dog, pause 10 seconds, and call them back. If your dog is more experienced, don't use your out, just use your no reward marker, stop your dog, pause 10 seconds, and call them back. Allowing a dog to work stock is a huge reinforcer, so don't allow your dog to work livestock in an incorrect manner.

 *If your experienced dog slices their flank on the outrun, use your NRM procedure; then call your dog back to repeat the outrun. Give your NRM verbal cue and stop the outrun as soon as your dog starts to slice in. If your foundation is solid, your dog will start to open up after being called back a few times.*

Set-out stock

Having a friend use their dog to set out stock for your dog to fetch is a valuable experience for your dog. Almost all trials use a set-out crew to move and hold stock so that every run starts at the same point. Some trials use crews with both dogs and horses. If you are going to a trial that sets out with horses, be sure and expose your dog to some horses being used for setting out.

If your dog has never seen another person, with or without a dog, next to the stock, they may hold the livestock to the set-out person instead of bringing them to you. Most dogs figure this out quite quickly but don't leave it to chance if you are planning on trialling your dog.

This picture shows my dog practicing long outruns with a friend and his dog holding sheep for my dog to fetch to me. My friend and the sheep are on the right side of the horizon and I am taking the picture.

When your dog becomes more advanced, a good learning experience is being part of the set-out crew at a trial. Your dog has to be able to let another dog come up and take control of the livestock they have been controlling and yield control to that dog. This is a situation that really tests your dog's self-control!

Silent gathers

A **silent gather** is a fetch with only one cue allowed, the fetch cue. You would send your dog and then remain silent. Silent gathers are a great way to identify the weak parts of your fetch. If your dog understands their job and has a strong foundation, they will complete the outrun, lift, and fetch without a problem. The stock should stay settled until your dog arrives behind them, calmly move off toward you as a group, travel a straight line at a moderate pace to you, and finally, arrive at your feet.

Any deviation from the ideal tells you where you need to concentrate your focus and training efforts. The silent gather puts all of the responsibility for a correct fetch on your dog.

If your dog does not have herding instinct, they will not be able to do silent gathers. You will have to cue all parts of the fetch; the outrun, lift, and fetch.

Blind gathers

A **blind gather** is a fetch where the animals to be gathered are out of sight. Before you try a blind gather be sure your dog can do a silent gather. If the stock is not in sight, you will not be able to help your dog with the lift or beginning of the fetch. Your dog must be able to work on their own, without cues from you, until the stock is in your sight.

Never send your dog for stock out of sight if you are not 100% sure that there is stock to be found.

To set your dog up for success doing blind gathers, always use your setup pattern for the outrun. Set your dog up at your feet and face where the livestock will be found. If you send your dog and there is no stock to be gathered, you start to break down the trust that you have built with your dog. It's okay if your dog comes back and does not locate the stock. Just go out closer to the stock and resend your dog.

In the next chapter, we will cover the look back and go over lifts and fetches in more detail. Those elements will complete your dog's training for getting the livestock in the paddock or field to your feet.

CHAPTER 12

Look back, lift, and fetch

When your dog is sent on a fetch, they are to bring all of the stock that is visible to them or search for stock if none is visible. If they start on their outrun focusing on a close group of animals, you may see them naturally kick out wider when they realize there are more animals in the area to gather.

Inexperienced dogs sometimes get focused on the closest group of animals and don't notice that there are other animals nearby. Thus, they will lift the close group and start fetching them. Since you don't want your dog to bring only part of the flock or herd, you need a cue to tell them to look back behind them for more animals. You need a look back cue. **Look back** means turn around and look for more animals. Once your dog turns around and spots the new set of stock, you will then cue a flank to tell your dog which direction you want them to go to pick up those animals.

If your dog knows how to look for stock, they are halfway to having a look back behavior.

This cue is only given after you have stopped your dog. The look back is more of a static behavior than a moving one, basically a change of focus and direction. Initially, you will want the second group of livestock to be visible to your dog, once your dog turns back to look for them. Once your dog understands the concept of looking back for more stock, you can send them for livestock out of sight, but you may need to cue an *out* if your dog starts to come in too much before getting behind the livestock.

Before you start – Stand at home base

Before training the look back, you need your dog standing perpendicular to you on home base. To train home base, take 20 to 30 treats and stand your dog. You may use a rug as a home base station but it is not required. Don't use a platform as a home base unless it is half an inch thick, or thinner.

As soon as you get your dog standing at home base, quickly feed a series of 5 to 10 treats, one at a time. Then start to feed treats at a slower pace, with more time in between each treat. You may verbally mark before each treat or just feed the treats without any marks. Continue stretching out the time between the treats, increasing duration, until your dog will stand still for 10 seconds between reinforcers. Be sure to ping-pong the amount of time you wait between treats so that you are not continually making it more difficult for your dog.

Move into a position perpendicular to your dog to start training the look back exercise. If your dog moves off of home base position, shape them to stand at home base with you standing perpendicular beside them. Pictures illustrating this exercise follow between the Look back Phase 1 and 2 instructions below.

Before you start – Target stick

To teach a look back you need your dog to follow a *target stick*. (See Chapter 12 in *Positive Herding 101* for target training.) For this exercise use a long target stick (at least 24 inches in length) and shape your dog to follow it, keeping their nose 6 to 12 inches from the target. Your dog should be able to follow the target by trotting in a circle around you, turning in a tight circle or spinning, and jumping up toward it, before you start this look back training. Your dog also needs to be able to stand in place for at least 5 seconds without offering to sit or move away from you.

I like my dogs to jump as they turn to look back but the important element of the behavior is a complete 180° turn, end for end. If you prefer, you can eliminate the jump as a criterion for the behavior.

As you start training this exercise, hide a treat in the hand that is on the same side that your dog is facing. Hold the target stick in your other hand. Once your dog is flipping past perpendicular, facing directly away from you, switch treat and target stick hands. You always want the treat hand closest to where you will be delivering the reinforcer.

Once your dog is flipping past 90°, you should be holding the target stick in your left hand, if your dog is spinning clockwise, and have a treat hidden in your right hand. If your dog is spinning counterclockwise you should now be holding the target stick in your right hand and have a treat hidden in your left hand. (See pictures below.)

You always want the hand hiding the treat to be closest to your dog's mouth when they have flipped completely around (180°). This setup helps to facilitate feeding the treat quickly and smoothly, once you have marked the behavior. Note that I usually use a verbal marker for training this behavior because both of my hands are full. One hand holds the target stick and the other a treat.

Look back – Step by step

Practice handling target stick and treats without your dog before starting this training!

Phase 1 – The flip
1. Grab some high-value treats, a treat pouch, and a target stick.
2. Stand facing your dog holding the target stick, but with the actual target behind your back.
3. Your dog stands perpendicular to you such that you are looking at their side.
4. If you have noted your dog likes to spin in a certain direction, clockwise or counter-clockwise, then use that direction for this behavior.

5. Lower the target within a few inches of the side of your dog's head, to the opposite side of your dog that you are standing next to. You will be extending the target stick handle over your dog's back.
6. When your dog turns their head to look at the target, mark, and reinforce by delivering a treat to your dog's mouth while it is near the target stick.
7. Lift the target back up and behind your back to reset, after you reinforce your dog.
8. Reset your dog to the initial starting position after every trial.

9. Shape your dog to move their feet and turn farther away from you until you are both looking in the same direction, with your dog in front of you.
10. Start to hold the target up high enough that your dog jumps to touch it as they turn toward it.
11. Continue shaping the turn until your dog is turning 180°, such that they end up pointed in the opposite direction from which they started.
12. Repeat until your dog is confidently turning end for end.

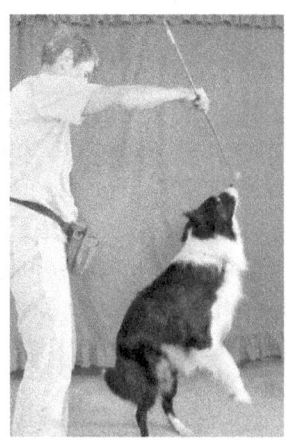

In this series, Sir has progressed to step 11. His starting position is perpendicular to me. Sir jumps as he turns to follow the target until he is facing the opposite direction from which he started.

13. To get a quicker turn throw the food after you mark the turn.
14. Switch from food to a toy or tug to further increase the speed of the turn.
15. Add the cue *look back* before you present the target.
16. Repeat until your dog is again confidently turning end for end. At this point, the verbal cue has no meaning for your dog.

Phase 2 – Fade target
1. Switch your target stick end for end or remove the target ball to begin fading the target stick.
2. Repeat until your dog is confidently turning end for end.
3. Now replace the target stick with your hand as the target. Mimic the movement of the target stick with your hand.

4. Decrease your hand movement until you can completely fade your hand out of the picture, so that you only use a verbal cue and no target movement as a cue.
5. Move farther away from your dog and generalize the behavior by ping-ponging your position closer and farther from your dog and at different angles from them.

From this point on, your dog must wait for a release cue before they move forward to get reinforcement. When looking back for livestock your dog needs to flip around away from you on cue but needs to wait for a flank cue to know which way to begin their fetch. If you set your dog up correctly during the look back, you can use your fetch cue, as it will be obvious to your dog which direction they need to go to fetch the livestock. More on that later!

CHAPTER 12 LOOK BACK, LIFT, AND FETCH | 165

This is the completion of the look back turn. I am now using my hand as the target. The next step is to fade and eliminate my hand movement.

Phase 3 – The look (Use large flirt pole)

1. Once your dog is flipping end for end, stand in front of your dog, hold the flirt pole handle, and place the rat on the ground about 4 feet behind your dog, such that when your dog flips around they are facing the rat. The rat should be positioned where you previously threw food or a tug.
2. Cue *look back* and when your dog flips around successfully, reinforce with the cue *yes*, and then cue *get it* and allow your dog to grab the rat. If your dog does not see the rat, use the flirt pole handle to make it move.
3. If your dog goes for the rat before you release them with *get it*, fly the rat back up into your free hand. You want your dog to wait for a release cue, after flipping around, before going for the rat.
4. Repeat by having your dog flip back to their starting position, with the rat already in place. Your dog will always flip around in the same direction, clockwise or counterclockwise.
5. Now your dog should be flipping on cue, looking at the rat, but waiting for a release cue before grabbing the rat.

Troubleshooting
- ***Dog doesn't wait for release cue*** – If your dog has trouble waiting for their release cue use a stop cue as the reinforcer for the flip instead of a verbal marker. For my dogs that would make the cue sequence: **look back > there > get it** (In phase 4, *get it* would be replaced with a flank cue.)
- ***Dog is confused by use of flirt pole*** – If your dog does not hook up to the rat, try using a tug or other toy instead of a flirt pole. You may even hold the tug behind your back to start and then throw it after your dog has flipped around. Eventually, start throwing the tug out before you ask your dog to flip.

Finally, your dog should be able to walk in to and then flank around the tug or flirt pole rat, when cued.

Phase 4 – The flank
1. Once your dog is watching the rat and waiting for their release cue before grabbing the rat, move your starting position such that you can place the rat on the ground 10 feet away from your dog once they have flipped around.
2. Cue *look back* and after your dog flips, allow them to find and focus on the rat out in front of them. If they don't see the rat, make it move a bit.
3. If your dog holds their position, cue the flank that would take them away from you such that you are not cueing an off-balance flank.
4. If your dog flanks out around the rat, cue *get it* and tug with your dog.
5. If your dog goes directly to grab the rat instead of flanking, whip the rat back into your free hand and start again.

---

6. Repeat until your dog can flip, pause, and then flank on cue.
7. Now change your position to the opposite side, so you are cueing the other flank, and repeat. (Your dog will still be flipping around the same direction no matter which flank cue you are using.)

LEFT: *At this point, I am waiting for Sir to flip around before throwing the tug.*

RIGHT: *I used a tug for this phase to show that it is a viable alternative to using a flirt pole. Use what works for you and your dog!*

LEFT: *The movement of the flying tug focused Sir on it as he waited for a cue.*

RIGHT: *I then cued come bye as I wanted him to flank away from me and not cross between me and the tug.*

Phase 5 – The sheep

1. Finally, take this exercise to sheep. Have two pens of sheep, separated by a good distance, 40 to 50 feet. Use very high-value treats as the reinforcer for this phase of the training.
2. Position your dog halfway between the two pens of sheep, but facing and hooked up on the stock in one pen. You stand to the side and slightly behind your dog.
3. Start with just asking for the flip by cueing look back. Your dog should flip around and face the other pen of sheep, but *not* move toward them. Mark and reinforce with food delivered directly to your dog's mouth.

4. When your dog is flipping back and forth between pens on cue you are ready to add a flank. The flank cue will now be the reinforcer for flipping around.
5. After your dog flanks around behind the penned sheep, stop them and recall them back to you. Reinforce the recall with food.
6. Fade yourself out of the picture by slowly moving away from your dog.

7. Now have your dog flip around, wait while focusing on the sheep, and flank around the sheep they are facing until they get behind those sheep. Then, stop your dog, flank them back the other way, and stop your dog directly between the two pens at their starting position.
8. Now have your dog look back at the other set of sheep and repeat the exercise.

9. Eventually, move the pens of sheep farther and farther apart.
10. Finally, secure helpers to hold each set of unpenned sheep at a good distance from each other. You and your dog will be on one point of a triangle and the sets of sheep will each be on the other two points.
11. Send your dog to gather one set of sheep.

12. When the sheep are at your feet have your dog look back for the other set.
13. Once your dog spots the new set, flank your dog around them. Remember, if you send your dog on a flank, you will have to tell them when to stop or turn in.

It's important that when you send your dog on their second outrun that your dog does not cross over in front of you. Be sure to flank your dog away from you and not around in front of you.

Above left and above: When you go to penned stock, begin near your dog and use high-value treats, just as you did when you started teaching the look back in your house.

Left: When your dog is looking back without prompting, start moving away to generalize the behavior.

To prevent a cross over, flank your dog to the side you are going to send them, to move them out from being directly between the two groups. So if you are going to send your dog come bye for the second group you would flank your dog away to me, while still

The final stage with penned stock is for your dog to flip, wait, and then flank around the penned stock in the direction you cue. It will take several training sessions to build this behavior to fluency but your dog should find flanking to be a high-value reinforcer for the look back.

hooked up on and working the first group, and stop your dog at about 10 o'clock. Now your dog is set up for a look back cue and then a come bye flank once they have spotted the second group.

If you set your dog up correctly by flanking them around to the correct position before asking them to look back, you should be able to just cue a fetch at that point and have your dog head in the correct direction.

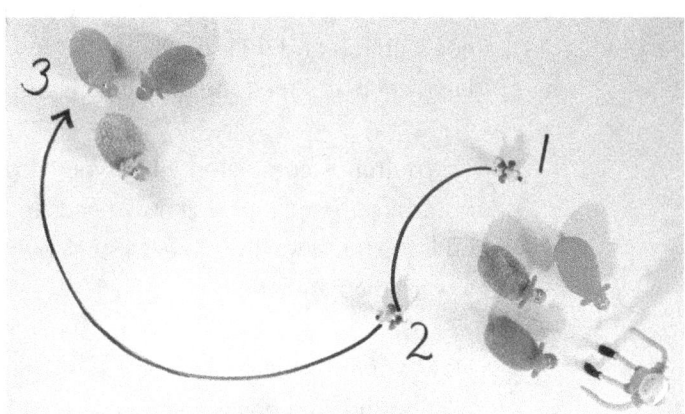

This diagram shows how to set up Dawg for a second fetch. In this scenario, Dawg is at point 1 and needs to fetch the farther group but due to constraints he must flank come bye on the fetch. He is hooked up on the closer flock so he would be flanked away to me and stopped at point 2. He would then be asked to look back and then sent come bye to point 3 or beyond to lift the stock.

Most times it is safer to cue a flank instead of a fetch and make sure that your dog starts their fetch in the correct direction to prevent them from crossing over between you and the second set of livestock.

Dogs love to work, so being cued that there are more animals to herd is like giving them a pass to herding heaven! The look back behavior comes in handy whenever your dog misses some stock while fetching. It is also necessary for completing an advanced trial element called the double lift. The **double lift** requires your dog to fetch one group of animals, look back for a second group, and then cast out and fetch the second group.

Look versus look back

Look and look back are very similar cues, both in how they sound and what they cue your dog to do – look for livestock. You may want to use different verbal cues for look back and look. When you transition your verbal cues to whistles you will definitely want a different whistle for each behavior.

I use look and look back without any problem primarily because they are situational cues. Look is only cued when my dog is standing next to me and look back is cued only when my dog is at a considerable distance from me.

With the look cue, your dog already knows which direction to fetch because they are standing beside you. With the look back cue, your dog has to be told which direction to flank. Having your dog pause between spotting stock and starting to flank is vital in order to have time to tell your dog which direction to go, after looking back and spotting the stock.

The lift

The most important part of your fetch is the lift. The lift is the transition between your dog's outrun and their fetch. The lift is where your dog and the stock have their first interaction and the tone of the fetch and possibly the entire run is set during the lift.

The outrun is completed when your dog successfully gets behind the stock without disturbing them. Your dog now needs to lift or get the stock moving toward you. The **lift** is the transition from the livestock being stationary and settled to calmly moving off toward the handler.

How your dog lifts the stock is extremely important because it determines the relationship your dog is going to have with the stock during this encounter. If your dog comes in fast and hard and startles the stock, they may get nervous and bunch tightly or split up. If your dog stalls and barely inches forward, the stock may challenge your dog, refuse to move, or wander off.

The first time your dog interacts with the stock sets the tone for how the stock will respond to your dog, during your run or the practical work you are trying to accomplish.

There is a difference between a dog that comes in fast and hard and a dog that has power. Sometimes a weak dog will come in and jam their stock due to fear, rather than power. Offense can be the best defense. If animals are running away, they are much less likely to stop and turn on a dog. A dog that has power will come in unhurriedly and apply unwavering pressure until the livestock moves off. Even if the livestock turn to face the dog, stamp their feet, or shake their heads, the dog with power will stay hooked up with laser focus on the stock's eyes. As the stock turns away the dog will allow them some space to move off and then fall in behind them.

A fearful dog may try several maneuvers to get the stock moving, including staring, inching forward, lowering their head, lunging, flanking back and forth, and even barking. Breed tendencies to bark vary, but for most border collies, barking is a desperate, last-ditch effort to get the livestock moving.

If your dog shows any fear or unease around stock, your most important job becomes bolstering their courage. You can help your dog by staying close to them in tight situations, making sure they always win when challenged by livestock, and initially training on light stock that is easy to move.

You can't always get a dog past their fear of stock, but you can almost always shatter the confidence of an inexperienced dog by putting them in over their heads too soon. Always err on the side of safety and concern about preserving your dog's confidence. You cannot give a dog power, but you can undermine the power that they have. Switch to lighter sheep, smaller calves, goats, or ducks, if your dog shows a lack of confidence.

The fetch

The **fetch** is the drive from the lift to your feet. If your dog lifts all of the animals in the group with calm authority, they will move off together and head toward you. Now is when you want your dog to pace themselves. You want the stock to move at a steady **pace**, which is a purposeful walk or calm trot. The stock should not be leisurely strolling and grabbing mouthfuls of grass, but instead, be walking with purpose or calmly trotting. If the stock gets **off line**, deviate from the direct path to you, your dog should flank over to bring them back on line. If your dog does not flank, allow them a chance to flank by pausing a moment, then cue the flank. When your dog has gone far enough to bring the stock back on line, ask your dog in.

By allowing your dog the latitude to flank to bring the stock back on line without you giving a flank cue, you prevent your dog from becoming mechanical. A **mechanical dog** always waits for a cue before moving.

Some dogs naturally hold a line once it is established. These dogs are referred to as line dogs.

Ideally, the fetch flows smoothly, with your dog bringing the stock at a steady pace, rather than starting and stopping. If your dog punches the stock and then has to be stopped, as the stock flush out away from them, the fetch becomes jerky. This can also happen if a dog is reticent to push stock and claps or stops as soon as the stock starts to move off. Every time your dog stops, they lose control of the stock and have to re-initiate contact with them.

Some dogs can get stock to **lean on** them or suck the stock back on themselves and thus can control the stock with almost imperceptible movements from behind. These dogs can often bring stock back on line without flanking out to cover them. Instead, they will use their eyes or drop a shoulder and pull the livestock back on line without flanking. Watching these dogs work gives you an even greater appreciation for their innate skills. You cannot teach a dog to drop a shoulder or pull livestock back onto themselves, but you can learn to see and value those instinctive skills when they appear.

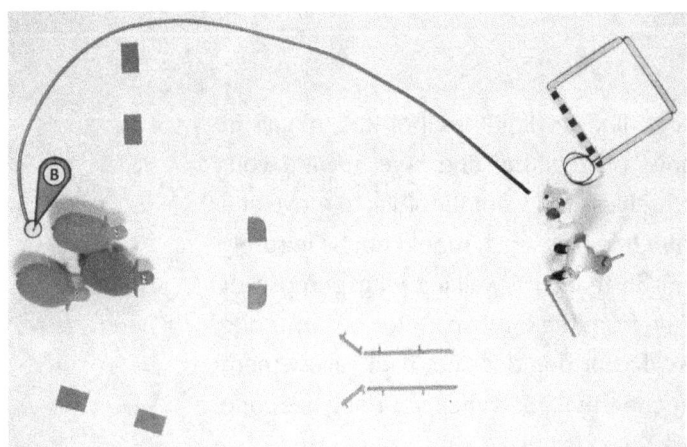

Path of outrun to balance. The point of balance is indicated by the "B" in the pointer behind the sheep.

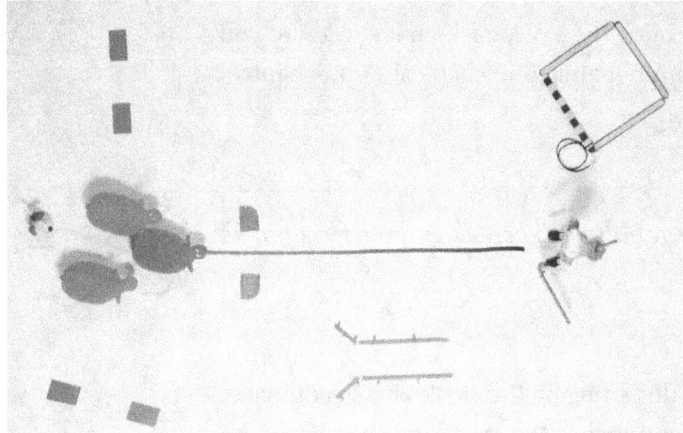

Dawg lifts the sheep to start the fetch.

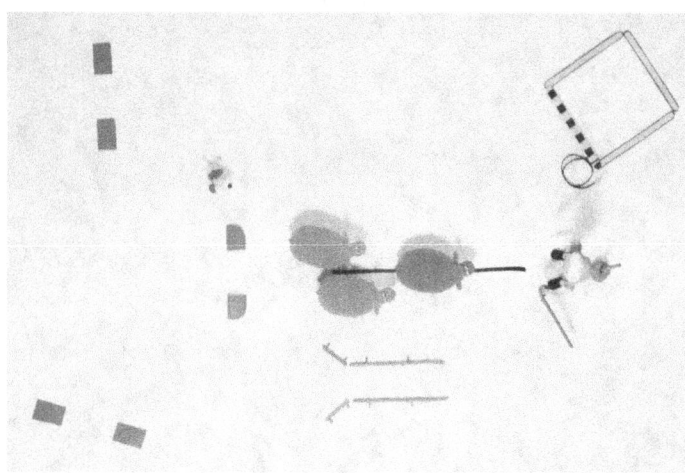

The sheep are fetched through the fetch panels and brought straight to the feet of the handler.

As your dog fetches farther distances be sure to allow them the opportunity to flank over and bring the stock that has wandered, back on line without a verbal cue. If you always jump in with a flank cue, your dog will likely come to wait for a cue and will not automatically bring off-line animals back on line. If you do not allow your dog to make any decisions about handling the stock, your dog will become mechanical. A mechanical dog waits to be told every move to make.

On the other hand, you don't want your dog flipping from side to side unnecessarily. Too much **wearing**, flanking back and forth, tends to unsettle the livestock. If your dog is working 3 to 5 head that stay together well, your dog should not flank excessively and instead should be able to walk straight into the group and bring them as one unit. If your dog is working 15 or more head or a small group that does not want to stay together, your dog will have to flank farther and more often to keep the group bunched and headed in the right direction.

Your dog should now have the basics of fetching stock from a greater distance in place, including the setup, outrun, lift, and fetch. Next, let's re-visit walking in and then we can move on to driving and cross driving.

CHAPTER 13

In, driving and cross-driving

Walking in is all about applying pressure to livestock and is the basis for many elements of herding. Herding elements related to applying pressure include the lift, fetch, drive, and cross-drive; pressure is also fundamental to shedding and penning. Herding is based on applying and releasing pressure. Not enough pressure and the stock will not move; too much pressure and the stock may blast in all directions. Knowing how to read stock and practicing good stockmanship are key to smooth, calm livestock movement.

Remember, there are times that you, as a predator, will also be applying and releasing pressure on the livestock. Anytime you are working a close-in element, such as penning, shedding, or putting the stock into a barn or trailer, teamwork becomes vital. Both you and your dog apply and release pressure in a coordinated effort to persuade the livestock to move as directed. Herding is always a game of pressure and angles.

Anticipation

Being a keen observer of your dog and livestock is one of the most important skills a handler can possess. All of your cues are based on what you see and what you anticipate is going to happen. If you wait for things to happen before you respond, you are almost always going to be late giving cues. Cues should be given just before your dog needs to respond to allow your dog time to respond.

You have to read the livestock movement or situation, formulate a cue, deliver the cue, *and* your dog has to have time to receive and respond to the given cue. Plus, each handler and dog have different latency or lag times between their ability to perceive a situation or stimulus and respond to it. The slower your dog's reaction times are, the sooner you have to cue your dog.

Sally says: *I noticed at some trials that even the handlers with good timing often misjudge the time it will take for their cue to actually reach the dog, if their dog is a long distance away (especially if the wind is against them).*

The best way to improve your timing is to practice herding different livestock in different situations and locations. Experience is a great teacher if you are willing and able to observe and change your behavior. Having a friend or teacher to guide you or studying your videos are also great ways to grow your abilities and confidence. Video is particularly helpful since you may not have access to a knowledgeable mentor and you can watch video in slow motion.

Timing is a matter of split seconds, so slowing down or stopping a video can make a murky situation crystal clear. If you struggle with timing, don't despair! I cannot tell you how many hundreds of times I had been told my cues were "too late" before I realized I had to anticipate my dog's and the stock's movement in order to give cues on time.

If you keep finding yourself cueing late, concentrate on anticipating when the livestock will turn their heads or start to move and how long it takes your dog to respond to your cues.

If you still struggle with timing, you may benefit from again working livestock without your dog. Taking your dog out of the equation frees you up to concentrate on reading the livestock and responding to their movement without worrying about what your dog is doing. There is a lot to keep track of when you, your dog, and the livestock are all interacting, so take advantage of every opportunity you get to grow your timing skills.

Adding a criterion to the in

As you work large groups of stock or smaller groups that don't flock or stay together well, one of your dog's main responsibilities is to fetch and drive *all* of the stock. You now need to add another criterion to the walk in behavior: drive all of the livestock.

Let's say you have a group of 20 goats in a small enclosure. You send your dog around behind them while you stand at an open gate. When your dog is in position behind them you ask your dog *in*. What you want your dog to do is to push the entire group forward and out the gate, which may mean your dog has to wear or flank a bit to get all the goats to move. What you don't want your dog to do is to push just the five or eight animals directly in front of them to the gate, while allowing the other goats to remain stationary or hang back in the enclosure.

Do not allow your dog to bring only part of a group while allowing the other animals to remain behind! In means to bring ALL of the livestock!

Establishing the line

Driving is based on lines. The shortest distance between two points is a straight line and in herding, especially trialling, driving is based on straight lines. To tell your dog what direction you want them to take the stock, you need to **establish the line of the drive**. To establish a line, you first have to determine where you want the livestock to go, the destination. Once you know where the stock is to go, you next need to determine where to ask your dog in to take the stock in the desired direction, where you ask your dog in will be the point of inception. Imagine a 20-foot alley along your drive line and strive to keep the stock within that imaginary alley during the drive.

Establishing the line would be rather simple if you did not have to take pull into consideration. Just as *your dog* has to adjust where they turn into the stock at the top of the outrun, depending on the pull in the situation, *you* have to consider the pull when you ask your dog in to establish a drive line.

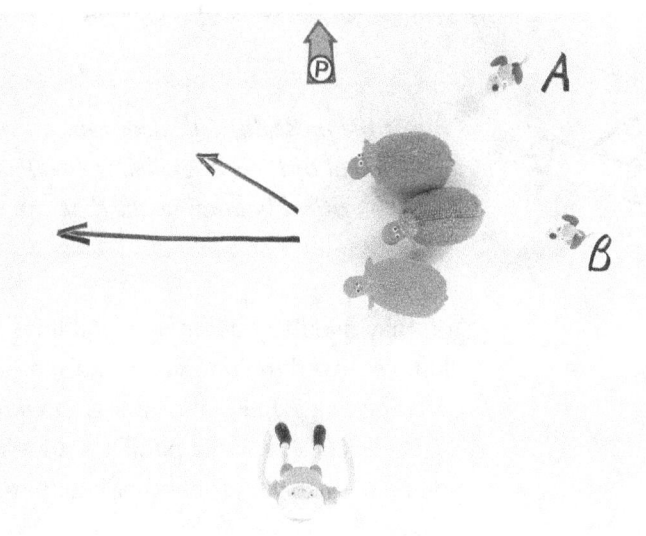

If the pull (P + short, wide arrow) is away from Shandler, would Dawg have to apply pressure at A or at B, to cross-drive the sheep? (The cross-drive path is the longer arrow.) Why would applying pressure at the other position take the sheep on the shorter path?

Sometimes, you will ask your dog in and then realize you were incorrect because the livestock is not heading in the desired direction. If this happens, you will have to flank your dog to re-set the line and ask your dog in again. Once the line is established, your dog should hold that line. **Line dogs** are dogs that hold a line instinctively, but most dogs have to learn through repeated experience. If the livestock starts to go off line, you should pause to give your dog the opportunity to flank and correct the off line movement before you give a flank cue to bring the stock back on line. If your dog does not spontaneously flank to bring the stock back on line, then you would cue your dog to flank and then ask them in again.

It is very important that you include the pause that allows your dog time to correct the stock's direction and bring them back on line. If you always cue a flank the moment the stock start to head a bit off line, your dog will not learn to take responsibility for holding the line and will always depend on you to tell them when to flank. Use your dog's instinctive abilities to the max and don't make your dog mechanical!

If your dog does not have a lot of herding instinct, you will have to read the pull and tell your dog not only where to turn in to establish the line but also when to flank during the drive to hold the line.

Once your dog takes over responsibility for holding the line, you still must be alert and flank your dog if they allow the stock to go off-line. The final responsibility for anything your dog does lies with you. If you don't like what your dog is doing, it is your responsibility to have them change their behavior.

One of the most difficult decisions an inexperienced handler makes is when to take control of their dog, give it cues, and when to let their dog work on instinct. This is a critical balancing act that can only be mastered through trial and error.

You may need to establish several lines in succession to get the stock to where you ultimately need them to go. In trials, the drives are usually to fetch or drive gates and each line to a gate is called a **leg**. On your acreage, you may need to establish a line to get the stock behind a pond, set another line to bring the stock along the side of the pond, and then set yet another line to move the livestock out a gate.

Tucking the corners

Another important herding concept is tucking the corners. A **corner** is the lateral edge of a group of animals during driving. There are two corners, one out to each back side of the group, for your dog to cover as they drive. To keep the group bunched together and moving your dog may need to flank out to a corner and tuck the animals there back into the group. This is called **tucking the corner**. Especially with a large group, your dog needs to flank or wear the stock to keep them together and moving in the same direction.

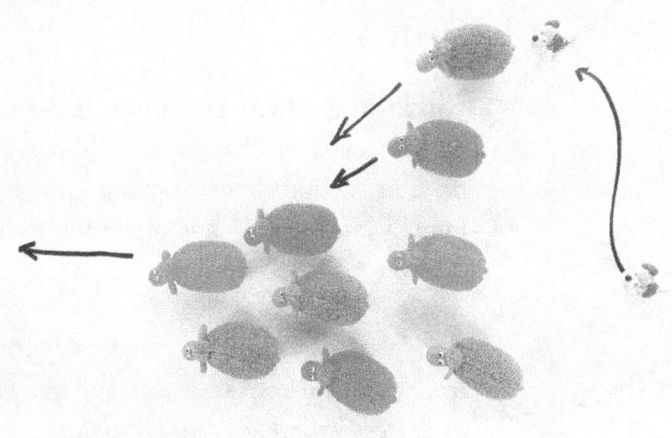

The two sheep at the top of the diagram are drifting away from the line of the drive. Dawg needs to move from directly behind the flock to tuck the upper corner and keep the flock together and moving in the correct direction.

If the corners are not tucked, animals will tend to fall behind or spread out in a long line perpendicular to the drive line, rather than come as a bunched group. It is much easier for your dog to control animals that are bunched as compared to those that are spread out. If the animals are spread out, your dog will have to flank much farther to get to the corners to push them ahead or change their direction. As your dog goes out to one side to influence the animals there, the animals on the other side will tend to slow down, stop, or wander.

Less confident, less experienced, or sideways-moving dogs may not want to apply pressure and thus will allow the stock to spread out and form a long line, side by side, rather than stay bunched in a group. Be on your toes with these dogs as they prefer not to push. Refrain from stopping these dogs as much as possible. If you do have to flank these dogs, don't stop them before you ask them in.

Flanks on the fly and flank directly to in

If your dog struggles with transitions and you have not worked transitioning without stopping your dog, now is a good time to do so. Driving and cross-driving require your dog to take their in, stop, and flank cues without hesitation. You may also need to work on your dog moving from flank to opposite flank or from flank to walk in, without stopping. Both scenarios are trained similarly because you are eliminating a stop between changing flank directions or between a flank and an in.

If you have a forward-moving dog you will transition from flank to flank and from flank to walk in much less than if you have a sideways-moving dog. A forward-moving dog tends to be pushy so you may need to use more stops and pauses, but a sideways-moving dog tends to be sticky, so you will want to eliminate as many stops as possible. If your dog has trouble transitioning between flanks and walking in see Transitions in Chapter 9.

Circle stock away from handler – again!

As mentioned in Chapter 9, an important exercise that your dog needs to know to drive in any direction is circling stock far enough away from you that they flank in front of you. Go back and revisit this exercise if your dog is not fluent performing this behavior.

Again, remember to start and end circling sessions with fetches! You always want to protect your dog's sense of balance and excessive circling can be detrimental to maintaining balance.

After your dog is comfortable flanking in front of you, start moving farther away from the stock and have your dog flank all the way around the livestock in both directions. Then move on to adding stops and changes of direction. Finally, add walking in.

It also bears repeating, that at no time should your dog begin orbiting or blindly circling the stock. Your dog should always be reading the stock. Watch to see that your dog is occasionally looking in at the stock as they flank around. If your dog starts to orbit, eliminate full circle flanking around the stock for a while.

Once your dog can flank completely around the livestock in both directions, flank off-balance, and take in, out, and stop cues you are ready to move on to cross-driving.

Cross-driving is primarily known for its use in trials but is also used any time you need to drive stock perpendicular to your position.

Cross-driving

Your dog must know their flanks and off-balance flanks to cross-drive. Once they are competent at driving stock to and away from you, you can combine the two skills, driving and flanking into cross-driving. **Cross-driving** is driving stock perpendicular to the direction you are facing. The stock will be driven either left to right or right to left, in front of you. Cross-driving is used in trials but is also very useful to move livestock to pens or out gates when you need to be positioned to the side of the stock.

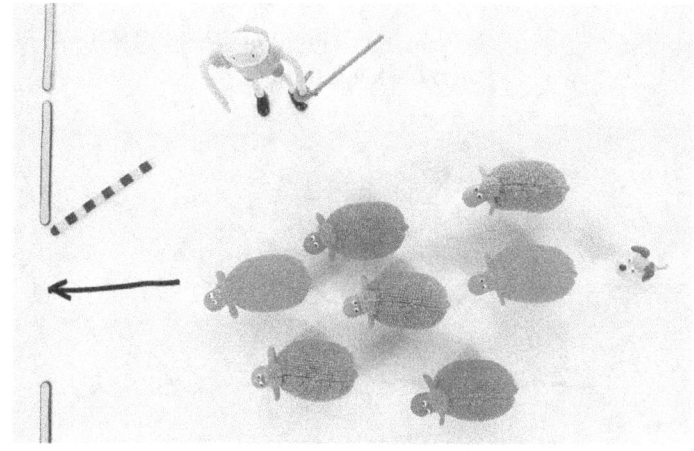

Cross-driving is an invaluable skill for everyday use or at trials. Many dogs struggle with cross-driving because their instinct is to fetch.

Here Dawg is cross-driving to put the sheep through the gate that Shandler has opened.

This is when establishing a line and having a dog that will hold that line comes in very handy. Your line will no longer be direct to or away from you, but from side to side in front of you, or at some angle in front of you. Your dog will most likely want to fetch the stock back to you when they begin cross-driving. If your dog goes behind the stock as they are cross-driving, which would send the stock back toward you, they are positioned **too high**. To correct this and bring your dog back into position, you need to flank them back toward you, an off-balance flank. If your dog comes too close to you while cross-driving, thereby sending the stock off line and away from you, they are positioned **too low**.

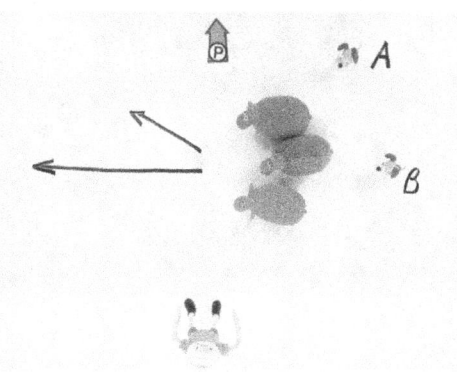

*In this diagram, Dawg is too low at position **B**, due to the pull away from the handler, so pressure at this point would send the stock off the cross-drive line and away from Shandler.*

182 | SECTION 2 ADVANCED HERDING SKILLS

Cross-driving along a fence

Have your dog start cross-driving fairly close to you. Be ready to give an off-balance flank cue. Start by having your dog drive the livestock along a fence, while you stand toward the center of the paddock. In this situation, your dog only has to hold one side of the stock as the fence is a barrier on the other side. You walk along and to the side of your stock. Slowly fade your movement so that your dog is eventually driving side to side in front of you, but still using the fence as a barrier on one side. Eventually, move farther and farther away from where your dog is driving the stock along the fence. Be sure to have your dog drive the stock in both directions in front of you, right to left and then back left to right.

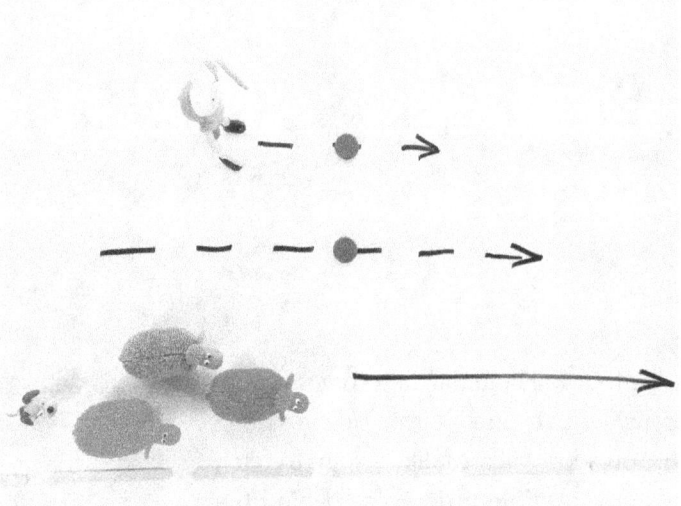

Start by walking alongside your dog almost the entire stretch of fence. As your dog gains confidence gradually decrease the distance you walk until you can stand still, indicated by the circles, while your dog drives the sheep along the entire fence.

Now, step back farther, from the fence and walk just far enough to support your dog's driving along the fence. Again, fade walking until you can stand still and your dog drives with confidence. Finally, move back farther, until you are at a substantial distance from your dog and they are driving back and forth in front of you.

Here Sir is driving along the fence while I just stand back and watch. Be sure to cross-drive in both directions. You may have to switch to a different fence line if the pull in one direction is so strong that the stock runs down the fence before your dog can get behind them.

If possible, move to another fence and repeat the same process. Eventually, you will end up standing a good distance from your dog as they drive the stock across in front of you.

Some dogs are very insecure about driving when they are not fetching to you, especially dogs with a lot of balance. Take all the time your dog needs to be comfortable and capable when cross-driving along a fence.

Be very patient, as it may take dogs with a lot of herding instinct quite a while to get comfortable with cross-driving. Do short drives and use a flank that swings your dog around away from the fence and behind the stock to stop and control the stock, as reinforcement for cross-driving. Then, do a short cross-drive in the opposite direction. Your dog will figure out cross-driving, but their instinct is to fetch the stock to you.

For your dog, cross-driving feels like they have lost control of the stock, so they want to flank around behind the livestock to regain that feeling of control. Your dog must trust you, so it is important that you initially set the exercise up in a way that the stock will NOT run away from your dog. If the stock starts running away, your dog will most likely panic, flank around to catch them, and then become much more reluctant to cross-drive.

Always end a cross-driving session with a fetch or two to keep your dog's sense of balance strong!

Cross-driving without a fence

When your dog is confident cross-driving along a fence, start setting your line such that the stock will no longer be driven along a fence. Start with very short drives and keep training sessions brief. Take breaks often, as cross-driving can be very stressful for your dog.

Have your dog drive a short cross-drive and then flank your dog around to drive back the other way or call them to you and send them to fetch the stock to you. Slowly extend the length of the cross-drives as your dog becomes proficient and confident doing them. If you find yourself becoming frustrated, go back to driving along a fence again and even walking along with your stock for a while, if need be.

Remember, cross-driving goes against your dog's innate herding instinct to control livestock. It takes time for your dog to trust that you will not put them in a position that will allow the stock to escape. Cross-driving is based on trust!

Cross-driving to panels

The last step, if you are interested in trials, is to cross-drive to a set of panels or gates. Again, start fairly close to the panels and make the distance between them generous, 30 feet or so. You will be amazed that once you back away from the gates it will become quite difficult to hit them! It is one thing to pick a spot or tree that you plan to drive to, but quite another to hit panels out in a field. Eventually, you will need to bring the gates closer together, until they are about 15 to 20 feet apart, similar to what they would be at a trial.

At a trial, you are always better off to miss the panels to the far side, the side away from you, rather than the near side, because if all of the animals miss to the near side, you will lose extra points for cutting the course.

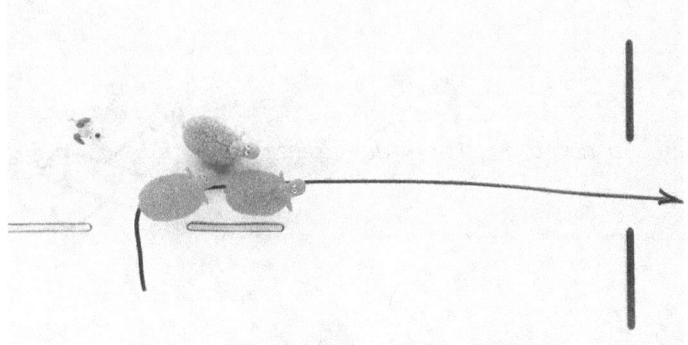

The lighter panels on the left would be drive gates and the darker on the right would be cross-drive gates. The goal is for the stock to go between the panels, the closer to the center the better. Also, try to turn the stock just as they pass through the panels without having them come back through the opening.

Trial fields are notoriously deceptive, in terms of judging the line necessary to take the stock through the cross-drive panels. It takes a lot of practice and keen depth perception, as well as great stockmanship, to drive a straight line on the cross-drive and take the livestock through the middle of the cross-drive gates. Pull is always in play and each set of livestock is unique in their reaction to the pull, the field, your dog, and you. The only way to get good at cross-driving is to practice, practice, practice! Use panels or gates set up in many different locations in your field and at many new locations with different livestock.

Driving a course

The final step to get ready to trial is setting up a course that includes fetch and drive gates. The goal is to calmly and steadily move the stock around the course while maintaining straight lines between all obstacles. Start with a small course and extend it as you and your dog gain competence.

Be sure to change your course periodically because the pull may be totally different when you send your dog from a different place in the field. You don't want your dog to develop any habits that only apply to your trial field, such as the pull always being to the same side or always being behind or in front of you.

If you run the same course with the same sheep, the sheep may become course broke and learn to run the course despite, rather than because, of your dog.

Also, be sure and go to other locations and set up a course comparable in size and, if possible, on similar topography to the field you will be trialling on. Generalize your herding skills as much as possible to give you and your dog the best possible chance to have a good trial experience.

That's it!

You are now the proud member of a competent herding team! You and your dog have the skills to control and handle livestock in a calm, competent manner. Your dog should be able to perform most herding trial obstacles and practical jobs around your acreage and be a big help to you with your livestock. If you are interested in going to some trials or doing everyday practical work around your acreage, you need to learn penning and chute work, found in Chapter 17. These final steps will prepare you and your dog to handle most chores around your acreage or compete at the novice or introductory level, at most trials.

Of course, there is still plenty you and your dog can learn that will help you handle stock more precisely and efficiently. If your dog is going to work at any distance from you, I encourage you to teach your dog whistle cues. Whistles are easier for your dog to hear at a distance and save you from having to yell when it is windy or your dog is working in tall grass. Next, you will learn about whistling while your dog works!

CHAPTER 14

Whistles

Why bother adding whistle cues when your dog already knows a full set of verbal herding cues, you don't need your dog to work great distances away from you, and whistling can be difficult to master? These are all good reasons to use only verbal cues. Why not save yourself the hassle of learning how to whistle and the time necessary to teach the various whistle cues to your dog?

You just might get away without whistle cues, if you never herd when the wind is blowing strongly toward you and away from your dog, your dog never has to run through tall grass, your dog never works a long way away from you, it never rains hard while you are working your dog, your dog never gets old and starts to lose their hearing, or you never lose your voice.

If you are going to be herding in all types of weather, in different terrain, and at a good distance from your dog, you need whistles on your dog. Almost all handlers that run dogs in trials, beyond the lowest levels or in field trials, use whistles. Once you start using whistles, you will quickly realize how much easier it is on your voice to not have to shout for your dog to hear your cues.

Another great advantage of having whistle cues on your dog is that you can finesse your whistle cues even when they have to be quite loud for your dog to hear them. It is difficult to encourage your dog to calm down and move slower when you are yelling your cue, no matter how slow and drawn out you give the cue. People also naturally tend to clip or shorten their verbal cues when they shout or get excited.

Sally says: *I regard my mastering of the sheepdog whistle as significant a victory as training the dog! It takes time to get the hang of using a whistle, so start practicing well before you need to actually use your whistle. The tricky part is, you can't whistle with your dog around because you don't want them to learn to ignore the sound. I used solo car journeys as my practice time and wondered what other road users were thinking as I huffed and puffed, all red-faced and frustrated. It is worth the effort though – I find that my dog responds better to whistle cues and, of course, I could never communicate with her over the distances I need to, with verbal cues.*

Types of whistles

There are three common ways to whistle: using solely your mouth, using your fingers in your mouth, or using a herding whistle. The main advantage of using your fingers is that you always have them with you. The disadvantages are that it is very difficult for most people to learn how to whistle using their fingers and fingers are often dirty when working with livestock. Unfortunately, learning to blow a herding whistle is also not easy.

Herding whistles come in two basic shapes, the half-moon and the A1. They may be made from many materials including silver, brass, aluminum, plastic, buffalo horn, and Corian (a material also used for countertops). Whistles can be plain or engraved and may be found in many different colors.

The half-moon and A1 shapes are the types most commonly used for herding whistles.

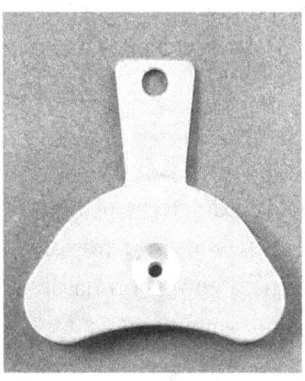

L<small>EFT</small>: *Half-moon whistle*

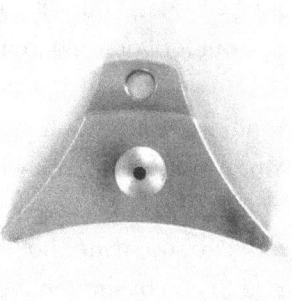

R<small>IGHT</small>: *A1*

Since herding whistles are fairly small, most people attach them to a lanyard that is worn around the neck. When not in use, the whistle hangs straight down on the lanyard or is placed in a shirt pocket, while still attached to the lanyard. The lanyard serves to keep the whistle close at hand and prevents its loss.

Lanyards also come in a myriad of colors, styles, and materials, to suit any taste or price range. They run the gamut from ordinary string to custom-made braided kangaroo leather. A lanyard is a must to keep track of your whistle.

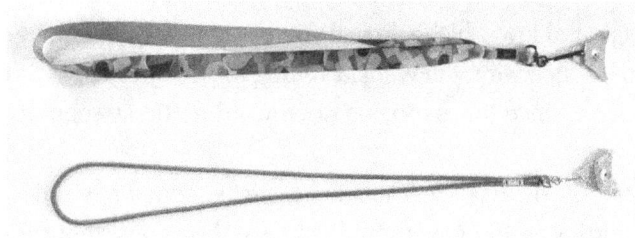

Lanyards range from simple and inexpensive to extravagant and costly.

Several online herding sites sell whistles, lanyards, and educational CDs or DVDs that teach whistling.

• •

In the first international trial held in South Africa, one of the older overseas competitors was seen frantically scrabbling around in the dirt next to the post. In his excitement he had whistled his false teeth completely out of his mouth!

Sally says

• •

Learning to whistle

I suggest you buy an inexpensive plastic whistle to start. If you have some shape preference get that style or get one of each shape to try and see which you like. If both styles feel equally strange in your mouth and difficult to blow, just grab one and start.

Never practice blowing a whistle where your dog can hear you!

Give yourself plenty of time to master blowing a whistle. You may get frustrated and quit honing your skill for a while before you get your whistle out again and redouble your efforts. Start early because it can take a long time to master blowing a whistle, learn the whistle cue equivalents of the verbal cues, and find time to practice where your dog cannot hear you.

Once you can produce a repeatable tone, move on to whistling a simple song. To move forward from there, you need to decide what whistle cue you will use for each verbal herding cue. There are CDs and Youtube videos that give examples of possible whistles to use and how to modify your delivery of the whistles to encourage the speed of movement you desire.

There are standard whistle cues that have been used traditionally in herding. You can use traditional whistles or come up with your own. Usually, flank whistles are two or three tones that move in the opposite direction for opposite flanks such as high – low – high and low – high – low. If you decide to use unique whistle cues, try to match them to the behavior you want your dog to perform. For example, use descending tones for a stop, since tones moving downward naturally seem to indicate slowing down.

When you have learned an entire system of whistles, record them. Listen to the whistles as you play them back. Are they consistent for each particular cue? Can you tell the whistles apart? If you cannot distinguish what behavior the whistles are cueing, your dog is going to be lost too.

When to add whistles

Start adding your new whistle cue for a behavior after your dog is proficient taking the verbal cue for that behavior. By waiting until your dog is nearing a 100% success rate before adding the whistle cue, your reinforcement history for the whistle cue should be almost 100%, once your dog learns the new cue. The old verbal cue may have had many mistakes associated with it but the new whistle cue should have very few. Thus, it becomes much more likely that your dog will respond correctly to the whistle cue with an even higher rate of success than the corresponding verbal cue.

Flank whistles may be trained just as you taught flank cues, in the house sitting on a stool. Just be sure to blow the whistles very quietly!

Adding whistle cues

Add whistle cues one at a time (stop or in) or one set at a time (flanks). For forward-moving dogs, I usually start with the stop whistle and for sideways-moving dogs with the walk in. After the initial cue is added, I usually introduce the flank cues and then fill in the rest, one at a time.

The whistle cues usually taught are **stop, walk in, flanks, easy, look back**, and the **final recall** off of stock (that'll do). Traditionally the easy or take time whistle is often a shortened stop whistle, but it is less confusing to your dog to have a unique whistle cue for each verbal cue.

That'll do is the traditional recall cue that is reserved for calling your dog off of the stock when you are done working for the training session, trial run, or day.

You may start adding whistle cues anytime during your training, as long as your dog is proficient at taking the verbal cue for that behavior. Some people like to add whistle cues early in training and others wait until the dog is quite experienced. I like to wait until my dog is proficient at taking their verbal cues before I add whistle cues.

To add whistle cues, use the same procedure that you would use to add any new cue: new cue, pause, old cue. When your dog is responding to the new cue immediately, you can drop the old cue. So for whistles, this might sound like: *High, low, high (whistle) – pause – come bye (verbal)*.

Whistles versus verbal cues

You may use all whistle cues when your dog knows them, or a combination of whistle and verbal cues. I was taught to use whistle cues for out work, your dog herding at a distance from you, and verbal cues for close work, your dog herding close at hand. **Close work** is herding you and your dog do as a team, such as penning and shedding. **Out work** is herding performed primarily by the dog alone, under your direction.

Some handlers use all whistle cues, some all verbal, and most a combination of whistle and verbal cues. Use what works for you and your dog, but keep in mind that whistle cues can be heard at a much greater distance than most verbal cues.

• •

One of South Africa's top handlers had his front teeth crowned just before the Nationals. To his horror he found that he could no longer produce a whistle. He was given advice and started whistling through his fingers – two months down the line his mouth whistle is slowly returning, but he notes that older handlers often lose the power of their mouth whistles due to the slackening of their jaw muscles.

Sally says

• •

Say what?

If your dog is working and looks back at you after you give a cue, they are often indicating that they did not hear the cue, don't understand the cue, or aren't sure about taking the cue. Your dog looking back toward you often means they need further direction or information. This is one time that it is totally acceptable to repeat a cue!

If your dog looks back at you after giving them a cue, they are usually asking for clarification or more information.

Sometimes, when your dog looks back at you after you have cued a flank, it may mean that they are looking for more information, but it may also mean that they want to take the opposite flank to maintain control of the stock. If you are confident you want your dog to flank the direction you cued, then just repeat the cue.

A common problem for inexperienced handlers is that they sometimes give the wrong flank cue and this leads to diminished confidence when cueing flanks. When their dog looks back at them after they have given them a flank cue, a bit of doubt creeps in and they wonder if they gave the correct flank. Does the dog need more information because they didn't hear the cue or was the wrong flank cue given? As they pause a moment to ponder this conundrum, the stock is likely to make their escape. This is part of the experience you gain as you grow as a trainer and handler. If you allow your dog to use their instincts, you may stumble more along the way, but you will eventually end up with a dog that easily handles livestock in situations where you might have had a train wreck.

When to cue your dog and when to allow them to take control of the livestock and situation instinctively is learned by experience. Too much cueing and you may end up with a mechanical dog, too little and you may end up with chaos.

Don't beat yourself up when you make mistakes, just learn what you can from the situation and move on. Don't expect your dog to be perfect either! You are both learning the new skills of herding and one of the most important parts of herding is teamwork. Teamwork is the name of the game in the next element of herding we examine, the shed. Shedding is separating and controlling one or more animals from a group – divide and conquer!

CHAPTER 15

Shedding without stock

At times, you will need to separate, sort, or divide a group of animals on your acreage. If you move into the upper-level herding classes, shedding will be required. **Shedding** is separating one or more animals from a group and maintaining control of those animals. Although it is a joint effort, the majority of the work is done by your dog. You set up the shed and then call your dog through the group to you. Your dog is to come straight toward you, create a hole or gap, then turn toward and drive the indicated animals away from the original group.

Shedding is an advanced skill that can be handy around an acreage but is usually taught in order to move into the Open or highest trial class. Shedding should be taught only after your dog is proficiently performing all of the other herding skills: fetching, flanking and off-balance flanking, driving, cross driving, and especially holding. It is vital, when shedding, that your dog moves out and close when cued, does not slice in on their flanks, and stops and stays stopped when cued.

Shedding is usually difficult for dogs because all of their previous herding experience has been geared toward controlling and bunching stock. Now their job is to come into the flock and separate one or more animals from the group.

Shedding demands different skills from both the handler and dog than have been covered previously. Penning and other trial obstacle negotiation will be covered later, but completing most trial obstacles require only basic herding skills. Shedding requires skills that are unique to shedding and are taught exclusively for shedding.

Qwest is across from me and the sheep are strung out between us, all heading the same direction. I reach my right hand and arm toward Qwest and cue him to cut. In the second picture, the sheep have split into two groups; two escaping to the right and two stopped and beginning to turn back to the left. In the third picture, the two pairs of sheep are exiting in opposite directions. Finally, in the last picture, Qwest turns toward the sheep I have indicated and drives them away.

There are two main schools of thought on how to teach your dog to shed. One depends on a bulletproof recall and the other is based on flanking. I use the method based on calling your dog to you and will explain that method in some detail. The flanking-based method will then be more briefly explained. Both methods, or a combination of the two, can be used to get your dog successfully shedding. You will probably find that one method works better for you and your dog than the other.

No matter what livestock you have trained on to this point, sheep are probably the best to work with when teaching shedding. Once your dog knows how to shed sheep, you can generalize the skill to shedding other livestock. From this point on, these instructions will assume you are training on sheep. It is also much, much easier to teach the shed if you have a larger group of sheep, 10 to 12 head or more. The more the better!

Initially, you will be training the shed with two sets of penned sheep. Next, you will move to one group of sheep in a corner pen with another group of sheep loose, the setup you used to train the hold in Chapter 10. Then you will move to a fence line with all loose sheep. The fence serves as a barrier to keep the sheep from curling behind you and reuniting before your dog can get between the two groups.

Before you start – Necessary skills

Shedding is an advanced skill that combines many herding skills into an entirely new skill. Your dog will not be successful shedding unless they have these component skills in place before you attempt to teach the shed. Probably the most important part of shedding, which cannot be taught, is having a confident, powerful dog. You can put your dog in bad situations and destroy their confidence but you cannot, to the same degree, give a fearful dog courage.

The best gauge of your dog's likelihood of being able to shed is how well they have mastered holding livestock that tenaciously attempts to get past them and back to their buddies. If your dog loves the challenge of holding animals that are determined to get past them, then they will likely shine at shedding. On the other hand, if your dog shies away from stopping and turning back animals that try to get by them, your dog is not ready to learn to shed.

There are six critical skills your dog needs before you start teaching the shed:
1. *Flanks* – Dog must stay out or maintain distance from stock when flanking.
2. *Stop* – Dog must stop and stay stopped when cued.
3. Hand target
4. *Recall* (near stock) – Dog must quickly come straight to handler.
5. Drive away from handler.
6. Hold

The three most critical skills are flanking, stopping, and recalling to you. The first two skills come in to play as you maneuver the stock, to set them up for the shed. Setting up the shed, while keeping your stock settled, is one key to getting a shed and is the **first part** of the shed. Your dog must maintain their distance while flanking when shedding or doing any close work. If your dog slices their flanks, they will force unwanted movement of the stock every time they flank.

Another critical skill is a solid stop. Your dog must stop when cued and remain stationary, even if the stock is starting to get away from them. Your dog has to be able to let one group of stock escape while focusing on the group you direct them to hold.

The final critical skill, the most important to accomplish the shed, is a direct and speedy recall to you to split the sheep. The splitting of the sheep is the **second part** of the shed. Once you have a hand target in place, as explained in the following paragraph, you need to practice calling your dog to you with your hand extended toward your dog. First, get a hand target well trained and then work on recalls without sheep and then near sheep. If necessary, see Chapter 12 in *Positive Herding 101* on teaching the stand for instructions on how to teach a hand target.

A recall, around stock, is essential because you will be using it to pull your dog to you in the early stages of teaching shedding. The recall for shedding will be new to your dog because your hand, arm, and body position will be different from your usual recall position. Your body position is part of the stimulus picture that your dog associates with your verbal recall cue. The body position you will use for shedding is one arm outstretched toward your dog with the hand pointing at your dog. Your body will be turned, so your side is to your dog, and you will bend your knees and hips to bring your hand down so that it is close to eye level with your dog.

Practice the recall using your new shedding posture and throw a tug or food beyond you as a reinforcer until your dog is consistently recalling to and past you at speed. At first, your dog may be hesitant to come to you with your hand stretched toward them. Practice recalls, having your dog come toward both your right and left hands, in many places until your dog comes to you at speed.

I cue my dog to stop, with a fair distance between us, then get into my stance, cue the shed (cut), and immediately give my recall cue (here). Once your dog comes to you at speed, you are ready to start training the shed *without* livestock.

The **third part** of the shed starts when your dog is between the two separated groups of stock and consists of your dog hooking up to and driving one group away from the other. To complete the shed your dog needs to be able to hold the two groups apart once they have been driven away from each other which is the final or **fourth part** of the shed.

As your dog drives one group of sheep away from the other, the driven sheep will probably try to get back to join up with the original flock. Your dog will need to be able to hold these sheep and prevent them from getting back to the other group. Also, note that the other group of sheep, that you have allowed to escape, may turn back and try to join the group you are driving away. So you need to keep track of both groups of sheep until the shed is completed.

The four-part shed
To recap, the shed consists of four major sections:
1. *Setup* – Getting the stock settled and ready to be split.
2. *Separation* – Dividing one or more selected sheep from the group.
3. *Drive away* – Driving the shed sheep away from the remaining sheep.
4. *Hold away* – Keeping the shed sheep separate from the other sheep.

The four parts of the shed happen fast, usually within seconds. All four parts are vital to complete the shed but the setup is the most critical part. If the sheep are not kept calm and handled gently, their arousal level skyrockets and they stick together as if their lives depend upon staying safe with the flock. A good setup doesn't ensure a clean, efficient shed but a poor setup often leads to shedding failure. Before you worry about completing the four parts of a shed, let's do some training away from livestock.

Sheep-less shedding
You will start training shedding only after your dog is recalling to you at speed, while you are in your shedding stance. Remember that the shedding stance is arm and hand outstretched toward your dog, knees and waist bent, and body turned sideways. When your dog will *consistently recall* to you *at speed* while you are in your shedding stance, you are ready to start sheep-less shedding. If at any time during the training, your dog recalls to you at a trot or walk, you need to go back and work on your dog's recall. You want a running recall throughout the entire shed training process.

Before attempting to shed live sheep, you should teach your dog the basics of shedding away from stock. For this exercise, you will need 6 cones and a toy or treats that can be thrown several feet. You will use a verbal marker instead of a clicker because both of your hands will be involved in training the sheep-less shed.

This exercise will add mass to your dog's behavior of coming directly to you, which will come in very handy once you move on to working with sheep. The goal of this exercise is to get your dog to come through a gap, toward you, and then turn the same direction you are facing, just as they would when shedding. Work this exercise in your yard and then in your paddock without sheep.

Be sure to practice the steps of the sheep-less shed *without* your dog until you have all of the mechanics mastered. Stop between major steps and practice the next series of steps without your dog. If you are confident teaching the steps of the exercise, your dog will benefit greatly and your training will go much more smoothly.

Sheep-less shed – Step by step

1. Set 6 cones out in a straight line, with about a yard (3 feet) between each cone.
2. Stand about 5 feet away from the line of cones and between the 3rd and 4th cone. Face your dog, who will be standing 5 feet away from the line of cones facing you. There should be 10 feet between you and your dog, with a line of cones between you. Adjust the distances from the line of cones as necessary to get your dog coming to you at a trot or faster.
3. Hide your tug behind your back or a large treat in your hand and recall your dog to you. Mark when your dog is coming through the line of cones and throw the reinforcer behind you so that your dog runs by you.
4. Repeat the call through, until your dog is coming to you on the run. Anytime during the training that your dog slows down to a trot or walk, you need to go back and work on your recall until your dog comes to you on the run. The shed depends on your dog coming in toward you quickly!

5. Now turn your body perpendicular to the line of cones and hide the reinforcer in your hand, away from your dog. If using a tug, hold your hand close to your side and behind you, to block your dog's view of the tug.
6. Extend your other arm and hand toward your dog and bend your knees. (Your shedding stance.)
7. Cue your dog to shed, followed immediately by your recall cue. (*Cut* and then *here*.)
8. Your dog should run through the line of cones toward your hand.
9. Mark just as your dog comes through the line of cones and throw the toy or treat in front of you, parallel to the line of cones but just on your side of the cones. You want your dog to turn as soon as they get past the cones and run parallel to the line of cones to get their reinforcer. (The direction your body is facing is the physical cue that tells your dog which direction they will be turning.)
10. Give your release cue and allow your dog to get the treat or tug.
11. Play with your dog! Use super high-value treats or have a rousing game with your dog as reinforcement. You want your dog to get excited and run after the thrown toy or treat.

12. Repeat this exercise 5 times.

13. If your dog starts to slow down as they come to you, do several reps of throwing your reinforcer behind you, such that your dog runs past you again.

14. Now turn the opposite way so that your other hand is extended toward your dog. Your dog will now come toward you and then turn and run in the opposite direction, while staying close and parallel to the line of cones.

15. Repeat 5 times.
16. Switch sides so you are now where your dog was and they are where you were, relative to the cone line.
17. Work your dog coming through the line of cones and turning in both directions. Repeat until your dog is confidently coming through to you and turning as indicated.

18. Now move along the cone line so that your dog is coming through the cones at different places. Change things up to generalize the behavior.
19. Finally, set up a line of trash cans, dog crates, barrels, etc. and repeat the exercise using larger props as sheep.

Cone setup for sheep-less shed, the recall. My tug is hidden behind my body.

Mark as your dog comes through the cone line and throw your reinforcer along the line in the direction you are facing.

This should be a fast and fun exercise with your dog. Add excitement to your verbal marker and release cue and include plenty of verbal reinforcement, in addition to the toy or treats you are using. Coming directly and quickly to you are keys to performing a shed, so you need your dog running straight to you before you begin shedding sheep. If your dog is not running to you, do more recalls while in your shedding stance, throwing a tug or treat behind you. Speed coming in between sheep is essential for shedding!

Here Sir is coming between dog crates. The larger objects help to generalize the recall and approximate the bulk of sheep.

Eventually I switched sides, direction, and which crates I called Sir to come between to further generalize the behavior.

Before you start using sheep

To teach the shed, based on your dog coming to you, your dog must have a great recall around livestock. This means that your dog comes directly to you when called, without hesitation, even if you are standing right next to your sheep with your hand extended toward your dog.

Take the time needed to get your dog comfortable and consistent coming quickly and directly to or past you as you stand next to sheep. Eventually, you will practice having your dog come to you with sheep on both your right and left, while standing near a fence.

Once you start shedding loose sheep, you will need to carry a crook or stock stick. Although one of your hands will be stretched out toward your dog, be sure that your crook, which will be in your other hand, is behind you and out of the way when you call your dog to you.

Never call your dog into your outstretched crook or stock stick. If you use a crook to help make a gap for your dog, you must pull it back out of the gap before you call your dog through the gap to you.

When doing the shed, in its final form, you will use your dog to position the sheep in front of you. As you set up the shed, your dog will be flanking back and forth opposite you, to position the sheep for the call-through. Your dog must flank far enough off of the sheep so that their movement does not cause the sheep to move significantly or push them over you, as they flank. If your dog slices in on their flanks, they may cause the sheep to move sideways or around and behind you, as they flank. Maintaining the same or more distance from the sheep, as your dog flanks back and forth, is imperative!

Let's head out to work shedding with some livestock in the next chapter on shedding.

CHAPTER 16

Shedding 1

The following training instructions for the shed work best for forward-moving dogs. Sideways-moving dogs do better with a method of shedding based on flanking. These step-by-step instructions should only be started when your dog is recalling directly and promptly to you, while you stand next to sheep. Try this method first and if your dog struggles, try the alternate approach found at the end of Chapter 17, Shedding 2.

If you have any sheep that want to fight or challenge your dog, remove them from the flock until your dog is confidently shedding.

Shed – Step by step
Phase 1 – Recall between penned sheep
1. Set up a small pen, against but on the outside of your paddock, if possible.
2. Call your dog to you as you run past the empty pen.
3. When your dog is running, both directions, past the empty pen, start calling your dog past the pen while you stand still and face your dog.
4. Repeat until your dog is consistently running to you, past the empty pen.

5. Put a few head of sheep in the pen and call your dog past the sheep to you.
6. Practice until your dog can run past the penned sheep to you.
7. Repeat but have your dog recall past the penned sheep in the opposite direction. (You may need to set up a barrier of panels to keep your dog from flanking out away from the sheep as your dog runs by them. You want your dog running close to the penned sheep.)

8. Set up two small pens about 30 feet from each other.
9. Practice calling your dog between the two empty pens.
10. Repeat until your dog is consistently running to you, past the empty pens.
11. Place at least two head of sheep in each pen.
12. Practice calling your dog between the two pens of sheep in both directions.
13. Take a long break. Celebrate!

When your dog is running to you on cue (*cut*, followed by *here*, if necessary) start moving the two pens closer to each other, 3 feet closer after each successful training session, until the pens are close together, about 4 to 6 feet apart. Take as long as it takes for your dog to be successful as you move the pens incrementally closer.

Sir is recalling to me near sheep that are penned on the outside of our normal working paddock. The barrier opposite the sheep helped Sir stay near the sheep rather than flanking out away from them.

I started in my shedding stance facing Sir but turned and ran away after calling him, to get him to run and chase me.

Next, I used two pens of sheep about 30 feet apart and called Sir to me, between the pens. As Sir was successful I moved the pens closer together. At this point in the training, the pens are about 10 feet apart. After each successful training session, I move one pen a few feet closer to the other, until they are finally about 4 feet apart.

Troubleshooting

- **Dog stalls out near sheep** – If your dog hooks up to the sheep and stops in front of them, try attaching a leash to their collar or harness. Start by walking with your dog past the sheep. If your dog stops, keep walking and let the leash tighten and give your dog a little tug. Go back and forth until your dog walks along with you without stopping. Mark and reinforce your dog moving freely past the sheep. Next, trot past the sheep and repeat the exercise. Finally, move on to running past the sheep with your dog on leash. (I did this with Sir and I never had to tug on the leash. He realized he was on leash and readily stayed with me at all three gaits.)

- ***Dog doesn't run past sheep when called*** – If your dog recalls slowly, turn and run away from them as soon as they start moving toward you. This should encourage your dog to chase you and speed up. Use lots of happy verbal reinforcement too.
- ***Dog flanks instead of running directly to handler*** – If your dog flanks or curves toward you instead of coming directly to you, try attaching a light long line to their collar or harness. Stand between the two pens of sheep, holding the long line. There should not be a lot of slack in the long line but it should not be tight. Call your dog, as soon as they start forward, turn and run away from them. The long line should guide them to you without yanking them. (Again, I used this with Sir and he came directly to me without the long line ever becoming tight.)

Phase 2 – Hold *(These steps should look familiar! If not, review Chapter 10 Putting it all together – Phase 2 Holding using two groups of sheep)*

1. Put several sheep in a small pen in the corner of a paddock and leave a few out in the paddock. The smaller loose group will most likely move toward the larger penned group to regroup. (Situate the pen in a corner by a gate or other draw to encourage the loose sheep to be strongly drawn to the penned sheep.)
2. Step in and help your dog push the loose sheep away from the penned group.
3. Move slightly away from the fence so that you are helping to hold the loose sheep along the fence. Your dog should be between the loose sheep and the penned sheep.
4. Walk a bit ahead of the loose sheep such that they turn back toward your dog and the penned sheep.
5. Cue your dog to hold.
6. If the sheep try to get past your dog, your dog should freely flank to prevent them from getting past. (Cue flanks only if necessary and drop cueing as soon as possible.)
7. If the sheep don't try to get past your dog, then you should attempt to push the sheep back past your dog.
8. When your dog actively prevents any sheep from getting past them and regrouping with the penned sheep, on only a hold cue, take a short break. Celebrate!
9. Reset and repeat until your dog will freely move to cover sheep attempting to get to the penned group on only the hold cue. (You should not need to give your dog flanks at this point unless they don't have herding instinct.)

The above exercise should have been a review of holding stock for your dog. Now, it is time for your dog to come between the penned and loose sheep, without your help.

Sir has come in between the penned and loose sheep right on the heads. Yay! He then stops momentarily, when cued before... driving the loose sheep away. In a perfect world, Sir would have driven the sheep back the way they had come, but he did drive them away from the pull to the corner and the other sheep.

Eventually, you will work both sides, such that your dog comes in and turns both right and left. You may need to move to the opposite side of your pen to set things up for your dog to come into the other side.

Work the next phase, Phase 3, for about 10 minutes and stop the session, no matter where you are in the steps. Take a long break and do another session, picking up where you left off. Both you and your dog will need time to process and relax between sessions. This phase is critical to teaching the shed since it is at this point that you are training your dog to create the gap between the two sets of sheep. Once your dog learns how to create a gap, they have acquired a crucial skill for shedding success.

Phase 3 – Hold becomes shed

1. You are still working with two groups of sheep, one group is penned in the corner of your paddock near a gate and the other is loose.
2. Stand by the corner pen, near one fence, having placed your dog out and away from the pen. Your dog will be coming to you, between the loose and penned sheep.
3. Face toward the loose sheep and hold out your target hand, as you did for sheepless shedding. Call your dog to you such that your dog comes toward you and between the penned and loose sheep. You may start by stepping forward to form

a gap and move the loose sheep away from the pen but gradually do less and have your dog make the gap.
4. When your dog is between the two groups, face the loose sheep, cue in, and walk with your dog as they drive the loose sheep several yards away from the penned sheep.
5. Call your dog off of the sheep and give lavish praise!

6. Reset and repeat until your dog is coming in between the two groups of sheep immediately when cued, without any help from you.
7. Add the new cue, *cut*, before the recall cue. (I keep using my recall cue until my dog is proficient at shedding because my *here* cue has years of strong reinforcement history while my shedding cue has only weeks of history.)
8. Repeat 10 more times or until your dog is proficient in making the gap and pushing the loose sheep away from the penned sheep.
9. Now change your positions so that your dog comes in and turns in the opposite direction to drive the sheep off and start back at step 3. (Your dog will now be coming in from the opposite side and turning in the opposite direction to drive the loose sheep away from the penned sheep.)
10. When your dog is confidently coming in and driving the loose sheep off, start to randomly switch sides with your dog.

In Phase 4 you will be working with only loose sheep. Now is when your dog's square flanks and solid stop become crucial. Any slicing of your dog's flanks or cheating on their stop and it will be impossible to set up the sheep for the shed. If you are becoming frustrated in this phase, try watching video of your training. Check specifically for flanks that start square, remain the same distance from the sheep, and for solid stops. Also, be sure your dog is opening up or coming closer when cued.

For this phase, you will just be calling your dog to you while both of you are standing to the side of your flock of sheep. The goal is for your dog to come straight to you at speed. Dogs often have trouble ignoring sheep nearby and focusing on running to the handler. Although you are essentially doing a recall, you will still use the cue *cut* for this exercise.

It is very difficult for your dog to hold their position when stock starts to escape, so a very solid stop is essential for shedding. Instinct tells dogs to stop the sheep from escaping while you are asking them to hold position.

Phase 4 – Call dog next to sheep *(This exercise is similar to calling your dog between two pens of sheep, but now all of the sheep will be loose and in one flock or group.)*

1. Stand next to your small flock along a fence with your back to the fence. You are next to the sheep, not directly behind them.
2. Your dog starts out standing about 15 or 20 feet in front of you with the sheep beside you and your dog. (Put the sheep in a corner if you cannot get them to settle within 10 feet of you and your dog.)
3. Allow your sheep to settle.

---

4. Turn sideways, facing toward the sheep, and reach your closest arm out toward your dog. Cue your dog to come to you using your cut cue. The sheep will probably move farther away as your dog comes to you. Use your recall cue as a follow-up cue.
5. Your dog's reinforcer, for coming to you, will be the chance to drive the sheep off and then flank around them.
6. Drive the sheep away, then flank your dog away from the fence and around the sheep. Stop your dog when the sheep move back to where they were originally settled.

---

7. When your dog is coming directly to you with speed, move to the opposite side of your flock and repeat.
8. Repeat steps 4 through 6 until your dog is coming directly to you at a trot or faster, on both sides of the flock.

Troubleshooting

- ***Dog comes in too slow (1)*** – If your dog will not at least trot to you, move farther away from the fence. Often dogs don't want to run up to a barrier (the fence), especially when the sheep will be moving farther from the fence as your dog approaches you.
- ***Dog comes in too slow (2)*** – Try moving farther down the fence and away from your sheep, before calling your dog to you. The closeness of the sheep may be too distracting for your dog. Once your dog is recalling at speed, slowly move your position toward the sheep until you are within 10 feet of the sheep.

Set your dog up for success in Phase 5 by picking a place along a fence in your paddock where your sheep will settle. You will next be making a gap for your dog to come through between the two flocks.

The following picture sequence gives you an idea of what Phase 5 entails. Slide along the fence behind the flock. Split the flock to make a gap for your dog to come through. By creating a gap for your dog to come through, you make the recall behavior much easier for your dog.

First, the sheep are strung out in front of me and heading for the gate in the corner of the paddock.

Sir is flanked come bye to stop the flow of the sheep.

One lamb turns back but four other sheep continue toward the gate.

I call Sir to me and he comes at a trot. The remaining sheep have turned back due to his approach.

I stop Sir for a moment before cueing him to walk in and drive the indicated sheep away from the others.

Phase 5 – Make gap and call dog

1. Stand next to your small flock of 10 to 12 sheep or more, if possible, along a fence with your back to the fence.
2. With your back to the fence, slide along it until you have about the same number of sheep on both sides of and in front of you. (You probably will have to flank your dog a time or two to keep the sheep in position.)

3. Position your dog across from you with the sheep in between.
4. Make a hole or gap between the two groups of sheep by stepping into the sheep or by using your crook. The larger the distance between the two groups the better. The gap should be at least 6 to 12 feet wide.
5. Pull your crook behind you, if you used it to form the gap, turn your body sideways toward the sheep you want your dog to turn onto. Now, extend your hand and arm, closest to your dog, and call your dog to your outstretched hand using your cut cue. (You will turn your body so you are calling your dog to your side with your hand and arm extended toward your dog.)
6. Step sideways and back out of the gap as your dog comes into it and toward you. (If you can determine which way each group of sheep will turn, possibly due to the pull in your paddock, then always have your dog turn toward heads rather than rumps. You want your dog to turn into the pressure and that means turning to face heads.)
7. When your dog gets almost to you, they should be between the two groups of sheep, cue your dog to walk in to the sheep you are facing. (The sheep may have turned away from you as your dog came into the gap.)
8. Walk with your dog as they drive this group of sheep away from the other group, at least 10 to 20 feet along the fence.
9. Stop your dog and tell them how brilliant they are! Celebrate!

10. Flank your dog out away from the fence, around the sheep they have just driven away, and have them put the two flocks back together.
11. Reset and repeat 5 times. If the sheep are not pulling in one direction, then alternate which group you turn toward. Alternating which way you face helps your dog to learn that they will turn toward the animals you are facing when you call them in and that they can turn in both directions.
12. Have a party and quit for the day!

Stay at this stage until your dog is coming into the gap at a trot or faster, turning onto the indicated group, and driving them off with confidence. This will take as long as it takes. Some dogs like to shed and will figure shedding out quite quickly. They find the challenge of holding pressure inherently reinforcing, so they come into the gap readily. Other dogs do not like to hold pressure and it may take longer for them to get comfortable being close to sheep and facing up to the pressure.

Troubleshooting
- **Sheep move when dog flanks** – If your sheep move excessively when your dog flanks back and forth to help position them, either there is too much pull and you

need to change your location or your dog is flanking too close to the sheep. Use your out to move your dog farther from the sheep.
- **Dog won't come in between groups** – If your dog doesn't want to come to you when cued, you need to make a bigger gap. If need be, pen each group along the fence and call your dog between the penned sheep a few times.
- **Dog works too far off of sheep** – If your dog is too far off of the flock they may not want to come in when called. Work at getting your dog to flank closer to the sheep using your close cue. Staying too far off may indicate your dog is not confident in this situation.
- **Sheep run past dog, from one group to the other** – If any sheep attempt to get past you and your dog, it is your responsibility to help your dog stop them and turn them back to the group they came from. This is the main reason you are carrying a crook. If this happens several times, despite your best efforts to help your dog stop them, you may need to use different sheep.
- **You are unsure which way to turn** – Always try to turn toward the heads of the sheep. If you cannot tell which way to turn because both groups are turning away from the gap, just pick a side and then alternate. This becomes more important over time. At this point, you just need to get your dog to understand that they use the direction your body is facing as a physical cue for which direction to turn. Your dog also needs to learn that you can ask them to turn in either direction, onto either flock.

If you are having trouble setting up for the shed, look closely at your dog's flanks and stops. Are they staying off of the sheep when flanking and stopping and staying stopped, especially while you are making a gap and when part of the sheep are escaping? Many dogs break their stop to cover the escaping sheep and maintain control of the situation which causes the shed to fail.

You and your dog have taken giant steps toward learning to shed! In the next chapter, I will add the finishing touches to the shed and offer an alternative method of teaching the shed. Shedding is not an easy skill to teach your dog, but it is a very useful skill for your dog to have. A dog that can shed is much more useful on an acreage and can compete at the highest level of trials.

Fortunately, the hardest work of teaching the shed is behind you, so press on!

CHAPTER 17

Shedding 2

The next step in shedding is having your dog make the gap as they come through the flock toward you. Again, the more sheep you have, the easier it is for your dog to be successful. Initially, your dog doesn't have to be precise in where they make the gap. Once your dog learns to make a gap, then work on your dog making the gap precisely where you want them to cut.

The setup for Phase 6 is the same as for Phase 5 in Chapter 16. You started out making the gap for your dog and now will slowly reduce the size of the gap you make, thus shaping your dog to take over responsibility for gap creation.

Phase 6 – Dog makes gap
1. Stand next to your small flock of 10 to 12 or more sheep along a fence with your back to the fence.
2. Your dog starts out standing about 15 or 20 feet in front of you.
3. Settle the sheep along the fence.
4. With your back to the fence slide along it until you have about the same number of sheep on both sides of you.
5. Position your dog across from you with the sheep in between.
6. Make a gap and call your dog through. Have your dog drive the indicated sheep off, bring the flock back together, and reset. Do not change the size of the gap until your dog is coming in with speed and confidence.

---

7. Start making a smaller gap, until there is no gap and your dog is making the gap. Your dog always comes into the hand you have extended, turns toward the sheep you are facing, and drives the indicated flock away from the other flock.

Work on this phase until your dog readily comes in and makes a gap or hole, turns onto the sheep you have indicated, and drives them off with confidence. Again, this takes as long as it takes. The more sheep you use in this phase of training the better.

When you call your dog through to make a gap you need them to be positioned just ahead of and catch the eye of the sheep you are bringing them in on.

In this sequence, Sir makes the gap by stopping the flow of the sheep. I have not stepped into the sheep to make a gap for him, but I would have, if necessary. For these first shedding sessions with all loose sheep, I am using a group of 18 head of ewes with older lambs.

Troubleshooting

- ***Dog does not want to come through without an existing gap (1)*** – If your dog is reticent to come to your hand, don't initially worry about where they come through. If you ask them to come and split the flock at the fifth sheep and they come in a sheep or two before or after where you indicated, don't worry about it at this point. The main thing is for your dog to start coming in with speed and making a gap. As they gain confidence, your dog will be able to come in where you indicate.

- ***Dog does not want to come through without an existing gap (2)*** – If your dog struggles to make a gap, you may want to use a much larger flock of sheep to teach your dog to make a hole. A flock of 100 or more light sheep works well.
    1. Flank your dog to the opposite side of the flock and call your dog to you while you move toward your dog.
    2. As you move toward each other, the sheep will form into two groups, with the flock shape going from an oval to an hourglass.
    3. When there are only 10 to 20 sheep between you and your dog, stop and encourage your dog to come through to you. (You may need to use and repeat your recall cue the first few times to encourage your dog to come all the way to you.)
    4. At this point, the last sheep between you and your dog will already be moving toward one side or the other to join up with one of the groups.
    5. Once your dog has split the flock, turn toward one group, and cue your dog to walk into that group.
    6. Have your dog drive the indicated group a short distance, while you walk with them, and then have your dog flank around and regroup the flock.
    7. Repeat this exercise, with you moving less and your dog coming farther into the sheep each time. Eventually, your dog will come through from their side to cut the flock into two flocks without any help from you. (Your dog may not need to come all the way to you, as the pressure point will be somewhere between the two flocks.)
    8. When your dog is confidently cutting the flock into two flocks, try having your dog cut one of the separated flocks into two groups. Instead of working with 100 sheep, you are now working with only 40 to 60 head.
    9. When your dog is coming through small groups, go back and work on Phase 6.
- ***Dog turns toward the wrong group after shed (1)*** – If your dog turns on the wrong group, not the group you indicated, do not allow them to drive this group off. Call your dog back to you and ask them to drive off the group you previously indicated by the direction you were facing. Your dog does not decide which group to take control of after the shed. Instead, you indicate the group they are to control by facing that group as you call your dog in to shed.
- ***Dog turns toward the wrong group after shed (2)*** – If you indicate the group that has gone past as your dog comes through, your dog is being asked to take the sheep on the rumps instead of on the heads. You may need to reassess the pull in your paddock. Your dog may be taking the unindicated sheep because they are facing your dog, thus your dog is turning into the pressure, which is correct.

Often, you will need to change where you shed in a paddock to practice your dog turning in both directions.

Once your dog has progressed this far, you should be using the cue *cut* for cueing your dog to come through the flock and shed. If you have not done it already, transition to the new cue by adding the new cue (*cut*) before the old cue (*here*). At this point, your dog is thinking shed. When the shed is set up, your dog should be ready to blast toward you, no matter what comes out of your mouth.

Shedding has a lot of moving parts and is not easy to learn. It is even more difficult to learn when neither you nor your dog knows how to shed. If possible, find an experienced handler who can work with you to learn this skill.

The last step in shaping the shed is moving the shed away from the fence and into the open field. The fence has been a barrier to prevent the sheep from curling around behind you and regrouping. The key to preventing this re-flocking behind you is having your dog come in and quickly make the cut while you step backward as your dog is cutting. You may need to use your crook or stock stick, behind your back, to prevent the two flocks from regrouping behind you.

Regrouping behind the handler is a bad habit for sheep to learn. Once your sheep figure out that they can regroup behind you, they will become almost impossible to shed. If you have the sheep regroup behind you twice, move back to shedding along a fence again.

Phase 7 – Move away from fence
1. Stand in your paddock, away from a fence, where you can get your sheep to settle in front of you. Use 10 to 12 or more sheep if possible.
2. Determine where the pull is.
3. Have your dog bring the sheep up as close as possible to you without pushing the sheep around and behind you.
4. Flank your dog back and forth, until you string the sheep out in a line in front of you, with the sheep facing toward the pull. (**String the sheep out** means maneuver them from a compact group to roughly single file. It will take you and your dog working together to string the sheep out. It takes practice to become proficient at setting sheep up for a shed. The more relaxed and calm your sheep are, the easier it will be to string them out.) Your dog will have to be slightly

ahead of the sheep because of the pull. If your dog were exactly opposite you, the sheep would take off toward the pull.

5. Position yourself so that you are facing away from the pull and toward the heads of the sheep in front of you. Often all of the sheep will be facing the same direction, toward the pull.
6. Use your body or crook to make a gap.

7. Call your dog through the gap. As your dog comes through, the sheep may try to curl behind you, as there is no longer a fence there as a barrier. The faster your dog comes through, the less likely the sheep are to curl behind you. (It is part of your responsibility, when shedding, to prevent the sheep from curling behind you by stepping backward and using your crook to prevent the sheep from regrouping behind you.)
8. When your dog has separated the sheep into two groups, immediately cue your dog to walk in and drive off the group you are facing.

9. Have your dog drive the sheep 15 to 20 feet while you walk with them. As soon as possible, have your dog drive the sheep off while you remain stationary. (Keep an eye on the sheep in the flock behind you as they may decide to try to join up with the group your dog is driving away.)
10. Over time, reduce the size of the gap you make until your dog makes the gap without your help. The gap should be at the place you indicate with your hand.
11. Do short shedding sessions, over many days, until your dog is keen to shed.

12. Now, reduce the number of sheep you are shedding down to only 4 or 6.
13. At this point, your dog must come through precisely at the point you indicate. (If you indicate a cut between sheep 3 and 4, you cannot accept your dog coming in between sheep 2 and 3. Use your no reward marker, pause 10 seconds, and reset if your dog makes the wrong cut.)

14. Finally, practice shedding off the last sheep in line, this is called a **single**. Singles are particularly difficult to hold because they feel very vulnerable by themselves. A single sheep will usually test your dog's ability to control them by strenuously trying to get past your dog and reunite with the other sheep. Don't dwell on shedding singles. Instead, practice singles only occasionally.

15. Practice with other sheep at different places or in other paddocks.
16. Work shedding in a marked shedding ring. The shed, split, and taking control of the shed sheep, must occur in the ring.

The last few steps in the above exercise generalize and increase the difficulty of the shed. Shedding different sheep also changes the dynamics of shedding. The breed of sheep and their previous experience with shedding make a big difference in how easy or difficult it will be to shed them.

The faster your dog cuts through the sheep, the less likely the sheep will curl behind you. If the sheep regroup a few times, you need to move back to a fence to prevent the sheep from acquiring the bad habit of regrouping behind you.

The key to a good shed is having your dog come quickly to you when cued. If you have made a gap, your dog should have no trouble shedding, but if there is no gap, your dog should make one.

In this shed, there was no gap. Qwest made the gap by cutting between the second and third ewes.

Shedding a single can be dangerous because being alone puts the animal in a particularly vulnerable position. A single desperately wants to get back to the safety of the other sheep. The single may run, challenge your dog, or try to jump over your dog to get back to the other sheep. As with any shedding, your dog has to drive the single off and show that they have control of it before the shed will be **called**, considered completed.

If you are shedding for practical reasons, your dog must hold the single or group shed until you can gain control of those animals by confining them in a pen, barn, or other enclosed area.

In competition shedding, you are never allowed to touch the sheep with your hand, foot, body, crook, or stock stick. You may jump, stomp, kick dirt, etc. but you may never physically touch the sheep.

Troubleshooting
- **Sheep will not string out** – If the sheep stay in a tight ball in front of you, try using your body and crook to put pressure on them from your side. Step into the sheep and sweep your crook along the ground. You and your dog should work as a team by simultaneously applying pressure to both sides of the flock.
- **Sheep curl behind handler (1)** – If the sheep start curling behind you, be ready to block them with your crook by waving it as a barrier, but don't use your stick to hit the sheep. You mustn't let the sheep get into the habit of curling behind you. Move back to the fence if they curl a few times.
- **Sheep curl behind handler (2)** – If your dog is *not* coming through fast to make the gap, they will tend to push the sheep over you instead of splitting them. Go back and work on getting your dog to come through to you quickly.

Don't over-practice shedding, even if your dog loves it. Shed often enough that your dog is confident shedding, but not so often that they begin to set up to shed whenever you bring sheep to your feet, such as at the pen or chute.

Shed – an alternate approach
Another way to teach the shed is to start by asking your dog to flank behind you through a large gap. This method may be preferable for sideways-moving dogs. For this method, you need a larger flock of sheep, 30 to 50 head, but two separate flocks of 10 to 15 head each are even better.

Separate flocks are flocks that are not used to being together in the same pasture or paddock. These flocks will initially tend to split themselves into their respective groups when combined, so shedding will be much easier for your dog. You might even use a flock of sheep and a flock of goats as your two small flocks.

To start, put the large flock, or two distinct smaller flocks, in your paddock. Flank your dog to the opposite side of the sheep and then make a huge 20- to 30-foot gap for your dog by separating the one larger flock into two smaller flocks. Face the group you want your dog to take control of and quickly flank your dog in around behind you and between the flocks. Use your *chit-chit* cue if your dog is flanking slowly to hurry your dog.

Initially, encourage your dog to flank completely through the gap, from side to side, at speed and continue around the flock. Then start to flank your dog in next to you and stop them in between the two flocks. When your dog is comfortable flanking in between the two flocks, ask them to walk in after they stop.

If you don't have a lot of sheep or other livestock, you may set up two pens with a small number of sheep in each pen, with about 25 feet between pens. Walk your dog into one set of penned stock. Then, flank them around that set while you stand between the two pens. You want your dog to flank around one pen and then continue flanking between the two pens. If your dog starts to open up to go around both pens, call your dog into you with your recall cue to give them practice flanking between the pens. Allow your dog to circle the pen they were walking into one complete additional revolution before stopping them. Now have them circle the same pen, in the other direction one revolution and then walk in.

Once your dog is circling one pen freely, turn them back on the other pen and have them flank around the second pen. Repeat the process you used with the first pen until your dog will circle the other pen freely in both directions.

At this point, if you don't have two flocks or groups that will easily separate, start working with one group and follow the training plans for shedding in Chapter 16. You will have to adapt the plans to fit your dog and livestock.

I used this setup for teaching the look back but it can also be used for teaching your dog to flank between two sets of livestock, a basic skill necessary for the alternate shedding method. You want your dog running as they flank between the two pens.

Now let's go back and pick up the exercise using two flocks of loose sheep that are not used to being together. Once your dog is comfortable rapidly flanking in behind you, both directions, step slightly out of between the flocks. You will be on one side with your dog opposite the large gap between the flocks.

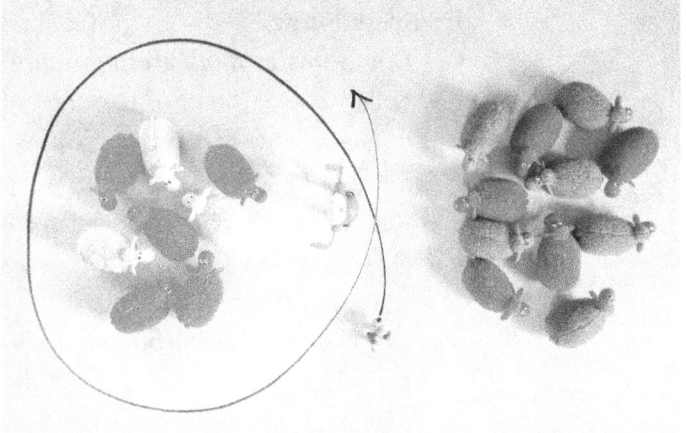

For the alternate shedding method, first have your dog flank completely around one set of stock, passing behind you as you face the group they are circling.

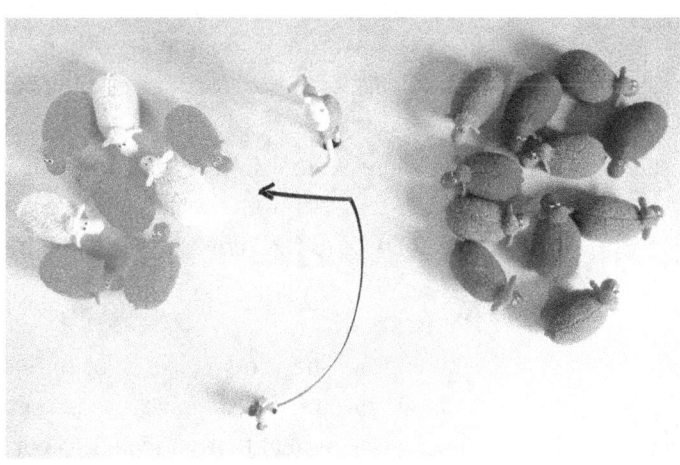

When your dog is flanking freely around each group in both directions, move to the outside a few steps, have your dog flank in toward you, then stop and walk into the designated flock when they are between the two flocks. Your dog will then drive one flock away from the other.

Flank your dog between the flocks and stop them as soon as they get between the flocks. Now ask them to walk into the flock they flanked around, just as you would have if you were standing directly between the flocks.

Once you get your dog to this point, you can start decreasing the distance between the flocks. Continue asking your dog to flank through the smaller and smaller gap until there is no gap and they have to make an opening themselves. At this point you should be ready to jump into the step-by-step instruction above at Phase 7 – Move away from fence.

The key to this method is getting your dog to become comfortable flanking quickly between the two flocks. Do not move on to asking your dog to walk in on one group until they are flanking at full speed as they flank between the flocks.

Troubleshooting
- **Dog wants to flank around both flocks (1)** – If your dog tries to flank around both groups instead of flanking between the groups, you need to extend the distance between the groups. If need be, put one group on the other side of a fence or in a pen. Both flocks will still be visible to your dog, but your dog will start to become comfortable flanking between them.
- **Dog wants to flank around both flocks (2)** – Be sure you are facing the flock you want your dog to flank around and start with two pens of sheep.
- **Dog wants to flank around both flocks (3)** – If your dog still tries to flank around both flocks, stop them and call them to you between the two flocks. Heavily reinforce! You want to increase the behavior of coming between the flocks. Eventually, change from a recall to a flank, once your dog finds coming between the two flocks reinforcing. Then, work on increasing the speed of your dog's flanks as they come between the flocks and follow the instructions provided.

There are several DVDs available that use this method to teach shedding. If you decide to use this method to teach your dog to shed, I suggest you invest in one of those DVDs as they cover this method in greater detail.

Why shed?
Training the shed seems like a lot of effort, so why bother? If you want to shed off animals around your acreage, the important thing is to get the job done. Maybe you have a sick animal that you want to cut out so you can move it to where it can be

treated or you want to pull a ram out of the ewe flock at the end of the breeding season. If you are doing practical work at home, feel free to set things up and help your dog as much as necessary to safely get the job done.

If you decide to learn to shed for trialling, there are a lot more do's and don'ts to keep in mind. Shedding is not for sissies! Usually, shedding is reserved for sheep and duck trials where the following rules generally apply. Be sure to know the exact rules for the association and class at the particular trial you participate in, as those rules supersede these general rules. At cattle trials, instead of a shed, they often require sorting of the cattle.

General rules of shedding at trials
1. The number of animals to be shed off will be predetermined and can vary from one animal, a single, to two or more.
2. Sometimes the animal(s) to be shed are marked with bright colored collars or a dab of color on their backs.
3. The dog sheds the stock. The handler helps set up the shed, but the dog separates and controls the livestock.
4. The dog comes in and turns onto the heads of the stock, called **shedding on the head**.
5. If the dog comes in and turns toward the rear ends of the escaping animals, it is not considered a shed and the animals must be regrouped and the shed repeated.
6. The dog must drive the shed animal(s) away from the rest of the group, maintaining control and not allowing any of the shed animals to rejoin the original group until the judge signals that the shed has been completed.
7. If shed animals are allowed to rejoin the unshed group, all of the animals must be regrouped and the shed completed again.
8. If animals that are allowed to escape (unshed) rejoin the shed animals, all of the animals must be regrouped and the shed completed again.
9. If there is a shedding ring, a circle marked on the field, the shed must occur in the ring.
10. The handler cannot enter the shedding ring until the first animal has stepped into the ring.
11. All animals must be inside the shedding ring to start the shed.
12. If the shed is completed outside of the shedding ring, the animals must be regrouped and the shed repeated within the ring. After the shed is accomplished the dog may drive the shed animals out of the shedding ring.
13. The judge indicates when the shed has been completed to their satisfaction.

14. After the shed, the animals shed off may be required to be driven to the pen and penned or they may be returned to the original group, depending on how the course is set up.
15. Every attempted and missed shed subtracts points off of the run's score.
16. Often, only two attempts are allowed to complete the shed. If the shed is not completed after the second attempt, the team must move on to the next obstacle.
17. Usually, the shed has to be attempted to move on to the next obstacle. You cannot skip the shed and move directly on to the pen or next obstacle without attempting to complete the shed.

Reading the shed

To shed you need to be able to read your sheep well and have a dog that will come in fast. Your responsibility is to set up the shed and help your dog complete it by holding your side. Your dog is responsible for maintaining distance while flanking, stopping, moving closer or farther away when cued, and coming in at full speed when asked. If you have calm sheep that will separate, you are halfway to completing a shed. Experience, for both you and your dog, is essential for learning to shed.

The shed is initially set up when your dog lifts the stock. The first contact between your dog and the stock sets the tone for their entire interaction or run.

If your dog comes in hard and fast on the lift, the stock will tend to be startled and stick tightly together for protection. If the lift is very slow and halting, the stock will tend to ignore your dog and be difficult to move. But if your dog comes in gently with authority, the livestock will likely move steadily and calmly away from your dog. A calm, authoritative start to the dog-stock relationship bodes well for successful shedding. Ideally, the stock remains relaxed enough during the entire run to string out so that a clean shed can be performed.

Your ability to read livestock is also crucial for setting up a successful shed. Stockmanship is the foundation that good handling is based upon. The best handlers are usually the best stockmen. Your ability to read stock is just as important as your dog's since you are controlling your dog the majority of the time. The better both you and your dog are at reading livestock, the better your team will be at herding. In the next chapter, we will take an in-depth look at stockmanship and how you can learn this essential herding skill.

Section 3
Stockmanship

Chapter 18 Stockmanship 101   231
Ewe move them   231
People are the ultimate predator   232
Reading stock   235
Contact   236
Physical adaptations – Pupil shape   237
Physical adaptations – Eye position   239
Physical adaptations – Smell and hearing   241
Instinctive behavior of livestock   241
Pull   242
Leaning on the dog   243
Pressure and release   244
Flight/tight/fight zones   245
Savvy stockmanship   247
Basics   248
Calmness   248
Flight zone   249
Pressure   249

CHAPTER 18

Stockmanship 101

The better you are at observing and understanding animal behavior, the more competent a stockman you will become. Now that you have a basic understanding of the instinctual foundations of animal behavior from *Positive Herding 101*, let's look more closely at balance, flight zones, and pressure and release, as it affects movement. Good stockmanship allows you to combine all of these elements to handle livestock safely, efficiently, and with minimal stress.

We will briefly examine some physical and instinctual characteristics of both dogs and livestock, predators and prey. Behavior is a function of form, instinct, and learning. All animals have evolved physically and behaviorally to survive. Animals do what works!

Ewe move them

Stockmanship is the rock-solid foundation upon which herding is precariously perched. The better you understand and implement stockmanship, the better your herding performance will be. **Stockmanship** is the art and science of reading and

Stockmanship is the rock-solid foundation upon which herding is precariously perched.

gently handling livestock. The safety and welfare of your dog and stock, as well as your safety, should be uppermost in your mind when handling livestock. Herding and stockmanship are woven together, but you can study the movement and control of livestock without a dog in the picture to gain a better understanding of and appreciation for the work your dog performs with stock.

Every time you are working with your animals, with or without your dog, you are training your livestock!

If you approach handling livestock with respect and compassion, you can usually gain their cooperation. There may be some individuals that, due to genetics, history, or personality, want to split off or fight. These individuals should initially be separated from the training flock or herd. Eventually, you can determine if they are suitable to rejoin the group or, instead, should be **culled**, removed from your herd or flock.

There are entire books written about stockmanship, yet many handlers remain woefully ignorant when it comes to understanding that stockmanship is based on the relationship between prey and predator. Learning as much as you can about stockmanship will significantly improve your ability to read and react to the prey/predator dance you see unfolding before you in your paddock or on the trial field.

People are the ultimate predator

You can easily see that your dog is a predator, but did you realize that you too are considered a predator by most livestock? Do sheep, cattle, ducks, chickens, hogs, and goats usually move away as you approach? Their movement away from you indicates that they perceive you as a predator. Since most of us eat meat we are the ultimate predator. Because your livestock perceives you as a predator, you can learn about reading and moving livestock without a dog in the picture.

When herding with your dog, you will be reading the stock and controlling your dog. To hone your livestock reading skills, you should spend a fair amount of time moving livestock *without* your dog. There is no way you can direct your dog if you don't have a clue about how the stock will react to pressure. Sheep are an excellent choice of stock to work with to learn how to move livestock without a dog. They are usually quite shy and non-threatening, flock well together, and move as one unit.

You are ultimately responsible for the safety and welfare of yourself, your dog, and your livestock!

The following exercises can be done with a few animals (3 to 6) or a large flock (50 to several hundred). Try to work with both a small flock and a much larger one, if possible. You will be amazed at how different variously sized groups react to you and how you have to adjust your actions to perform the same maneuvers with different sized flocks.

Some handler-only exercises, no dog involved, include:
- Move the stock along a fence.
- Move the stock through a gate.
- Move the stock into a pen, barn, or chute.
- Drive the stock in a figure 8 pattern.
- Stop the stock and keep it stationary.
- Divide the flock into two flocks and hold them apart.
- Divide the flock into two flocks and drive one flock through a gate or into a pen.
- Shed off a few head and drive them through a gate or into a pen.
- Shed off a single animal and drive it through a gate or into a pen.

Be creative and try these exercises, and others you devise, to further your knowledge of stockmanship. Also, repeat some of the exercises with different stock or use the same stock but work them on a different day or in a different paddock.

Reading livestock comes in handy many times during herding training.

First I put two ewes in one pen.

Then I put two in the other pen. Note that the sheep are looking at my dog, who is not in the picture.

With limited help from my dog, I penned two sets of sheep in preparation for training shedding.

Now, grab a friend and work the same exercises with two handlers but no dog. Initially, *don't* talk to each other once you have determined where you want the stock to go. Is it easier or more difficult to work with another handler? It may be easier or more difficult to control and move the livestock, depending on how experienced you and your friend are at reading and responding to the stock.

Finally, go back to the same exercises and designate one person as the "handler" and the other as the "dog". Again, no real dog is involved. The "dog" is only to move as cued and not to react to the livestock unless cued to do so. The "dog" is free to hold a line when asked in, to cover a ewe that tries to break away, or to use their instinctual understanding of balance. If asked to flank, the "dog" should respond as cued and not flank in the opposite direction because they realize that is what the handler needs them to do to complete an obstacle. The "dog" should not stop, walk in, or perform any cued behavior unless cued by the handler.

For even more fun, don't tell the "dog" what obstacle or exercise the handler is going to attempt. That way the "dog" will not be tempted to add uncued movements. The "dog" may walk in too slow or quick, flank too close or far off, flank too slow or fast, or behave in any way that a real dog might when herding.

Then switch roles and the handler becomes the "dog" and the "dog" becomes the handler. I guarantee you will learn a lot and have a lot of fun by moving livestock without a real dog in sight!

Moving livestock without a real dog is one of the most fun and educational exercises an inexperienced handler can participate in. If you move stock as a learning exercise, I guarantee that you will laugh, but if you wait and move them by necessity, I guarantee that you will swear, or want to!

Reading stock

How did you do moving livestock without a real dog? What did you learn? What else? Reading livestock is about being able to anticipate, from what you see, what the stock will do next.

Anticipation is the key. If you wait for something to happen before you act, you will be too late. You want to see the behavior that tips you off as to what the livestock intends to do next. Only by anticipating and acting on that knowledge will you be able to be in the right place, or give your dog a cue promptly, to have them positioned where they need to be.

Here are a few things that you may have learned or noticed about livestock:
- The fewer animals handled as a group, the more flighty or touchy they tend to be.
- The more animals handled as a group, the more settled or calm they tend to be.
- Ears and heads are primary indicators of anticipated behavior.
- Raised, lowered, or shaken heads indicate concern.
- Lowered heads and pawing may indicate the animal will charge.
- Turned heads indicate likely changes of direction.
- Ears tell you what the animal is focusing on and their level of concern.
- All animals, even those in the same group, do not act alike.
- Some animals tend to be leaders and some followers.
- Animals will change their behavior depending on how they are handled.
- A single animal is unpredictable and will act erratically, especially when separated from a group.
- Animals do not react exactly the same to two different people (or dogs).
- Stock can be **heavy**, slow or difficult to move or **light**, quick and effortless to move.
- Different breeds, species, sexes, or individuals may react differently from their peers.

Many factors influence how the stock reacts in different situations. Different dogs, individual animals, weather, time of day, locations, smells, handler experience, pulls, topography, handler posture and speed of movements, shadows, sounds, presence of offspring, and more, can influence how the stock will react at any given moment.

Contact

Contact happens when the prey and the predator initially notice, hook up to each other, and begin mutual communication. Until the stock notices your dog, there will not be any communication from your dog to them. Prey may notice your dog before your dog notices them.

A dog making contact with stock is different from them entering the flight zone. **Contact** is when your dog, who is already hooked up to the stock, is noticed and focused on by the livestock. At this point, your dog is usually at a distance and is not applying pressure to the stock.

Your dog enters the flight zone when they start to put pressure on the livestock. Both contact and entering the flight zone can happen simultaneously if your dog is not noticed by the stock until they are within the stock's flight zone.

- *Hook up* – Predator notices and remains focused on the prey or prey notices and remains focused on the predator.
- *Contact* – Prey and predator become mutually hooked up.
- *Entering flight zone* – Predator applies pressure to the prey.

When your dog first makes contact, the stock will raise and turn their heads and ears toward your dog. As your dog approaches the flight zone, the stock will turn away from your dog in preparation for moving away. A dog flanking around a flock should stay in contact with them, but should not be within their flight zone. Thus, the stock should notice your dog flanking, but not move away from your dog as they flank.

Hook up goes in both directions, from predator to prey and from prey to predator. Predators read and react to prey, just as prey read and react to predators.

If your dog is too far away from the stock, especially when flanking, they will be out of contact and no communication will happen. If they are too close to the stock, they may cause the livestock to panic. This communication is based on what attributes each player, stock or dog, possesses.

Laser focus!

How your dog reacts to livestock is based on their confidence, instincts, modal action patterns, physical attributes, and training. How livestock reacts to your dog is also based on their instincts, physical attributes, and previous interaction with predators. Animals have evolved to survive by changing physically and instinctually. Their behavior also changes as they learn.

Sheep, as defenseless prey, read predatory behavior at least as well as dogs, armed predators, read them, in order to survive.

So what are the major physical and instinctual attributes that dogs, as predators, and livestock, as prey, bring to the paddock?

Physical adaptations – Pupil shape

Both prey and predators have developed unique and extremely useful visual traits, in the form of the shape of their pupils, for increasing their odds of success in capturing or eluding capture. A **pupil** is an aperture or opening in the eye that allows light to enter it.

- *Horizontal pupils* Sheep, cattle, horses, and goats are herbivores and have a horizontal pupil that gathers light from the front, back, and sides but limits light from above, thus reducing the amount of direct sunlight that can enter. This configuration helps them to see predators approaching and also see the ground well, for good vision while running.

Sheep see better to the side and rear than they do to the front, although they do have a blind spot directly behind them. Woolly sheep may also have trouble seeing due to wool covering their eyes, which is known as **wool blindness**.

Sheep have large rectangular pupils which give them panoramic vision, allowing them to survey the horizon for potential threats. Their eyes are placed more to the side of the head, which gives them a wide field of vision

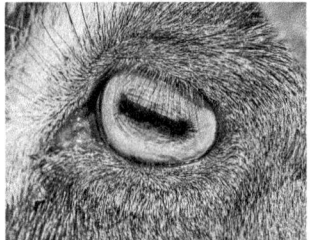
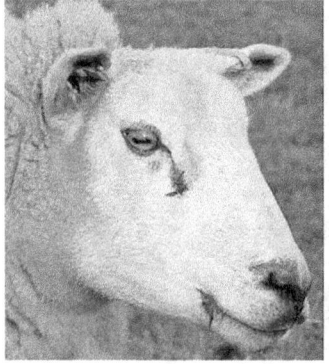

Goat's eye
Note the horizontal shape of the pupil.

Prey animals with horizontal pupils also have **cyclovergence**, *the ability to rotate their eyes to keep their pupils horizontal, no matter what position their head is in, up or down.*

Herbivores focus on the ground when their heads are down, but because they have very limited binocular vision, their depth perception is poor, especially at ground level. Because of this, they tend to balk at shadows on the ground and fear entering dark alleys or barns.

Left to right:
Cat's eyes,
Tiger's eyes
Dog's eyes

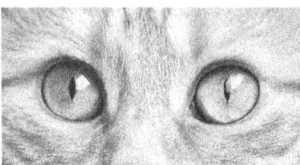
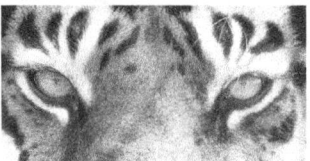

- ***Vertical pupils*** – Some predators have pupils that are vertical such as cats and foxes. These predators are classified as ambush predators and they hunt both day and night. Surprisingly, big cats such as lions and tigers have round pupils similar to dogs and humans.
- ***Round pupils*** – Predators with round pupils include dogs and humans as well as big cats. These animals are known as active foragers or predators that chase down prey.

Top middle & right: Sheep grazing ©Gordon Love, Durham University
https://phys.org/news/2015-08-pupil-linked-animals-ecological-niche.html

Physical adaptations – Eye position

Besides the difference in pupil shape, the position of the eyes on the head is markedly different between prey and predator. Eyes on the sides of the head versus eyes on the front of the head affect the size of the field of vision and the amount of binocular and monocular fields of vision. It all goes back to what eye position best suits the needs of the animal, as the hunter or hunted.

Eyes on the side of the head are found in prey animals, with each eye seeing individually and only a small amount of **binocular vision**, where eyesight from both eyes overlap.

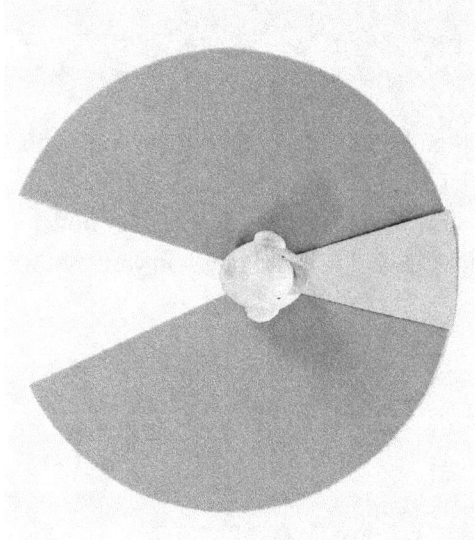

Duck

Birds, prey animals, have small areas of binocular vision with large areas of monocular vision.

The light grey areas in each diagram indicate the binocular field of vision and the dark grey areas indicate the monocular field of vision.

Cat

Cats, predators, are the opposite with large areas of binocular vision and small areas of monocular vision.

Prey animals tend to have small **blind spots**, areas behind them that they cannot see, and small areas of binocular vision. The advantage they have is an increased monocular panoramic field of vision. These characteristics aid prey animals in spotting and running from predators. Sheep can spot predators approaching when the predators are from 1,200 to 1,500 yards away!

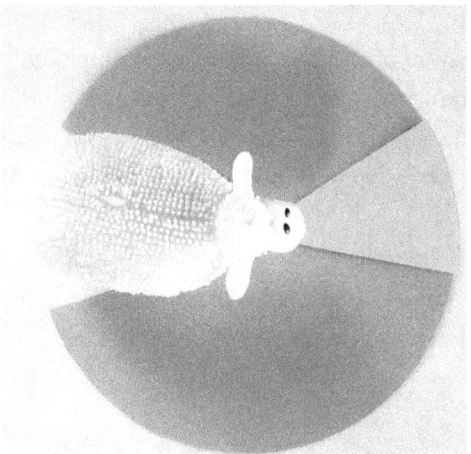

Sheep and cattle have small areas of binocular vision, 25–50°, with large areas of monocular vision. They also have a blind spot directly behind them.

On the other hand, predators tend to have large blind spots behind their bodies and larger areas of binocular vision, for better depth perception. Both of these characteristics aid them in locating and catching prey. Predators also have the advantage of noticing and targeting movement. Dogs have approximately a 240° field of vision with 30–60° of binocular vision.

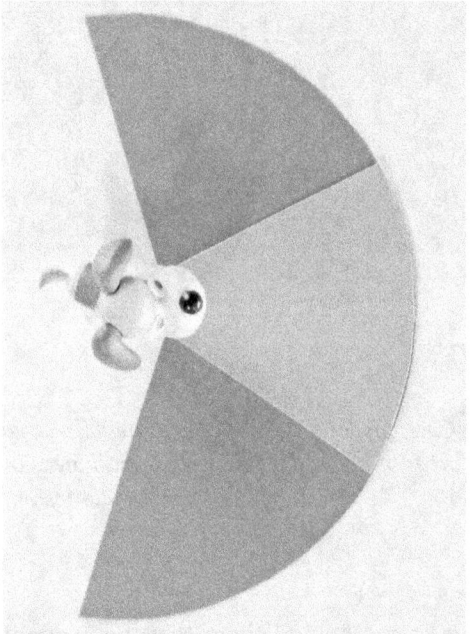 

Dawg has a larger monocular field of vision than Shandler while also having a smaller binocular field of vision. Dawg can also see more to the side than Shandler due to the shape of his head and the placement of his eyes.

Humans, as predators, are closer to dogs and big cats than sheep or cattle in their visual configuration with a 180° field of vision that includes 120° of binocular vision.

Physical adaptations – Smell and hearing

Both prey and predators usually have very well-developed senses of smell. Dogs generally have a sense of smell that is 40 times greater than that of humans. Sheep use smell to locate water and lambs, while rams also use smell to identify ewes in season. Sheep can also identify predators by smell. Cattle can detect odors up to five miles away and can also hear both low and high-frequency sounds beyond human capability.

Other predators and prey also have highly developed senses of hearing. Dogs can hear sounds at four times the distance a human can and can also hear higher-pitched sounds than humans. Sheep also have well-developed hearing and are especially attuned to high-pitched or loud noises.

Because dogs, sheep, and other livestock can hear, smell, and see better than humans, they sometimes react to stimuli that we cannot discern. If your dog or livestock displays unusual or abnormal behavior, it may be because they are reacting to a sight, sound, or smell that you cannot perceive.

Instinctive behavior of livestock

There have been many studies done and much has been written about the instinct of dogs, but prey animals also have instincts and modal action patterns that affect how they react to you and your dog as predators.

Instinctive predator avoidance patterns

- *Herding or flocking* – Since there is safety in numbers, most grazing stock will bunch together when a dog or other predator is noticed. Sheep and goats, having few means of protection, tend to group together more noticeably than cattle.
- *Facing toward or away from predator* – If a predator approaches, but is outside of the livestock's flight zone, the stock will turn toward the threat and focus on it. Once the predator enters the stock's flight zone, they will turn and move away from the threat.
- *Sticking together* – The more threatened a flock or herd feels, the more tightly they will stay together and the less likely they are to string out.
- *Milling* – When confused or cornered, a flock or herd may panic and start tightly circling. In this situation, the dominant animals will move to the center because the center is the safest place, farthest from the predator.

As a predator approaches an animal, the diagram shows how its position applies pressure and determines how the prey will react.

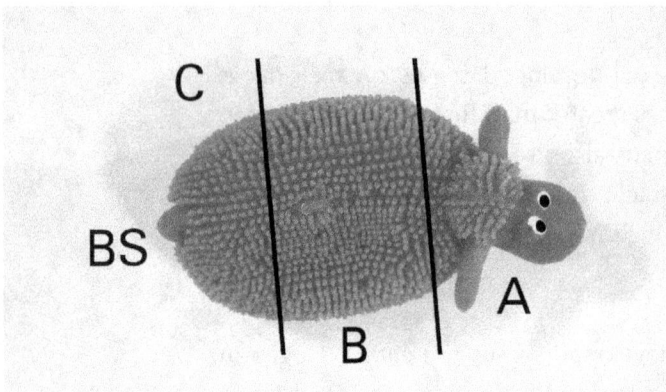

A – *Predator position that stops or turns prey*

B – *Predator position that moves prey forward or slightly turns prey*

C – *Predator position that moves prey forward*

BS – *Blind spot behind prey*

Temple Grandin is a professor of animal science, consultant to the livestock industry, author of several books, and a spokesperson for autism. She designs low-stress animal handling facilities and is known for looking at setups "through the eyes" of the animals that will be using them.

Livestock reacts to the approach of dogs based on their instincts. Some typical stock reactions include:
- *Flocking or herding together* – Sheep tend to flock more tightly than goats but different breeds and situations can affect the degree of flocking. Cattle tend to herd together more loosely than sheep or goats.
- *Snorting* – Sheep often use a snort to alert other sheep to danger.
- *Raising heads* – Animals will raise their heads to get a better look at an approaching threat.
- *Moving ears* – Animals will turn their ears toward danger.
- *Tail carriage* – Cattle will switch their tails when nervous. Sheep normally carry their tails down while goats carry theirs up.
- *Flapping wings* – Ducks will stand tall and flap their wings when alarmed and may try to fly or run.

Pull

As defined previously, **balance** is the point your dog instinctively seeks to control the livestock or to bring the stock straight to you. The point of balance is determined by what pull or draw the livestock feels. Stock is always looking for safety and comfort.

Pull or draw is the desire to move toward perceived safety and comfort. If threatened, the pull is to safety. Safety may be sought with other animals of their species or where they last felt safe. If uncomfortable, because hot or thirsty, animals will be drawn to water or shade, but if cold, the pull will be to shelter or windbreaks.

Safety trumps comfort! When animals feel threatened their first priority will be survival through avoidance of or escape from danger.

Always consider livestock that is visible to, or can be heard or smelled by, the stock you are working as a potentially strong draw. There is safety in numbers and stock wants to be in large herds or flocks when feeling threatened. Livestock will also be drawn back to where they last felt safe – a pen, paddock, or pasture. That is why stock is usually drawn to gates they have used to enter a paddock, they are looking to escape from a perceived threat.

Leaning on the dog

There is another use of the word **pull** in herding, and that is the pull that some dogs have on their stock, especially sheep. When the sheep draw back toward the dog and are comfortable with the dog quite close, it is said that they are **leaning on the dog** or the dog has pull on them. It is almost as if the dog has a set of invisible reins attached to the sheep and guides them effortlessly to wherever the dog wants them to go.

A dog that approaches and drives stock with an even, workmanlike pace will usually keep their livestock calm, but when sheep lean on a dog it is almost magical to watch the dog and sheep move as a single unit. The flight zone of the sheep, in this situation, seems to shrink for a brief time as they don't seem to perceive the dog as a significant threat.

Some dogs can get sheep to lean on them quite often, but most dogs never can. This is one behavior you cannot train and have to see demonstrated to comprehend and appreciate.

Pressure and release

Pressure, as it relates to herding, is the opposite of pull. **Pressure** is the desire to move away from perceived threats. Almost anything livestock considers threatening, such as a dog, an unfamiliar object, a person, a strange animal or smell, an obstacle, or a barrier such as a fence, can put pressure on stock. Pull draws animals toward something and pressure pushes animals away from something. Both pull and pressure affect where livestock wants to go and where you or your dog will have to be to move them where you want them to go.

Herding is based on pressure and release of that pressure on livestock. You and your dog apply and release pressure, but there are also pulls and pressure in the environment. Stock is constantly evaluating and reacting to the myriad pressures and pulls in their surroundings. Thus, herding is very dynamic and scenarios can change in nanoseconds!

Your dog may instinctively be an expert at applying and releasing pressure. Dogs apply pressure to get livestock moving and release pressure to slow or stop movement. Dogs may also move to a different position to stop or control movement. If the stock is heavy, your dog may need to apply significant pressure to get them moving, while they may need to apply much less pressure to get light stock moving.

One reason you need to work your dog on different livestock at different places is so that they can learn to adjust the amount of pressure they apply to unfamiliar stock. This is particularly important if you plan to trial with your dog.

Too little pressure and the stock won't move, but too much and the stock may explode and run away from or over you or your dog. Sheep are particularly apt to panic if threatened. They will raise their heads and draw their ears back and close to their heads, as they run. If panicked, they will run blindly into fences or people. If run excessively or panicked, some sheep may go down and stay lying on the ground until they calm down.

The concept of pressure and release is based on Negative Reinforcement. Pressure is applied by the dog (an aversive) and release is secured by the sheep by moving away from the dog (a reinforcer).

Flight/tight/fight zones

The **flight zone** is the stock's comfort or safety zone. It is often thought of as a bubble that a threat can approach without causing movement, but if breached, the animal will respond to the threat by escaping or fighting. The flight zone is not a perfect circle around an animal or group of animals. The flight zone is narrower on the sides and wider to the front and back of livestock. Flight zones are dynamic and change with the situation and previous experience.

The flight zone can be divided into three areas or zones; flight, tight, and fight. The tight zone is the next area that your dog would enter as they move through the flight zone toward the fight zone.

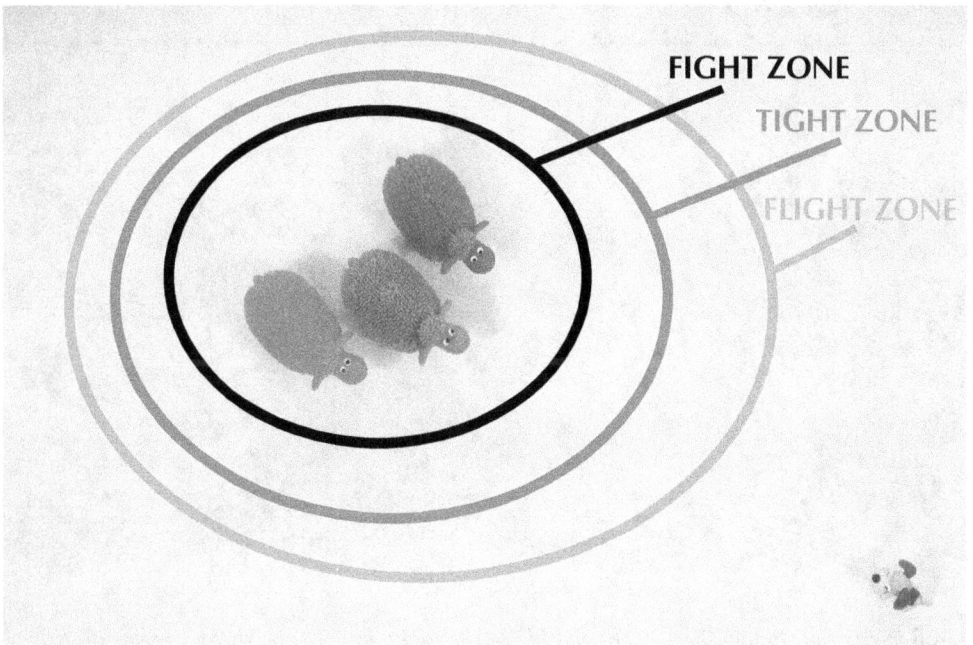

Your dog would have to enter the tight zone in order to move stock into a pen or other enclosure where the stock feels trapped. The **tight zone** is between the flight and fight zones and, like the flight and fight zones, changes in size depending on the situation.

Finally, if your dog continues moving toward the stock, they would enter the fight zone. The **fight zone** is the area around the livestock that is so close to the stock that the livestock will fight your dog. If stock is trapped in a corner, has young with them, or decides they are not going to move off of your dog no matter how close your dog approaches them, then the stock will most likely fight your dog. The stock also may explode in all directions, jump over you or your dog, or crash into a fence or gate.

Usually, your dog can approach and barely breach the flight zone to move livestock, but that is not always possible. Sometimes your dog will need to enter the tight zone and occasionally the fight zone. You will notice that your dog usually slows down as they move from the flight zone toward the fight zone as they realize that the stock is becoming concerned and the situation touchy. Your dog slows down to evaluate and be ready to react to the response of the stock. If your dog does not have herding instinct, then you will have to monitor your dog's approach to the stock and slow your dog down as they move closer to the tight and then fight zones.

Wild stock can usually be tamed down by using good stockmanship practices when handling them, thus shrinking their flight zone.

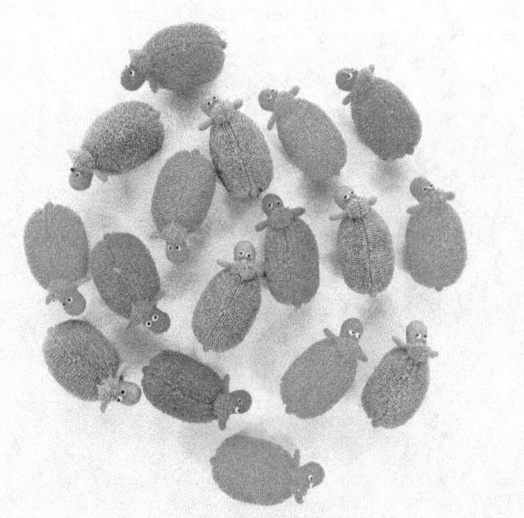

Sheep and cattle will mill, *circle tightly together, when confused or upset. It can be difficult to move a flock once they begin milling.*

The bubble of the flight zone of the sheep in relation to Shandler.

One key to good stockmanship is allowing stock the time necessary to process new situations before attempting to force them to move into unfamiliar environments. A few moments or minutes allowing animals to investigate and settle can save a lot of headaches.

Livestock that is forced into a situation that they feel they cannot escape from will fight for their lives. Females, and some males, will fight to protect their young. Some males will fight other males in an attempt to drive off what they perceive as competition for breeding females.

> **Warning!**
> Handle all intact male stock and female livestock accompanied by young with extreme caution!

Stock that is being penned or held in a corner may feel threatened and climb onto or run into fences, explode in all directions, or run into or jump over you or your dog to escape to safety.

Some warning signs stock display when feeling threatened include:
- Bobbing head
- Swishing tail – cattle
- Shaking head
- Pawing or stomping
- Snorting
- Lowering head while tucking nose – especially horned cattle, bulls, rams, or bucks
- Backing away while continuing to face the threat – bulls, rams, or bucks
- Turning to kick – cattle
- Turning sideways – bulls

Ruminants, such as sheep, cattle, and goats, have only lower incisors or front teeth, with a dental pad on their upper jaw in place of front teeth. Since they have no upper front teeth, they will not attempt to bite when threatened. Horses have both upper and lower front teeth and use their bite primarily for offense.

So how do you incorporate all the characteristics of prey and predators into a usable strategy for working with livestock? It all comes down to stockmanship.

Savvy stockmanship

Good stockmanship allows you to safely work your dog to move and control livestock. When you work with stock, the safety of you, your dog, and the stock should always be uppermost in your mind. Also, you always want to protect your dog's confidence and help them safely win livestock encounters.

There are some general rules that you can use to start building a good stockmanship foundation. Each scenario is different, but these general guidelines will give you a head start on developing your stock sense. Remember that there is no replacement for experience.

Basics

Every group has a lead animal which usually determines the group's initial response to a threat. The lead animal also acts as the "head" of the herd, with the rest of the animals becoming the "body." Where the head or lead animal goes, the others usually follow.

Stock is excellent at reading the intent of predators by their behavior. A coyote trotting by on its way to hunt mice will elicit a very different reaction from one stalking a flock. The same stock will also respond differently to various predators, such as dogs and people.

While grazing, stock will generally position themselves just behind the shoulder of the animal in front of them as a protective measure. An animal may also hide pain, in the presence of a predator, to remain unnoticed and not become a target. Even when grazing in the same pasture, sheep and cattle will maintain separate groups.

Calmness

Calm livestock naturally follow a leader and relaxed stock will often walk single file to water or bed down, but one **hawky** or nervous animal can upset the entire herd or flock. By being too pushy, your dog can also upset the flock. Calm animals are easier to move, lose less weight, and are more amenable to moving smoothly away from your dog, instead of fighting or blindly fleeing.

Generally, the fewer the head of stock worked, the lighter they tend to be, the more head, the calmer. Wild stock needs to be "dog broke" by experienced dogs before working inexperienced dogs on them. **Dog broke** means that the stock has learned to respect and move away from pressure applied by dogs. If done correctly, dog breaking of stock will make the stock less flighty and more settled in the presence of dogs.

Dog breaking stock, especially heavy sheep or cattle, should be done with an experienced dog. Use light stock that moves easily off of your dog for initial training.

Flight zone

The stock's flight zone size decreases with calm, consistent dog behavior and increases with erratic or excessively aggressive behavior. Remember that livestock read dogs as well as, if not better than, dogs read them.

When cornered or feeling extremely threatened, some stock will run directly into or jump over people or dogs, so care must be taken when penning or loading livestock. If the stock gets away while you are trying to pen or load them, they will learn that they can escape and will become much more difficult to confine.

One of the most dangerous situations your dog will encounter is handling **singles**, lone animals, that break away or have been shed from a flock or herd. To safely reunite the group, take the group to the single or move your dog out of the way so that the single can rejoin the group.

Pressure

Sheep, goats, and ducks are generally much more responsive to pressure from a dog than cattle. You always want to gather all livestock together before applying pressure to initiate movement of the group. Move stock by driving from behind or with the handler ahead and the dog behind. Very tame livestock may respond better to being led than driven. Always avoid approaching or remaining in the stock's blind spot.

A herd of cattle may chase off an unfamiliar dog. Cattle need to be "dog broke", worked by competent dogs, until they respect and move off of dogs before they are suitable for working with young or inexperienced dogs.

Certainly, these guidelines just scratch the surface of a true stockman's knowledge that has been gained through years of experience. As long as you keep safety uppermost in your mind and strive to have your dog handle stock as efficiently and with the least amount of stress possible, you will not go too far wrong.

The best way to become a good stockman is to learn all you can about the instincts and behavior of your dog and the stock they will be handling, work with and observe stock, and if possible, work with a seasoned stockman. There is so much to learn about herding that goes beyond training your dog. Figuring out how pull, balance, stock movement, pressure, and instinct all relate to herding can be overwhelming. Seek out an experienced handler to guide you if you become confused or frustrated.

Herding is a complex and fascinating endeavor! There is always more to learn. Some advanced layers of learning will not be accessible to you until you have a strong foundational framework in place. If you can find a mentor to help you along the way, I encourage you to avail yourself of their experience and expertise. Just remember to keep safety and fun at the top of your priority list.

Enjoy the journey.

Section 4
Trials and On-farm Skills

Chapter 19 Getting ready to trial   255
Do practical work with your dog   256
Set up a course at home   256
Hit the road   257
Types of trials   258
Watch some trials   259
Know the rules   260
Enter a trial   264
Arriving at the trial   264
Handlers' meeting   265
Potty your dog   266
Warm-up your dog   266
Watch other runs   267

Video your run   268
Ready, set, go   268

Chapter 20 Trial elements and obstacles   271
Problems at trials   272
Outrun   272
Lift   273
Fetch   275
Turning the post   276
Drive   277
Cross drive   278
Pen   280
Bump flanks   283

Chute or bridge   285
Maltese cross   286
Shed   287
Figure 8   289
Restricted handler movement   290
Ending the run   290
Cool down your dog   291
Setting out at trials   291
Judged versus timed trials   291
Trial dog or farm dog?   292

Chapter 21 Farm and ranch skills   295
Doing chores   295
Holding stock off feeders and at gates   296
Moving stock to new places   297
Gathering livestock   297
Penning or corralling   298
Sorting using a gate   299
Chutes   301
Loading into a trailer   301
Working multiple dogs   302
Working mothers with young   304

CHAPTER 19

Getting ready to trial

This chapter is not meant to be the final word on trials, but rather a compendium of what I have learned in my years of going to trials. I admit I enjoy the training of herding dogs more than I relish the thrill of competition. I do like to compete and win, but my real fascination is watching good dogs work and training dogs to use their instincts to herd.

Your goal at a trial should be to handle and move the stock with efficiency and minimal stress. In other words, a trial should be a demonstration of good stockmanship.

My best advice about trialing is to always compete first with yourself. If you can come off of the trial field and know that you and your dog worked to your current level of capability, you can be proud, no matter if you walk off with first prize or nothing. I guarantee that 99.9% of the time you will feel that if you could re-run the course, you and your dog would do better!

If your only goal is to win trials, you will miss out on a lot of fun and camaraderie. Going to trials takes a lot of time, travel, and money, and you have no control over the quality of judging or livestock that you draw for your run. To win trials you have to be well prepared, have a competent dog, and compete in many trails to gain experience and hone your handling skills.

Do practical work with your dog
One of the best ways to get ready for a trial is to use your dog to do chores and practical work at home. Chores and practical work seem to automatically make sense to a dog. They thrive on the repetition of repeated chores if criteria are maintained. Both partners can gain a sense of accomplishment for a job well done.

Types of chores that can be helpful include:
- Gathering livestock to check or work them.
- Holding stock off of feed bunks while grain is fed.
- Moving stock to different paddocks or pastures.
- Bringing in animals for milking.
- Holding stock at gateways.
- Running stock through a footbath.

Take the time to make sure your dog is meeting criteria for *every* cue. It is easy to get in a hurry and allow your dog to slice their flanks or cheat on their stops when you are just trying to get something done. "Good enough" may get the chore done, but when you later ask your dog to be precise, you will find that you have a fair amount of work to do on cleaning up criteria.

Your dog will figure out and anticipate the next move on almost every chore that you do regularly. It won't take long before your dog will start to perform chores on auto-pilot, needing virtually no cues from you. This can be good and bad. I always like my dog listening for my cues and not taking initiative, unless I ask them to.

To prevent my dog from going on auto-pilot when doing familiar routines, I try to observe what cue my dog is anticipating and then cue the opposite behavior. If my dog is used to going come bye to gather the rams, then I will send them away to me. The main reason I like my dogs listening, even when doing familiar chores, is because something can change in the environment so that a chore needs to be done in a new way. I may need my dog to break their routine to readily perform the chore differently.

Set up a course at home
It is always helpful to set up at least a bare-bones course at home. It certainly doesn't need to be fancy and should not be completed over and over again in the same direction. Try to set the course so that you can move to different starting points and can send your dog both directions on their outrun. You don't want your stock to become course broke. **Course broke** means that the stock has learned to perform the course with minimal direction from your dog.

You also don't want your dog to become accustomed to always gathering in one direction, driving the same path, and then penning or shedding. Running a course over and over again will be like completing a chore for your dog and they will start to anticipate what they need to do and tune you out. If you repeatedly run the same course with the same docile sheep, you will defeat the purpose of practicing the course.

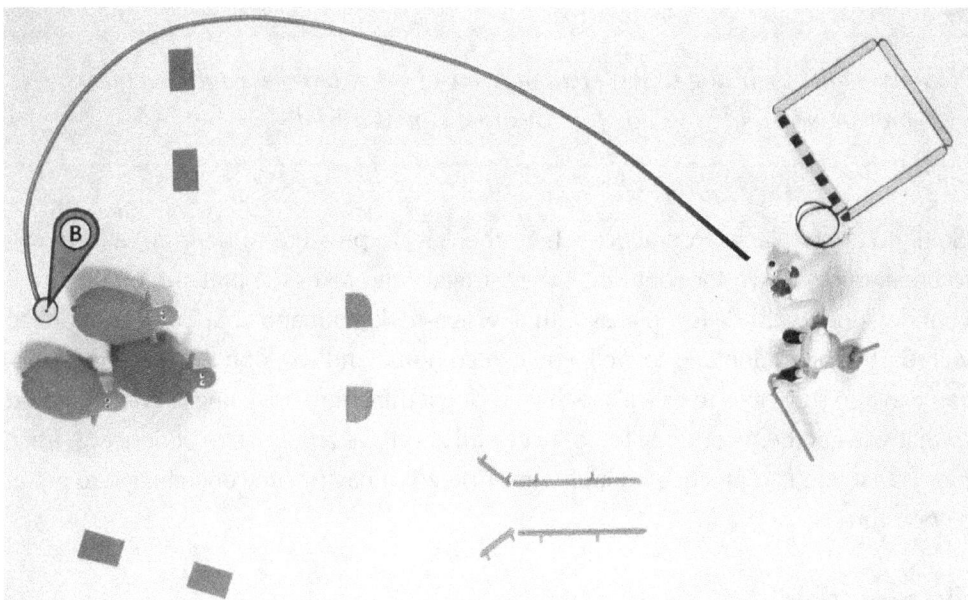

A typical mid-level trial course might include a post, drive and cross-drive gates, chute, and pen. An upper-level course may also have a shedding ring. The 'B' indicates the point of balance.

The goal is for you to learn how to judge the pull, to hit gates, etc., not to just complete the course. When you get to a trial, the course and sheep will be completely different and usually not very amenable to running the course just because your dog shows up behind them. If you have enough stock, rotate different groups through your practice sessions to keep them fresh and your dog on their toes.

Hit the road

Before you even think about going to a trial, be sure to take your dog to a few new places to work livestock that is similar to what you will be working at a trial. If you plan to trial, learn about the venues that you intend to compete at and practice at a friend's or a fun day before you attempt to compete with your dog. You need to generalize all of your dog's herding behaviors to new locations and new livestock. Some dogs adapt easily to novel places and livestock and some not so readily.

You also need to work with someone who can set livestock out for you, if the stock will be set out at the trial you intend to go to. A green dog will sometimes try to fetch sheep or cattle to the set-out person or may be intimidated when they get to the stock and find another dog nearby. If they set out with horses, you need to practice with someone on horseback near the stock as well. Don't have the first time your dog sees a set-out person be at their first trial!

Nobody wants their dog to look bad in front of other handlers and spectators, so over-prepare you and your dog for your first run at a trial!

Going to a few places to practice where there is no pressure to perform, allows you to break things down for your dog if they struggle and takes the pressure off of you. If your dog does well at a few places with new livestock, your and your dog's confidence will soar! If things don't go so well, you can go home and work on the problem areas. You can also stay close to or walk with your dog if things are not going as well as hoped so that you can help your dog to be successful and have a positive experience. A huge plus is that you can practice multiple runs instead of having only one chance to get in a good run.

Types of trials
There are many different types of trials in the United States put on by associations including, but not limited to:
- USBCHA – United States Border Collie Herding Association
- AKC – American Kennel Club (may also offer instinct testing)
- AHBA – All Herding Breeds Association
- ASCA – Australian Shepherd Club of America

Many breeds have their own herding associations

Countries all over the world hold herding trials and have classes, major trials, herding associations, and unique awards.

Most trials offer runs of sheep or cattle. Other trials offer classes of sheep, cattle, ducks, or some combination of the three, but species of animals are never mixed for a run. Trials also usually offer different levels of classes.

Classes in the United States are broken down many ways and the trial may include some combination of the following:
- Novice–novice = Novice dog and novice handler (no open handlers or open dogs)
- Pro–novice = Novice dog and experienced handler
- Ranch = Level between pro-novice and open
- Open ranch = Usually longer outrun and farther drives than ranch
- Open = Experienced handlers – open to any handler and any dog
- Nursery = Usually dogs under 3 or 4 years of age running an open course
- Juniors = Young handlers (under a certain age) running any dog

These designations are for American trials. In other countries, they often name their classes differently. In South Africa, the South African Sheepdog Association (SASDA) uses the following class names: Beginners, Juniors, Seniors, and Top Dogs, with Juniors referring to the experience level of the dog and handler, not the age of the handler.

Even in the US, some associations use other names for their classes. The American Kennel Club (AKC) has its own unique course designations – courses A through C, with A being the lowest and B the highest level herding course while course C is a tending course.

In some associations, you can earn titles with your dog. Some trials are only for dogs in certain registries and some are open to any dog. Because there are so many different class designations, depending on the sponsoring association, you need to investigate what is available in your area and the rules that pertain to those trials.

Some trials are field trials that are run on big fields with outruns of 500 yards or more, some are small arena trials, and some trial venues are in between. Some are judged and some are based on time and points. In **time and points trials** you earn points for each animal that completes an obstacle, such as passing through a set of panels, and the handler/dog team with the most points wins. If there are ties in points earned, then the team with the fastest time wins.

Watch some trials

Once you have identified a potential trial, be sure to go to a similar trial or two before you plan to run your dog. Scoping out a trial venue allows you to get a feel for what will be expected of you and your dog without any pressure to perform. Reading or talking about a trial versus attending a trial are very different things. There is no substitute for experience!

Talk to handlers at the trial. Most handlers are glad to share their knowledge, as long as they are not preparing to run their dog. Find out where handlers wait **on deck** to run and avoid that area. Most handlers are preparing themselves mentally and watching the run or two in front of theirs. They need this time before their run to focus on mentally preparing themselves to do their best. Ask handlers sitting and watching runs if you may ask them a few questions. Most handlers will be more than happy to talk herding!

You may want to ask if they know of any experienced handlers in your area who give lessons or have fun days. Watch not only the beginner classes but the more advanced classes as well. This is your chance to learn all that you can about what skills your dog will need to be successful in their future runs. You can also see how the more advanced teams perform. Take a chair and hat along, as most trials do not have bleacher seating, and you will most likely be sitting out in the open with no shade.

Take your dog with you to the trial, if allowed, and let them get accustomed to the sights, sounds, and smells of the trial scene. There is usually a lot of activity and dogs are everywhere. Going to a fun day, if you can locate one, is one of the best ways to introduce your dog to the trial atmosphere and is a great intermediate step between working at home and running at a trial.

Dogs are not welcome near the trial field or arena as their presence may apply pressure to the livestock being run.

Be aware that if your dog is already turned on to stock, they may become very excited watching the other dogs run and the stock move. Always keep your dog on leash and be prepared to retire to a safe distance or put your dog into a crate where they cannot see the action, if they become over-aroused.

Know the rules

Before you go to a specific trial look up the rules by getting a rule book or going online. Most associations detail the elements of each course or level and some have diagrams of the standard course for each level. It is helpful to understand the courses you will see being run. Some trials have announcers who detail the course and narrate the runs but most do not.

*Often announcers will **not** narrate runs as they occur because the narration could interfere with the communication between the handler and their dog.*

Most courses are not complicated. If you are unfamiliar with the course and the first handlers you watch struggle, then it may take you a while to figure out how the course is supposed to be run. Sometimes a course diagram is posted on-site or you can ask another spectator if they know how the course is supposed to be run.

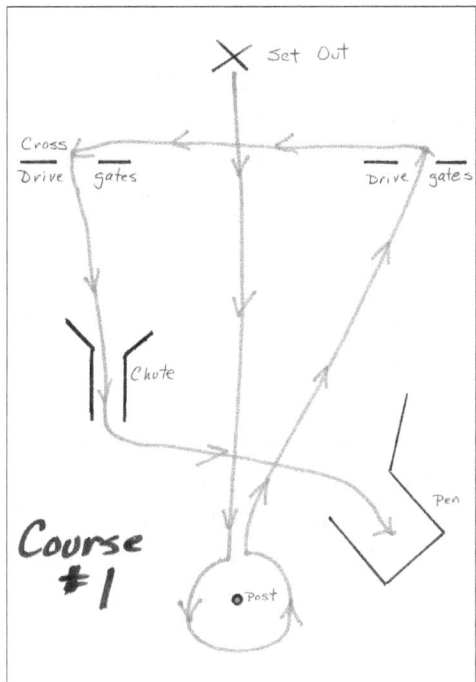

*Trial course sample drawing showing the path, and direction, the **livestock** is to follow. Not all trials provide drawings of the course.*

A good dog and handler team makes a course look easy, but if a team struggles, you begin to understand how much skill is necessary to put in a good run.

Most trials have a posted running order, and some announce who is **up** or running and who is **on deck** or next to run. Some trials post scores as runs are completed and some do not. If you have read the rules, you will also have a better idea of why points are deducted.

Usually, scores for judged trials are determined by assigning a set number of points to each element or obstacle and then subtracting points for mistakes or missed obstacles. A team might lose points on the outrun for crossing over, running too tight or too straight toward the livestock, running too wide and losing contact with the livestock, having to be redirected, and other infractions. There are many, many ways to lose points!

At some trials, scores are posted or announced and some trial committees pass out score sheets at the end of the trial. Often no scores are given, instead only placings are announced.

There is also usually a time limit on each run, and some trials will call handlers off if they fail to make progress. **Failure to progress** means that the livestock is not advancing around the course in a reasonable fashion or in a reasonable amount of time. This could mean that the dog failed to get the livestock moving on the lift, could not bring the stock to the handler, got stuck and was unable to negotiate an obstacle such as a chute or pen, or lost the stock back to the set-out pens multiple times. Only the judge can decide to call off a run for failure to progress, but they may excuse a team for various other reasons as well, at their discretion.

In time and points trials the score is usually calculated by adding a point for each animal that completes an element or obstacle. If the dog is working 3 head of cattle and only 2 pass between a set of drive panels, the handler would receive only 2, instead of 3, points for that obstacle. Some time and points trials require all animals to complete each obstacle before the team can move on to the next obstacle. Learn the rules for the class you are running. In time and points trials tie scores are usually broken by a time recorded at a certain point in the run. The fastest time gets the higher placing.

In judged trials, there is only one attempt allowed per element or obstacle. If 1 sheep goes through a chute and two pass by the chute, the handler cannot bring back the two sheep to re-try the chute once those sheep have passed the plane across the exit of the chute. (See diagram showing the plane of the exit below.)

Almost all courses have a time limit, even judged trials. Some trials will give the judge the responsibility of calling off handlers whose dogs are not making progress and some will allow the handler to continue the run as long as they have time and the stock is not being mishandled. Mishandling could include running stock into fences, losing the stock off of the course, etc.

CHAPTER 19 GETTING READY TO TRIAL | 263

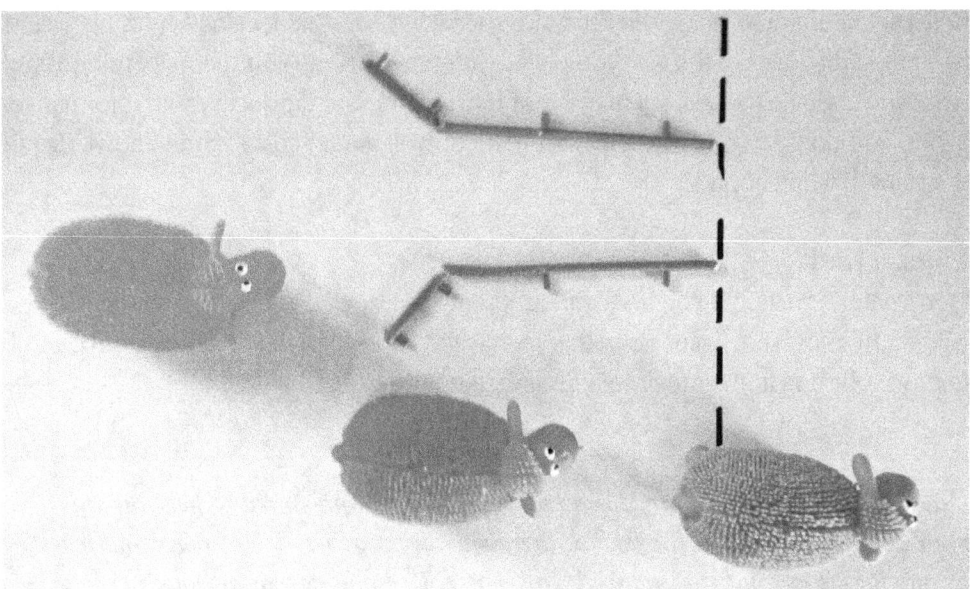

This diagram shows the plane of exit of a chute, which is indicated by a dashed line. The first sheep has crossed the plane and cannot be brought back to retry the chute. The second sheep can be turned around and put through the chute to avoid loss of chute points.

If your dog is struggling and your run has deteriorated to train wreck status, call or stop your run! Do not allow your dog to rehearse unwanted behaviors just because you have paid for your time and want to get your money's worth. In this situation, you are doing more damage than good to your dog's training!

There are also rules about when the handler may leave the post and help their dog. In lower-level classes, the handler is allowed to help their dog a considerable amount, while less help is allowed in higher-level classes. There may also be an imaginary line that the handler is not allowed to cross or the team will be penalized. In most judged trials the dog is not supposed to cross between the handler and the stock, **crossing the line of the drive**, or again the team will be penalized.

Many regional stockdog associations have year-end high point awards. To be eligible to earn points toward those awards, you have to be a paid member of the association. Any points earned before you are a paid member will not count toward the year-end awards.

Because there are so many rules that are specific to each association's trials, you must learn the basic rules of the trial you plan to attend. The time you spend learning about what you are going to see will make your day much more productive and informative. When you do go to run your dog at a trial you will already have some knowledge of the rules that will apply.

Enter a trial

Don't enter a trial until you are confident that your dog can complete the course you will be running. You want your dog to have a good experience and be successful. Putting your dog in over their head is a recipe for disaster.

Once you send in your entry for a trial, you can feel pressured to get you and your dog up to speed as the trial date quickly approaches. Try to relax and learn as much as you can from the trial experience. Remember that although this is your first trial, it most likely won't be your last.

Even if you are confident that your dog can handle the course, there are always unforeseen problems that arise at a trial. Cantankerous stock, blowing flags, crowd noise, extreme temperatures, and obstacle malfunctions are just a few of the unknowns that you and your dog may face.

Be prepared for your first run by over-training rather than just hoping your dog will be able to cope with the situation. Remember that you and your dog will be excited and a bit overwhelmed at the start of your trialing career. Getting around the course is your first goal. Once you are confidently completing the course you can work on becoming competitive.

Arriving at the trial

You have taken your dog to several new places and have successfully worked them on the type of stock that you expect to trial on. After finding a trial, learning the basic rules, and attending a trial, you now feel comfortable enough to enter your dog in a class. Most trials in the US require you to submit an entry form, along with payment for classes entered, prior to the trial. Many trials have a date that entries close and some have limited spots available with waiting lists.

Once you get signed up for a trial, be sure to arrive early to give you and your dog time to relax and scope everything out. Often there is a blind where you will stand with your dog when you are next to run. The **blind** is a blocking structure that allows you to be close to the course but does not allow your dog to watch the run. The main reason you don't want your dog to watch the run is that the last thing your dog would see would be the sheep being exhausted. Often if a dog sees the stock as they are leaving the trial course, they will fixate on the exhaust area and not look up the field to where the sheep or cattle will be set out.

If you are at an arena trial, don't let your dog lie ringside all day and watch runs. Most inexperienced dogs get too aroused watching other dogs work and cannot relax at ringside. Have a place, usually at your vehicle, that is located away from the arena where your dog can be crated or tied comfortably.

Handlers' meeting

Throughout the day the judge or trial committee will hold handlers' meetings for each class. Every class should have a handlers' meeting directly preceding it.

*Handlers' meetings are critical. Do **not** miss your handlers' meeting!*

In the handlers' meeting, the judge will go over the course, tell you what they expect, and answer questions. The judge's instructions supersede any previous rules or information you have been given.

*You are **not** allowed to bring your dog with you to the handlers' meeting!*

During the handlers' meeting, you are usually allowed to walk around the course and look everything over. You may want to open and shut the pen so that you are familiar with how difficult the gate is to swing and how the rope is fastened to the gate.

If you have any questions, feel free to ask the judge during the handlers' meeting. This is your chance to get clarification! If you have a question, it is likely others are wondering the same thing. Don't be shy as you want to give your dog the advantage of your knowing what you and your dog are trying to accomplish. The judge will usually also tell you if there is a time limit per run, if they will call you off for failure to make progress, how many head of stock you will be running, and any specific things they may be looking for in the runs.

Your dog will usually be disqualified for biting sheep or excessively biting cattle. Any dog that runs livestock into an arena fence or is not demonstrating reasonable self-control in handling the stock will also be disqualified.

Potty your dog

Shortly before your run make sure you take the time to potty your dog in the designated area. Some trials expect you to clean up after your dog and some do not. Be sure to have supplies on hand, just in case. A dog that stops to relieve itself during a run not only loses control of its livestock while it stops and is an embarrassment to you as a handler, but also will most likely lose points or be disqualified for stopping.

Some dogs will eat manure, sniff the ground, or stop to relieve themselves on the trial field because they are anxious. If your dog displays any of these behaviors consistently, they are not ready to go to a trial.

Many trial venues have a lot of people walking around, so be considerate and pick up after your dog if they have an accident on the public grounds. Most trials with a lot of spectators require that you keep your dog leashed, except when running a course.

Warm up your dog

Depending on how long each run is taking, figure out when you should warm up your dog. Plan to warm your dog up about 10 to 15 minutes before your run. Warming up your dog will help to prevent injuries and prolong your dog's competitive career and life. A warm-up may include active stretches, spins to each side, and some trotting or running. Ask your vet to help you develop an everyday warm-up routine you can use before you work your dog on stock. If you don't normally warm up your dog, at least walk and trot your dog before you run them.

*Be on the lookout for **heatstroke** in your dog. If your dog gets too hot they may stagger, have muscle tremors, or have a seizure, as well as several other symptoms. Learn the signs of heatstroke and if you think your dog may have it, immediately contact a veterinarian. Cool your dog as quickly as possible by getting them into a tub of water or running a cool stream of water over them from a hose.*

After your run, don't forget to cool your dog down. Walk your dog and cool them out just as you would a horse. Walk your dog briskly and then more slowly, until they quit panting heavily. Don't be in a hurry to put your dog into a crate or dog trailer where they may not be able to dissipate heat.

Although almost every trial has a tub of water available to cool dogs down, don't use the tub as the only method to cool down your dog. Instead, walk your dog for a while. When your dog starts to get back to breathing normally, allow them to jump in the tub for a few moments. Then finish your cooldown by continuing to walk your dog until they have returned to their normal resting heart and respiration rates.

Never run a lame dog! Many dogs are so focused on livestock that they will continue to appear sound after an injury. If your dog gets kicked or butted hard, call or end your run, take our dog off of the course, and check for injuries.

A dog that is lame will sometimes appear sound if allowed to herd. Running a lame dog will only exacerbate their lameness and prolong their recovery period. Also, be sure your dog is in condition to run the distance and time the course requires in the current weather conditions.

Watch other runs

Once you have attended the handlers' meeting and know where you are in the running order, you can either get your dog out, if you run early, or if you run later, take the time to watch other teams run.

Watching other teams run helps you to determine the pull and may give you insight on which way to send your dog, what problems may occur during the run, how the livestock are working, and some strategies for negotiating obstacles.

You know your dog better than anyone, so don't follow what others do just because everyone is doing it. It may be the best way to approach the situation, but then again it may not. Have confidence in your dog and do the best that you can. Experience is a great teacher and you can only learn how to run a dog at trials by running dogs at trials. No matter how many runs you watch, you have to get out and run a dog to become accomplished at trialing.

If you only watch runs at trials, you don't become a proficient handler, you only become a proficient watcher.

The more trials you run in, the easier it becomes to relax and do your best. Performing in front of people, especially people you admire, is never easy, but it does get easier as you gain experience and competency.

Video your run

If at all possible, coordinate with a friend or spectator to take a video of your run. This video will be priceless when you go back to determine what went well and what not so great. Often you will be so excited that your memory of the run will only be a blur. Having a video will allow you to watch your run as an observer and learn what you need to work on to improve your and your dog's performance.

You will be amazed at how often your impression of your run and the actual run are completely different! When you watch your video, look for what went well, don't just focus on errors. Your video will be a valuable learning tool.

Ready, set, go

When there are between 3 and 5 runs ahead of yours, it is time to get your dog out and ready to run. You want to be prepared to run your dog a bit early in case a team in front of you is disqualified and their run is significantly shortened or a team doesn't show up for their run. It is unnerving to have to race around and get ready for your run while the judge or trial committee is waiting for you and your dog to appear. Been there, done that!

Be sure to have your crook or stock stick, hat, glasses, whistle, and anything else you need at hand. A checklist is an easy way to bolster your confidence that you will not get caught out when you get to the trial or step onto the course.

When you are new to trialing it is easy to forget something as you prepare yourself and your dog for your run. You don't want to get into the middle of your run and realize you forgot to bring your crook or other essential aid with you. People forget things all of the time, especially if they are new to trialing or if someone comes up and talks to them while they are preparing for their run. Forgetting something is also easy to do if you are rushed by arriving late at the trial or misjudged how soon you will be called to run.

Usually, dogs are kept on leash until they enter the trial field. Take your leash off just as you head toward the post or enter the arena. Give your and your dog's names to the judge or other trial official. Heel with your dog on the side you intend to send them as you go to the post. The post is usually a fence post, the area in front of the pen, or a designated spot on the trial field. If possible, check the rope on the pen to make sure it is not tangled or caught before you start your run.

Usually, you must stay within arm's length of the post until you are allowed to leave to assist your dog or you will be penalized.

Set your dog up on the side you are going to send them and pointing slightly out to that side. When you are ready, wave your hand to indicate that the livestock may be released, if it is an arena trial. For field trials, the set-out person will usually indicate with a wave that the stock is in position and you can send your dog on their outrun.

Send your dog!

CHAPTER 20

Trial elements and obstacles

Your dog has started their outrun on your trial run. It's time to examine the key elements and most common obstacles found in herding courses and how to negotiate them.

Many beginner classes consist of only a fetch and a pen. This chapter includes all of the most common elements and obstacles found in upper-level courses.

Most courses start with an outrun, lift, and fetch, but after that, there are many possible configurations of courses with many types of obstacles. The lowest levels usually have little or no driving or cross driving, but most upper levels do. Almost all courses include a pen and only higher-level courses have a shed.

There are very high-level courses that may include a **double lift**, gathering two separate sets of stock and then running the course with the entire group, and an **international shed**, separating off marked or collared sheep, usually 5 or 8 out of 20. These highly advanced elements are beyond the scope of this book and will not be covered.

There are three ways a run usually ends. You can complete the course, be disqualified (DQ), or retire (RET). If the judge asks you to leave the course you have been **disqualified**. If you decide to **retire**, call your run for any reason, call your dog to you and acknowledge the judge as you leave the field or arena. If your dog gets in over their head, it is better to call your run than to have your dog rehearse unwanted behaviors such as chasing stock or ignoring cues. Also, if you believe your dog may have suffered an injury, call your run. You may call your run and retire for *any* reason.

If there is some outside interference that affects your run, such as an umbrella blowing onto the course or a sudden, extremely loud noise, you may be given a **rerun**. Sometimes an animal jumps back into the set-out pen or over an arena wall. If the judge determines that you or your dog were not responsible for the action of the animal(s) you may be allowed to rerun the course with different livestock. Reruns are given solely at the discretion of the judge.

Usually, a rerun is added at the end of the class to allow your dog to rest and to allow the class to continue as the run order prescribes. If you have just started your run and something untoward happens, the judge may give you a rerun immediately.

TRIAL TIP: If you have a sideways-moving dog, try to stop them as little as possible during your run so that they do not release pressure on the stock. You may want to stop them more to keep things under control but you then run the risk of having your dog get sticky. Keep transitions limited to ins and flanks, if at all possible, and avoid stops.

Problems at trials

If during a run at a trial or a friend's field you discover your dog lacks a major skill necessary to complete the course, stop the run and leave the field or arena. Later, work on the weak skill at home before you return to running courses.

Certainly, you should run courses as practice to see where your dog needs work and to hone your handling skills but allowing a train wreck at a trial because you have "paid for the time" does a disservice to your dog, the spectators, and the other participants.

There is no shame in calling or stopping your run and retiring from the field with dignity. Been there, done that!

Outrun

Set your dog up on the side you want to send them and give your fetch cue. Your dog should cast out around the stock without disturbing it. Depending on the venue, field or arena trial, your dog will either run a pear-shaped outrun, the small end of the pear toward you, or more of a half-circle outrun. In larger fields, you don't want your dog to run a big half-circle outrun because it will take a lot of unnecessary effort to cast out that far. Instead, they should start casting out to the side and when they start to feel the pressure from the stock they should open up and cast out even farther to get around the stock without disturbing them and finally come in behind them.

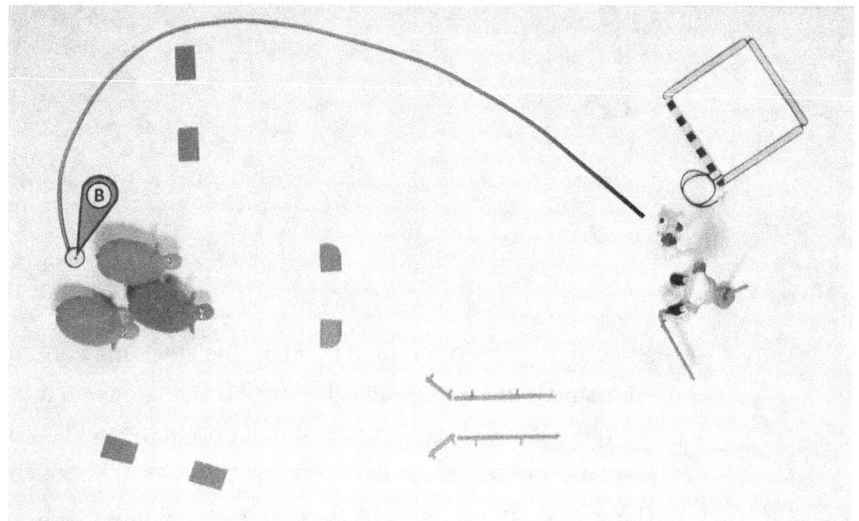

The outrun in an arena will usually be half of a circle rather than pear-shaped because your dog is going a short distance and there is limited room for them to get off of the livestock.

In an arena, your dog is limited to the confines of the arena and will usually cast out to the arena wall and follow it around to stay as far off of the stock as the situation allows. In arena trials the stock usually pulls back to the arena wall or gate where they entered the arena if there is not a set-out person or dog to hold them. Your dog may not be able to get behind the stock without pushing them off to the side as they go between the arena wall and the livestock. If your dog pushes the stock to the side as they go behind them, you will have to drive the stock back to the fetch line to start your drive to the fetch gates, if fetch gates are present. The **fetch line** is from the set-out point to the fetch panels and usually straight to you. If there are no fetch panels the fetch line is from the set-out point straight to you.

Lift

The lift is probably the most important part of your run. The lift is when your dog makes contact with the stock and establishes the relationship they will have with the stock for the rest of your run.

A perfect lift occurs when your dog comes in at the point of balance and gently **lifts** or starts the stock moving toward you without startling them. Your dog is neither sticky nor pushy but comes in with confidence and presence. In this scenario, the livestock moves calmly off toward you as your dog approaches and your dog has taken control of the stock in a respectful way.

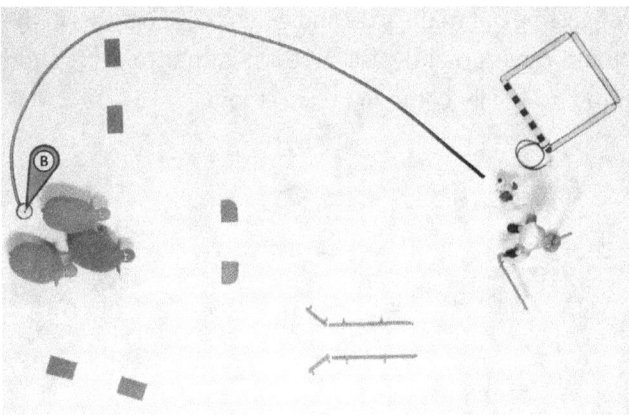

The lift is the first direct interaction your dog has with the stock and often determines the relationship between your dog and the stock for the entire run. The lift usually occurs when the dog is on balance (point B) and applies pressure to the stock.

If your dog creeps in, inch by inch, the stock may not notice your dog or feel enough pressure to move. Usually, the stock is being moved away from other nearby livestock so there is a lot of pull to stay at that end of the field or arena. Some dogs will get stuck and just eye the stock, in which case it is almost impossible to get the livestock moving. One last-ditch strategy to overcome this standoff is to flank your dog back and forth behind the stock. Just the motion of your dog flanking nearby may be enough added pressure to get the stock moving.

Some dogs get stuck lifting because they have too much eye and some because they lack confidence. You cannot decrease eye, but you can build confidence.

If your dog blasts in on their lift, the stock will likely startle and head in several directions or come to you on the run. Once the stock is upset and running it is very difficult to settle them and have a good run. Prevention is the best antidote for whirled-up stock. When the stock is running there is little you can do to slow them down on the fetch. If your dog tends to lift too abruptly, you may need to stop them on top to control the speed of the lift. You can also work on modifying how fast your dog comes in on top by teaching a slowdown cue.

The lift largely determines the success of close work and the shed, which come at the end of the run. If sheep are alarmed, they tend to become unsettled and stick tightly together for protection. This makes it very difficult to string them out to complete the shed or control them for penning or putting them through a chute.

Fetch

The line of the **fetch** is from the set-out point to you and is often through a set of fetch gates or panels.

If your dog pushes the stock away from the set-out point you must immediately drive them back to the set-out point to start your fetch.

The **fetch line** is from the set-out point, through the fetch gates, if present, and to the handler. The longer and farther the livestock deviates from that line, the more points you will lose on your fetch.

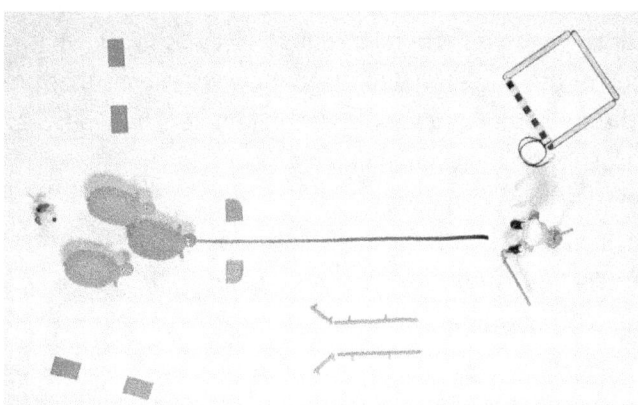

The fetch line is through the middle of the fetch gates and straight to the handler at the post.

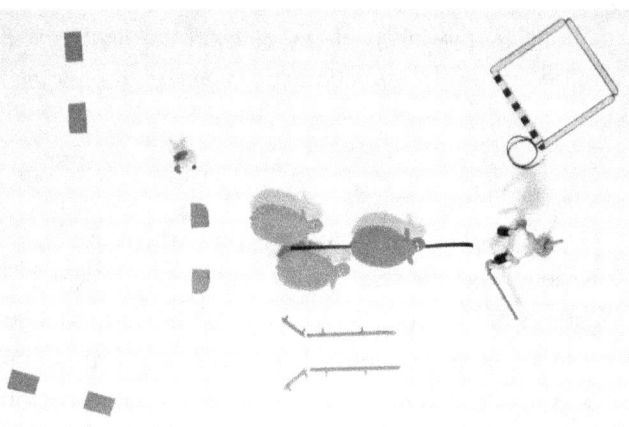

Unless the rules require all animals to complete an obstacle before moving on, you only have one attempt allowed per obstacle. This means that if you are running five sheep and they go past the sides of the fetch panels, not through them, you have completed the fetch gates. If all or none of the stock go through the panels you have completed the obstacle once the animal(s) cross the plane of the fetch gates.

Unless otherwise designated by the course rules, you are allowed only one attempt to complete an obstacle. Once an animal crosses the plane of the exit of the obstacle they cannot be brought back to re-try the obstacle.

Lines are very important in judged trials! The goal is for the stock to move in a straight line, at a good pace, from obstacle to obstacle around the course. The first line is from the set-out point of the lift to the center of the fetch panels. The course is usually set up so that if your dog lifts near the set-out point they will fetch on a straight line from the lift, through the fetch gates, to you. There is some leeway as far as what is considered a straight line. Think of the lines as 10 to 20-foot alleys or lanes that the stock needs to stay within. If the stock move beyond those parameters they need to be brought back on line or back into the imaginary lane.

The longer and farther the livestock travel off line the more points that will be deducted from the fetch, drive, or cross-drive.

The goal of the fetch is to bring the stock to your feet while you remain at the post. Once the stock is at your feet, about 10 feet away depending on the lightness of the stock, you will take them around you in the direction specified in the handler's meeting.

Turning the post

You must **turn the post,** take the stock around you and the post while you stand within arm's length of the post, in the correct direction. How tightly you can turn the post depends primarily on the lightness of the stock. Wild stock will not approach as close to you as more tame stock will. If you have been able to watch a few runs, you will have some idea of what stock you will be running and how tight a post turn you can attempt. The goal is to turn the post as tightly or as close to you as possible.

To turn the post, the stock comes in front of you and turns around you tightly, either clockwise or counter-clockwise and heads off toward the drive gates when they are directly between the post and the drive panels.

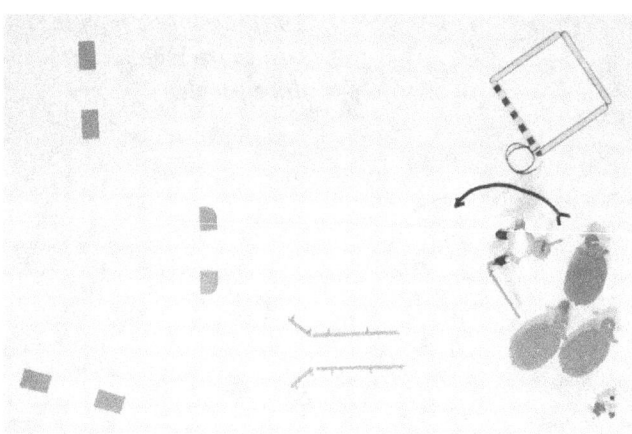

The stock will go around and behind you as you stand within arm's length of the post. If they go around in the wrong direction, they must re-turn the post in the correct direction before heading to the drive gates.

*If the stock goes the wrong way around the post you **must** unwind them and take them back around in the correct direction before starting the first leg of the drive to the drive panels.*

If you are standing in front of the post, the stock must go around both you and the post. If some livestock don't go around but some do, you may or may not have to re-turn the post. Ask the judge or consult the rules for clarification. Most trials allow you to proceed if at least one animal turns the post in the designated direction. Rules vary so consult the judge for clarification.

Drive

After turning the post your dog will drive the livestock to and through the center of the drive panels. Again the line the stock takes, as well as the pace of the drive, determines your score. Ideally, the sheep are moving around the course at a fast walk or slow trot. If the stock go off line, you need to bring them back on line as soon as possible.

If the stock moves at a reasonable pace, not running nor stopping to graze, you should have sufficient time to complete the course.

It is best to have your dog moving and in contact while driving. If you allow the stock to drift and stop, you will have a choppy drive and your dog will not be in control of the livestock at all times. You want your run to flow from one leg or obstacle to the next element.

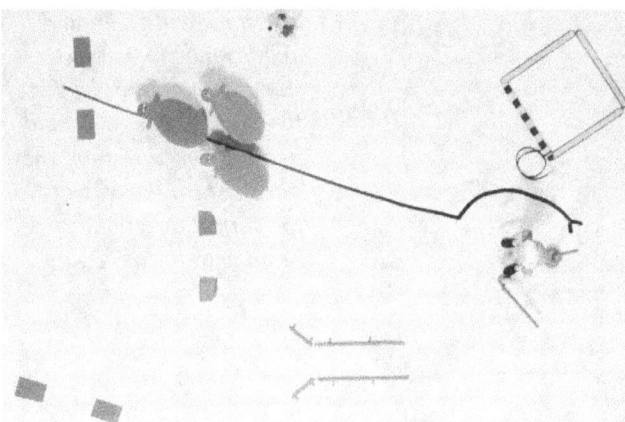

The drive line is from the post to the middle of the drive panels.

It is very difficult to have a good run if you ping pong the stock, move and stop your dog, watch the response of the stock, then move and stop your dog again. Instead, you want your dog up and in contact with the stock while moving them around the course.

Every time you allow the livestock to stop, your dog has to lift them again and initiate movement. This is a very inefficient way to drive stock and precludes having any flow to your run.

Cross drive

The **cross drive** is from the drive panels to the cross-drive panels. This drive is across the field or arena from one side to the other. The drive is completed when the stock clears the drive gates. Once the stock is through the drive panels the livestock should then be turned, as tightly as possible without pushing any animals back through the drive panels, and then driven in a straight line to the cross-drive gates.

Many inexperienced handlers have problems with the cross drive because their dog wants to fetch the livestock back to them instead of driving them across the field. As with all training, start close to where your dog is cross driving and slowly extend the distance from them by moving yourself back away from the path your dog is to drive the stock.

The cross drive is scored very similar to the drive and fetch, based on lines and pace. If the livestock wanders off line, always bring the stock back on line as soon as possible.

This might entail your dog flanking out and bring the stock directly back to the line such that the stock's path and the line are at 90° angles.

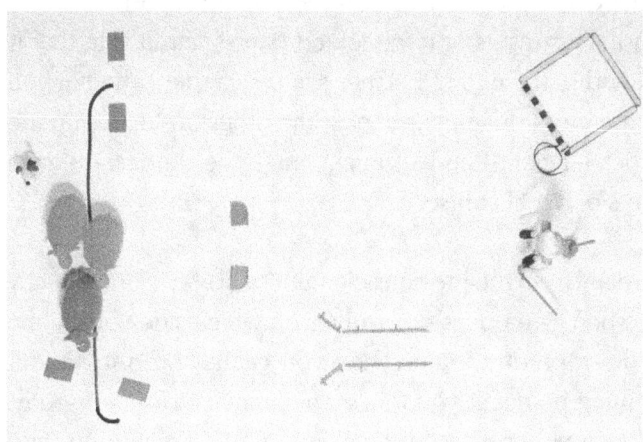

The cross drive begins as soon as the livestock clear the drive panels. The cross drive should be a straight line through the cross-drive panels, then turn, and head back toward you.

One of the most difficult parts of the cross drive is judging if the stock is on line to go through the gates. It may be difficult to tell if the livestock is too high or low until they are almost to the panels. Experience and good depth perception help! When you visualize the cross drive try to identify visual markers that will indicate that the stock is on line. Possible markers may include bare spots, dips or humps, changes in vegetation, etc.

After the stock has cleared the cross-drive panels you want a tight turn back toward the handler's post. Again the line of travel and pace of the livestock are critical criteria for keeping points. Since this will be another fetch to you, it is usually easier for your dog to accomplish than the drive-away and cross-drive legs of the course.

If you are going to miss the cross-drive panels try to have the stock go past them to the backside so that you do not lose more points for cutting the course.

When you drive through panels or gates, your goal is to have the stock go through the middle of the opening, make a tight turn close to the gates, and head off in a straight line toward the next drive panels, obstacle, or fetch straight back to you.

Pen

Sometimes, the area directly in front of the pen is used as the handler's post. Penning may come before the shed, depending on how the course is set up and if a shed is part of the course. The **pen** usually consists of three joined panels and a gate that is free standing with a rope attached to the end of it. Lines still play a role, whether you go to the pen from the shed, the cross-drive panels, or some other obstacle. You are always looking to move the stock efficiently and a straight line is the shortest distance between two points or elements of a trial course.

The goal is to take the stock directly from the previous element or obstacle and directly into the pen. The direction the pen gate opens determines on which side you will be standing. Once you pick up the rope on the pen gate, you cannot drop it without losing all or some of your penning points. If you touch any animals with your body, crook, or stock stick, you will lose points or be disqualified. If an animal jumps into you or brushes past you and inadvertently touches you, there is usually no penalty.

Teaching your dog a "hold" cue (Chapter 10) comes in handy at the pen and chutes. Usually hold is taught during practical work around the farm, to keep stock off of feeders while grain is put out or at gateways to prevent stock from coming through the gate while hay or grain is fed.

Penning is about blocking escape routes and applying pressure. You and your dog work as a team to pen the stock. Position your dog on the perimeter, using flanks, before asking your dog to walk in to the stock. You want your dog in position to control the stock before you put pressure on the livestock. If you miscalculate, you can always use a flank, out, or back cue to move your dog away from the stock into a better position.

Open the gate so that it is parallel with the panel it is hinged to. Aim the stock for where the gate hinges to the pen. Step back and away from the pen and have your dog bring the stock up into the **throat of the pen** – the area from the end of the gate to the end of the opposite gate panel, where the gate will eventually close. Once the stock is in the throat you may step forward to help control the stock from your side.

This is a video of Mattie, Sir's granddam, penning: https://www.youtube.com/watch?v=6ge7Tdn1McM&ab_channel=PositiveHerdingDog

The throat of the pen is where the two sheep are side by side. Once all of the sheep are in the throat of the pen, you step forward and behind the sheep. You should stand even farther back away from and behind the gate, than shown in the diagram, until all of the sheep are in the mouth of the pen.

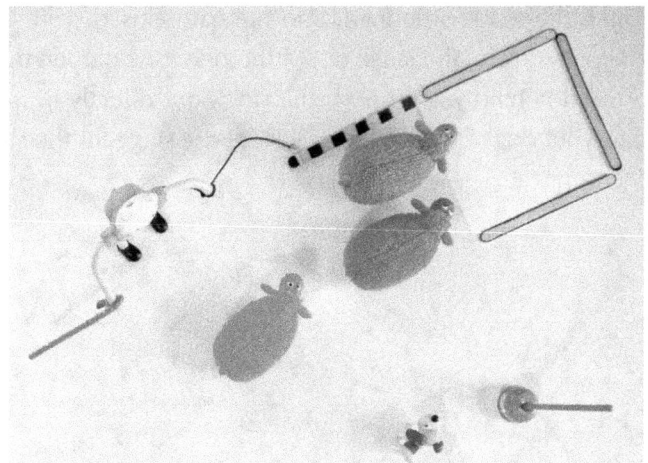

Finally, use your dog to push the sheep into the pen while you hold your position.

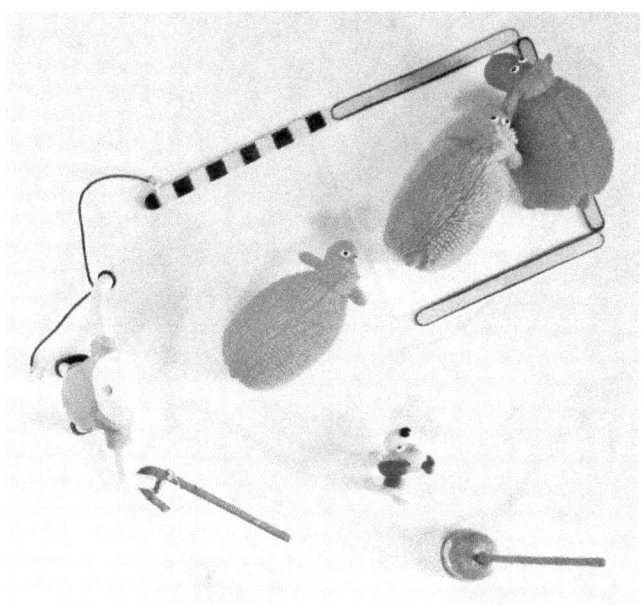

Don't forget that you can always step back if you feel that your presence is putting too much pressure on the stock. The pen rope will determine how far back you can move from the throat of the pen.

Penning is a situation where you may need to use your *back* cue if your dog is in too close. You want your dog to release pressure on the stock but to maintain hook up with and in control of the livestock. You will also probably need to use bump flanks to micromanage your dog's position while penning.

Once the stock is penned, and the gate closed, you should send your dog around the pen to push the stock out of the pen as you open the gate. Always send your dog around behind you to push the stock out directly in front of you and between you and your dog. This maneuver will set the stage for the shed, if a shed is required after the pen.

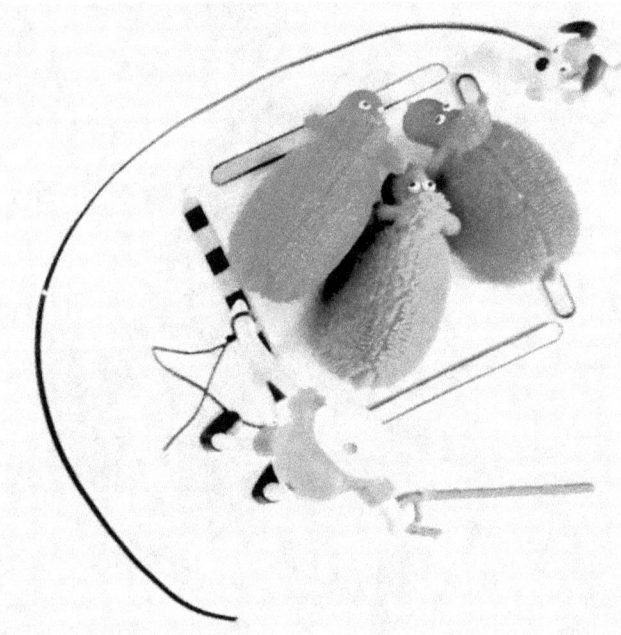

Always send your dog out around and behind you to push the stock out of the pen.

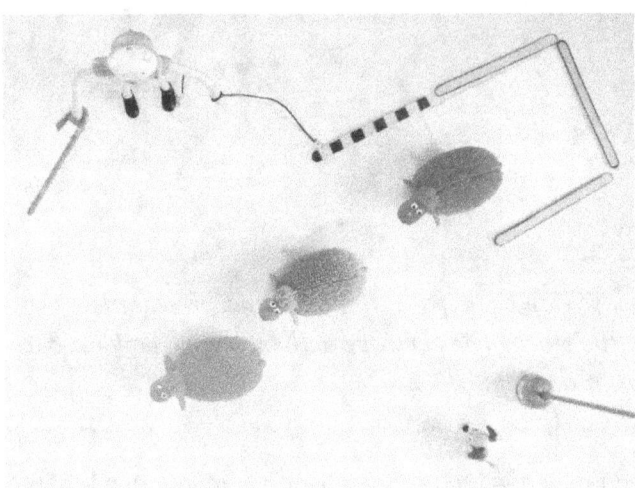

Then open the gate and the sheep will come out in front of you and ready for shedding.

Practice the pen at home and other locations until you and your dog are proficient at penning before entering a trial. Even the lowest trial levels have a pen, although some trials have a fence-line pen, a pen along the fence instead of a free-standing pen, which makes it fairly easy to complete. The pen is considered completed when you close the gate with all of the stock in the pen but note that a fence-line pen does not have a gate. For a fence-line pen the stock need to be in the pen and beyond where a gate would be if it were shut for the pen to be complete.

Bump flanks

Bump flanks range from your dog taking a step or two sideways, while continuing to face the stock, to just shifting their weight from one front foot to the other. Bump flanks are used in all close work, such as penning and shedding. For step-by-step instructions on training the bump flank, see Chapter 10.

The tricky part of bump flanking is that you are asking for a very short flank without using a stop cue to end the flank. With a regular flank, you are asking your dog to continue flanking until cued to do another behavior.

Bump flanks are cued with *to me* and *bye*, said slowly and softly. They are used primarily in tight situations where inches are critical. As your dog reads the situation, they will learn to feel the pressure and react cautiously. Next, let's take a closer look at penning and some strategies for success.

When practicing penning, the livestock may get away from your dog and run quite a distance. This is a good time to send your dog and have them learn that if they allow the stock to escape, they are going to have to go retrieve them.

Penning, like most herding, takes experience to learn and become proficient at. Once you do a fair amount of penning, your dog will start to learn the game and will cover escape attempts spontaneously. That is when the fun begins!

One issue to look out for is that your dog may attempt to hold the stock to you, instead of pushing them into the pen. If you do a lot of shedding or fetching to you, you may have inadvertently trained your dog to hold stock to you.

Be patient as you work with your dog to teach them penning. Some dogs may show reluctance to flank off-balance at the pen, but your dog must be able to flank off-balance and maintain their distance from the stock as they flank, in order to pen.

Shut the gate of the pen only after all of the stock has completely entered the pen. In other words, don't shut the gate until all of the stock is past where the gate will be when it is closed. Using the gate to push the stock into the pen may result in a loss of points if the gate touches the stock.

You can clap, stomp, jump up and down, snap your fingers, kick dirt, use your crook to sweep back and forth, tap on the ground, or use your voice to encourage the stock into the pen, as long as you do not physically touch the stock. Remember if the stock is flighty, doing any of these maneuvers may cause them to panic and explode back toward you or jump over the pen.

If you lay your dog down or step in front of them and pen the stock yourself, you may, and should, lose pen points. Your dog should be controlling and pushing the stock into the pen while you assist them.

Once stock escapes and circles the pen, they become exponentially more difficult to pen because they have learned that they can avoid going into the pen. Take things slowly rather than allow the stock to escape and circle the pen.

The point penalty for the stock circling the pen is usually one point per animal, per circle. It is possible to lose all of your pen points due to the stock circling the pen. Once you have lost all of your pen points, you will be asked to move on to the next obstacle even though you have not completed the pen. If you do get the stock penned, after losing all of the pen points, you will receive no points for the pen.

If you are to shed after the pen be sure and flank your dog to your side, the side with the gate hinges, and behind the pen to push the stock out of the pen. This will help to ensure that the stock comes out in front of you with your dog on the opposite side, which sets things up nicely for the shed that follows.

To get your dog opposite you for the shed you will flank them all of the way around behind the pen and to the other side of the livestock. If there is a strong pull to your side you may not be able to send your dog opposite you. Instead, you will have to flank your dog in behind you. Once the pen gate is shut you can move to the side away from the pull and have your dog control the side of the stock toward the pull.

Chute or bridge

Chutes or bridges are completed as you would a pen, but not all courses have these obstacles. Chutes and bridges are just enclosures (pens) without a back wall. As when penning, you hold one side of the obstacle and your dog holds the other.

You should always have your dog hold the side with the strongest pull. Your dog will be able to control stock that you would never be able to hold.

Some chutes have wings or extensions on them, that make it easier to funnel the stock into the chute, and others are wingless. Start out practicing putting stock through a chute using wings that are opened wide. The chute should be just wide enough for one animal to go through at a time. As you and your dog gain experience, close the wings down so that the chute becomes more difficult. Eventually, you will be working chutes without wings which makes chutes with wings much easier.

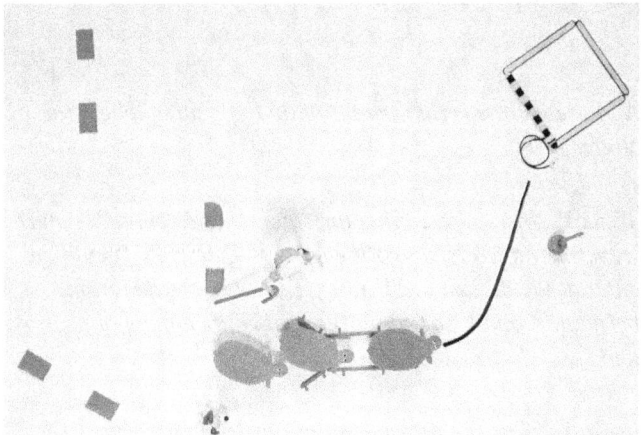

As with the pen, you hold your side and your dog holds the other side of the chute. If possible, have your dog hold the side toward the pull as it is more difficult to hold that side. In this setup, the drive line would be from the end of the chute straight to the mouth of the pen.

As with the drive gates, once an animal passes the plane of the exit of the chute or bridge, it can no longer be brought back to re-try the obstacle. If all animals cross the plane, then you must go on to the next obstacle unless required to complete all obstacles with one or all animals, as noted in the course rules.

There are also T chutes you may encounter. (See diagram below.) Usually, the stock enters the T chute at A and the judge determines if the livestock exit at B or C. The judge will tell you which way the stock is to exit during the handler's meeting.

The T chute is more difficult, as compared to a regular chute, because the livestock cannot see an exit as they enter the chute. To the livestock, this type of chute looks more like a pen than a chute. The difficulty is also increased because the stock has to be turned, to exit in the correct direction.

Maltese cross

The Maltese cross is similar to a chute without wings except there is an alley in the center of the chute where the stock may head in the wrong direction. Often the Maltese cross is used in arena trials in place of a shed. The handler is only allowed to stand in one quadrant, the area between alleys, and may not change quadrants. The handler may not enter the cross but the dog may. The dog may move anywhere, in or around the cross, while working it. The judge designates which opening the stock will enter. If the stock does not pass straight across the cross, or if only part of the livestock goes through the cross, points are deducted.

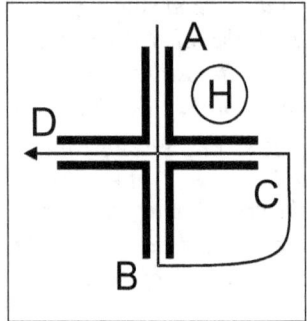

A Maltese cross is two chutes with an opening where the chutes meet.

To work this Maltese cross the stock enters "chute" A and travels completely across the cross to exit at B. They then enter at C and exit at D. You (H) stay in the quadrant between A and C, between the two chute entry points of A and C.

You would stay in the quadrant between A and C so that you are available to help your dog move the stock into both "chute" entries. The judge will usually designate which quadrant you are to stay within.

Depending on where the pull is on the field or in the arena, you may have to move your dog and/or yourself to prevent the stock from taking a 90° turn at the center of the cross.

Sometimes the stock will get into the cross, feel safe, and not want to come out. Again, you may not touch the stock with your body, crook, or stock stick. Another problem that commonly arises is that an animal or two will enter the cross, but others will balk. While you are working to persuade the last animals to enter, the ones already in the cross may decide to exit out the side chute instead of going straight through.

As long as the animals have not crossed the plane of the exit "chute" they may be brought back to enter, but once they are past that plane they must move on to the next entrance.

Shed

The shed is only required in the highest level classes. The shedding ring, if one is used, is usually marked with either a circle of powdered chalk/ground limestone on the ground or small ground markers in a circular pattern. You are usually not allowed to leave the post until the stock enters the shedding ring. Again check the rules at the trial you are running your dog in. Some trials have no shedding ring marking and instead designate an area between certain obstacles. If you have any questions on shedding, be sure to ask the judge at the handler's meeting.

The judge should call the shed when completed. If you are running 4 head of stock, usually sheep, the judge may say that the last 2 sheep should be shed on the head. This means that you are to split the sheep into two equal groups. When your dog comes in they are to turn toward the heads of the last 2 sheep and drive them away

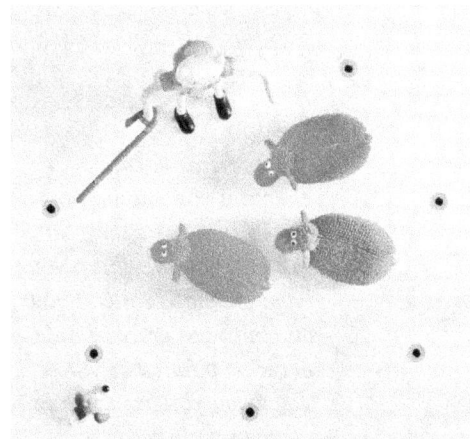

Once the stock exit the pen you may need to block them while your dog gets in position to control them. You also may need to move your crook or stock stick to your other hand during the shed.

until the shed is called by the judge. If you are to take a single on the head, that means that you are to shed off the last sheep. Your dog is to come into its head, drive it off, and maintain control of it until called off.

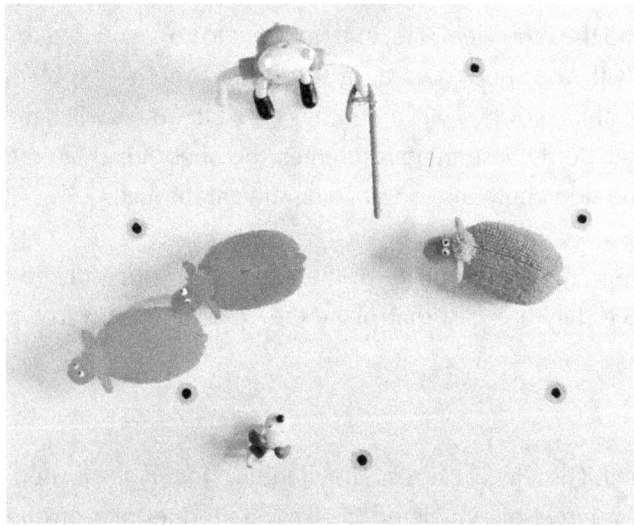

The shed has to happen within the shedding ring to count. You may use your crook to help set up the shed but need to pull it back out of the way when you are ready to call your dog through to you. If you leave your crook pointed at the place you want your dog to shed, your dog will be reluctant to come in, make a gap, and take control of the sheep they are to shed.

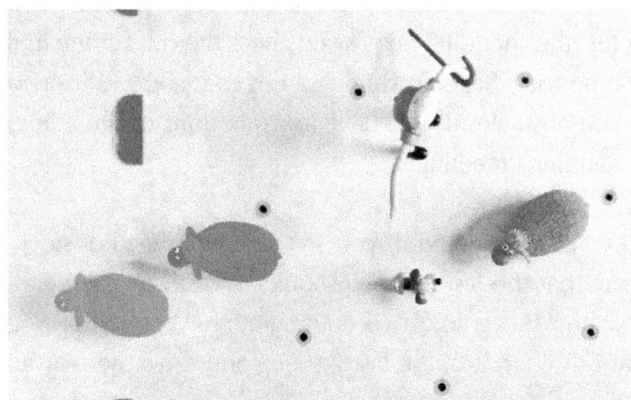

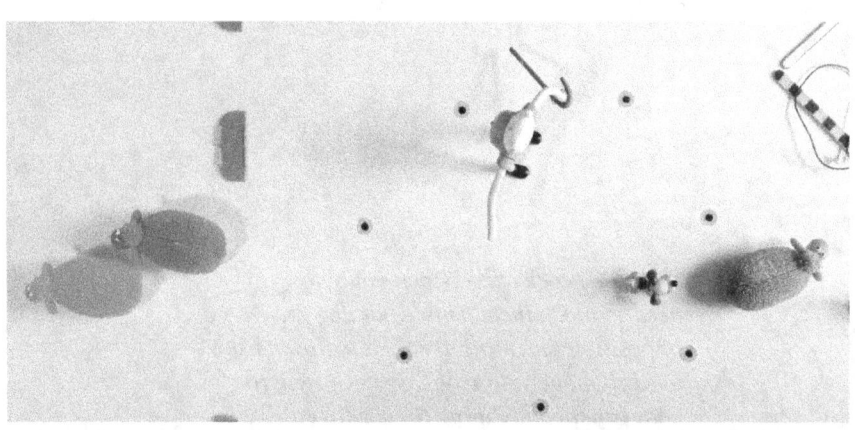

Remember to face the direction you want your dog to turn once they enter the gap. You may keep your hand extended toward your dog but your crook should never be pointed at your dog when you ask them to come in and shed.

If you split the sheep, when asked to shed on the head, and turn your dog on to the sheep already escaping, you have turned your dog on to the rears and the shed will not be accepted.

If the sheep exit the shedding ring before the separation or cut is made, the entire group must be re-gathered in the shedding ring before another attempt to shed can be made.

Shedding is an element of judged trials and isn't found in time and points trials. It is an advanced element that is good to train and practice, but it may be some time before you are ready to add shedding to your trial repertoire.

Some trials limit the number of attempts you can make at shedding to 2 or 3. If you call your dog through a specified number of times and don't complete the shed, you have to move on to the next obstacle and forfeit all shed points.

Some trials have you shed off 2 or 3 sheep and then pen only the shed sheep, allowing the other sheep to wander off, usually to the exhaust. If you are only penning part of the group you need to keep track of the other animals from the group as they may try to rejoin the shed sheep!

Since the idea of a shed is to separate stock for doctoring or confining, your dog must control the shed-off animals and not allow them to return to the others, until you cue them to. If your dog separates the designated animals, but then allows one of them to rejoin the other group before the shed is called complete, the shed will not count.

Figure 8

Some arena courses will include two barrels with the course being an S or a figure 8 around the barrels. This is an element that you can practice at home, but I would recommend you only practice this if you know it will be an obstacle at a trial you intend to enter. Usually, you want your dog to hold straight lines when driving.

The course will determine where you start the S or figure 8, which direction you go, and where you exit. The pull in the arena and the complacency of the stock determine the difficulty level of this obstacle.

Warning! – If you work cattle doing a figure 8 you may find the cattle will start to fight your dog after completing the first S of the 8. The reason they will fight is that once they turn back to go across the center of the 8, they realize there is no escape from the dog. No matter which way they turn, your dog blocks them.

I see no relevance of the figure 8 obstacle to any practical livestock handling and discourage the use of it as an element of a trial course.

Restricted handler movement
Some courses will set up lines, either real or imaginary, or barriers to restrict handler movement around the course. Sometimes an area is designated where the handler must stay or a line is drawn that the handler is not allowed to cross. This is usually done to downplay the handler's part in controlling the stock and showcase the dogs' abilities to handle the livestock. Often the handlers are dissatisfied with this arrangement, but if everyone has to adhere to the same restrictions the grumbling is usually minimal.

Nobody likes a whiner. There will be times at trials when you will feel you were shortchanged and times when you will feel you were dealt with more than fairly. It all averages out over time. Get over it!

Ending the run
Your run is over when you have completed the course. Usually, you will exhaust the stock. If the last element of the course is the pen, you will complete the pen by shutting the gate. Pause for a second, take a deep breath, praise your dog, and then open the pen and release the stock. Flank your dog around behind you to the back of the pen to push the stock out of the pen.

Have your dog drive the stock over to the exhaust pen and assist the exhaust crew until your set of livestock has been ushered into the exhaust pen. Call your dog and exit the field or arena! *Success!* Now is a great time to praise your dog for a job well done. Completing a trial course is a huge accomplishment for an inexperienced dog and handler team so give yourself a big pat on the back too!

Cool down your dog
In your excitement don't forget to cool off your dog by walking it and using a tub of water as noted in Chapter 19. While you are cooling your dog off you have some time to reflect on your run. What went right, wrong? Be sure to collect your phone or camera from whoever videoed your run for you. The video of your run will be invaluable for you to analyze later. Your memory of your run will probably be quite different from the video. In fact, you may not remember much at all about your run!

Setting out at trials
At trials where there are set-out and exhaust crews they are always looking for good help. If your dog can drive, will reliably hold, and then release stock to another dog, you may enjoy helping with the set-out crew. You can learn a lot from watching other dogs as they lift the livestock and begin their fetch.

Don't set out with an inexperienced dog! Wait until you and your dog have a fair amount of trial experience before volunteering to set out or exhaust stock.

It is important that all handlers get the same opportunity to showcase their dog's abilities at the trial. The set-out crew plays a vital role in giving everyone a fair chance by setting out the stock in a consistent manner.

Don't forget to thank all of the people who work the trial for all of their time and hard work. Putting on a trial takes a lot of planning, expense, and work!

Judged versus timed trials
I have a personal bias against timed trials because I feel that they encourage poor stockmanship. In time and points trials, the only way to win is to complete the course reasonably well and as fast as possible. This encourages running of the livestock, which is not how I want my stock to be handled.

Trials are showcases for handlers and herding dogs. If people in the audience come away with the belief that ramming livestock around is the preferred method when using a dog, they are much less likely to pursue learning more about or acquiring a herding dog.

Timed trials may be more exciting for spectators, but I believe stockmanship trumps that excitement and the welfare of the livestock is of ultimate importance.

Judged and timed trials both need judges, but their responsibilities vary depending on the type of trial. To continue to have sufficient numbers of competent judges available, I encourage you to think about eventually learning to judge. Judges have a lot of responsibility and sometimes take a lot of guff. If you don't like the judge at a trial, don't complain. Instead, don't go to trials where they are going to judge. If you have any interest in judging, consider becoming a judge once you have gained proficiency as an open or advanced handler.

Trial dog or farm dog?

Many people mistakenly believe that a dog can be a trial dog or a farm dog, but not both. A good farm or ranch dog needs the same skills as a trial dog. Dogs can work proficiently in both practical and trial situations. Having a lot of practical experience gives a good farm or ranch dog a leg up on dogs that only participate in trials. There is nothing like practical work to hone a dog's abilities to read and control livestock in tough situations.

Let's look at some skills that come in handy in practical situations on the farm or ranch.

CHAPTER 21

Farm and ranch skills

There is no difference between training a farm or ranch dog versus training a trial dog. Both dogs will benefit from precise training. Some dogs will be better suited to practical work, just as some people will enjoy having a helper around the farm but have no interest in trials. Other people will buy livestock solely to train their dogs for trials.

Don't believe that a dog used solely on a ranch or farm is an inferior helper as compared to a trial dog, that they need less training, or should be held to lower standards. Dogs that work for a living are indispensable helpmates and companions. They are ready and willing to do whatever needs to be done around the ranch in any kind of weather. They don't ask for payment and are happy, willing workers. A good farm dog is worth more than a hired hand in many situations.

Since cattle are usually less responsive to a dog's pressure than sheep, there is a tendency for cattle dog handlers to allow their dogs to get into the habit of slicing flanks. Just because a dog can get away with sloppy criteria is no reason to allow substandard work.

Doing chores

Many people use dogs to help them with chores on their farm, ranch, or small acreage. Some chores are done daily, some yearly, and others as often as needed.

If you often do the same chores with your dog, your dog will quickly start anticipating what needs to be done and will complete the chore without needing to be cued. This is a dangerous habit to allow your dog to get into. If you notice your dog falling into this habit, start giving them cues that are opposite of what they are expecting.

The reason you don't want your dog to do chores on autopilot is that they are no longer tuned in to you. When something changes in the environment, such as a bull getting added to the herd or ewes lambing, your dog may be at risk of injury if they attempt to complete the chore as they always have.

You always want your dog tuned in and listening to you!

This does not mean that you have to tell your dog every move to make when completing chores. It does mean that you should throw in a different cue occasionally to make sure your dog has one ear on the stock and one ear on you.

Holding stock off feeders and at gates

If you are feeding livestock grain in feed bunks, over time they can become quite pushy. If you are feeding on foot using 5-gallon buckets, they may shove you aside, step on your feet, or knock you down. Even if you are feeding hay with a truck or tractor you may not want your livestock to approach the hay until you have finished feeding it.

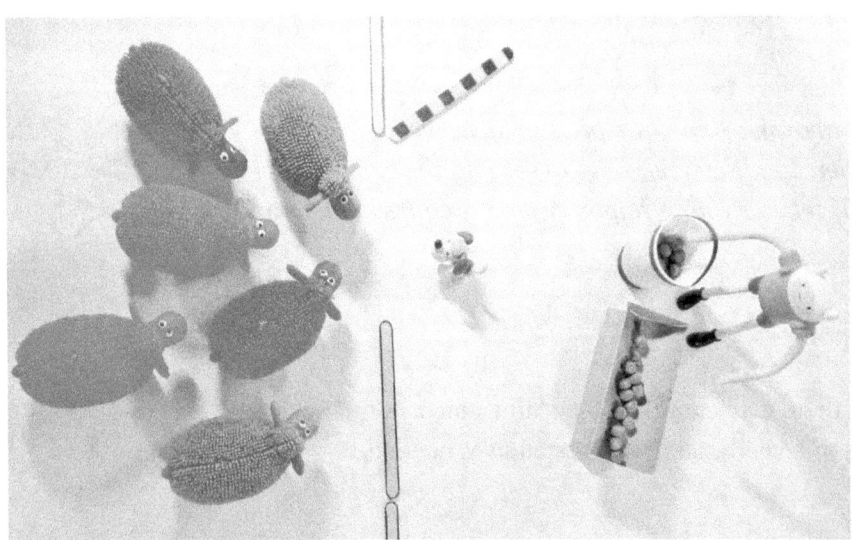

Holding stock off of a feeder or at a gate can make it much safer for you to feed grain or hay to hungry animals. A dog who knows their job will not let any animals through a gate or up to a feeder until they are given the cue to release the stock. That'll do is the usual release cue in this situation.

These are good times to use your *hold* cue, as taught in Chapter 10. Your dog will quickly learn that their job is to hold the livestock off of the feed bunk or area you are feeding in until you call them off. Your dog should know how to hold before you try to use this cue around hungry animals.

Remember that your dog is free to flank and walk in or bite livestock while holding. If they stay in one place after being cued to hold and the livestock start to go around them, you need to step in and cue a flank. Once your dog has covered the stock, re-cue the hold rather than a stop. After a few experiences holding the stock, your dog will start to cover without the need for cues from you.

Another place that dogs often help hold livestock is at gateways. Again, if your dog stays stationary after being cued to hold and the stock starts to go around them through the gate, then flank your dog. When they cover the stock, you may re-cue the hold.

Your dog is free to stand, sit, or lie down while they hold. As long as they move to cover trespassing livestock and don't allow them to get by, they are doing their job.

Moving stock to new places

If you need to move your stock to a new pasture or area, your dog should have all of the skills needed to complete the task. If you have tame livestock, you may want to lead them and have your dog behind the stock. If they are less tame, probably both you and your dog will be covering a flank and your dog will be driving them, depending on the size of the group.

If you are going to move your stock often to new pastures that are adjacent to each other or connected, you can go ahead of the stock and call them into the new pasture. Your dog can come behind the stock to encourage stragglers to keep up.

*If you do rotational grazing it is much easier to call your stock into a new paddock than to drive them into it. With **rotational grazing**, you give your livestock access to a fresh paddock to graze at frequent intervals.*

Gathering livestock

Unless you are going to gather a very large herd or flock, your dog should have all the skills they need to accomplish this task. If the stock is spread out in a hilly pasture, your dog may have to do a blind outrun where your dog cannot see part or all of the stock from where they start. If they go partway on the fetch, stop, and look back at you, you may need to walk out closer to the livestock and send your dog again.

Never send your dog on a blind outrun unless you are positive that there is stock in the pasture for your dog to gather.

If the stock is spread out, you may have to stop your dog from bringing only part of the stock and have them *look back* for the rest. Don't allow your dog to bring only part of the livestock as this can be the beginning of a bad habit.

After a few blind outruns your dog will learn to bring all of the stock. They will sweep out wide as they flank to make sure that they find all of the livestock in the paddock.

Penning or corralling

There are many reasons you may need to confine your livestock in a pen, corral, or barn. If you are only working a few head of livestock, then penning, as explained for trials in Chapter 20, will be useful. If you are going to pen or corral a large flock or herd, you will have much better luck if you can set up some panels or gates to form an alley that will funnel them into the enclosure. The alley should be wide where the animals enter and become more narrow as they travel along it to the pen or corral. Try to set up the alley in a corner of a field or extend one side of the alley to form a corner. It is extremely difficult to get animals to go through a gate or into the start of an alley that isn't in a corner unless the animals have previous experience entering the gate or alley.

As in trial penning, the key is to block all of the escape routes and then apply just enough pressure to encourage the stock to enter the gate or alley.

Allow livestock to settle and find the entrance to the alley or pen. Too much pressure can cause more harm than good.

Think of the flock or herd as one animal. If you can get a leader to go through the gate or into the alley the rest will usually follow. This is especially true for sheep.

Milling is counterproductive and means that the animals are highly agitated. Allow them to settle, if possible, before having your dog apply more pressure.

If you have the option, feed your livestock in the corral or pen daily for a week or two before you need them confined. Once they get used to entering the enclosure, you should have no problem luring them into the pen when necessary. Use your dog to encourage stragglers to enter the enclosure.

A barn can be a bit of a problem to get livestock to enter because not only may it be unfamiliar but it is usually dark inside. Animals do not like going into places where they cannot see what is inside, or places that they feel confined. Again, if there is any way you can feed the animals near the barn for a week or so and slowly move the feeders or feed into the barn, you will save yourself a lot of frustration. If you do need to push the animals into a barn, set up gates to funnel them inside.

Sorting using a gate

If you need to sort a lot of animals, using a gate is much handier than shedding. In this situation, you would swing the gate and your dog would initially hold the stock off of you and the gate. You would then need to flank your dog as necessary to string out the stock and bring small groups up to the gate for you to sort. Gates that are hung so that they swing freely are much easier to use for sorting than gates that must be dragged over the ground. Gates are usually easier to use for sorting than are cattle panels. Panels are too flexible and the stock can easily see through them, making them a poor barrier to use for sorting.

Gate cut refers to sorting only by the number of animals. If you buy livestock using gate cut, it means that you will not be able to pick individual animals. Instead, the first animals that go through the gate are the ones that you get.

When sorting, it is really helpful if you can easily identify the animals that you want to separate. If you can mark animals before you need to separate them, it will make the job much easier. To have the markings be helpful when sorting cattle, the marks need to be either on the head or ears, as this is the part of the animal that will be facing you.

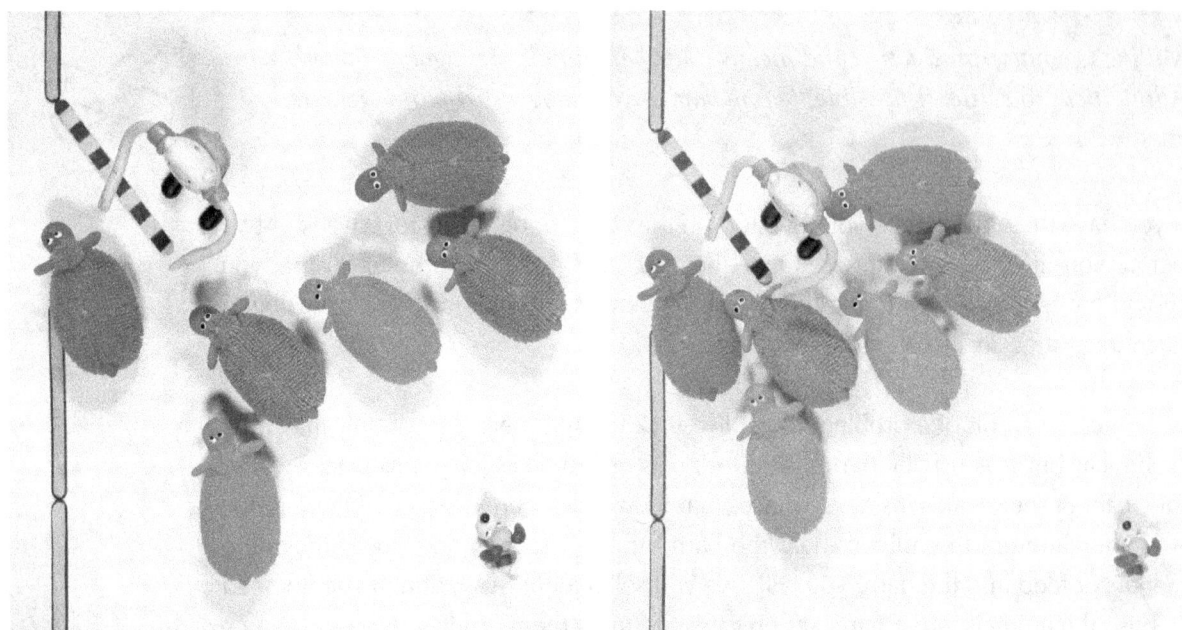

Your dog should be positioned to hold the stock off of you and the gate, allowing only an animal or two to approach the gate (L). You don't want your dog jamming the stock onto you and the gate (R).

Ear tags, plastic or metal tags in animals' ears, are usually numbered and are available in different colors. Ear tags or different colored livestock marker stripes on an animal's head make life a lot easier when you are sorting stock.

For smaller livestock, such as sheep or goats, the tags or markings should be either on the head, ears, or back. With small stock, you can easily see colored marks on the animals' backs as you look down at them.

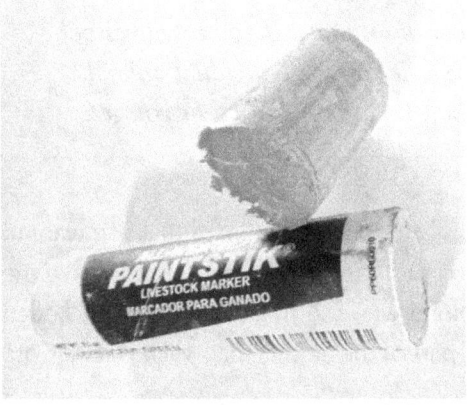

A Paintstik is similar to a large crayon and a marker that we often use. It comes in many colors and can be applied on heads, backs, or legs. The marks last for a few days and then wear off.

Chutes

Chutes are used on farms and ranches for two basic purposes. The first is to confine and individually treat animals, especially when an entire herd or flock will be processed, such as for worming, castration, dehorning, or vaccination. These chutes usually have a pen or **tub** that a small group of animals is put into. From the tub, they go down a chute in single file and are caught in a head catch for treatment.

Your dog can help move the livestock into the pen or tub from a larger pen or area. Some people like to use dogs to push cattle down a chute to the headgate, but this can be quite dangerous for the dogs. I would advise against using dogs to push cattle down chutes. It is much less dangerous for your dog to push sheep, but if you are not aware, your dog may become overly aggressive in biting the stock.

Use great care if you use your dog to push livestock down chutes.

Another type of chute is found on larger ranches and farms and is used to load livestock into trailers or semi-trailers. These chutes are usually permanent structures that are part of a corral system, but there are also movable chutes on wheels.

Again, you can use your dog to get animals into the pen that leads to the chute, but these chutes usually have solid sidewalls and are no place for a dog to be working.

Loading into a trailer

If you have livestock, they probably arrived and will leave your acreage in a trailer. You may also use a trailer to move stock around your farmstead at times. Loading stock into a trailer is just penning, with the trailer being the pen. The problem with getting livestock into a trailer is often that the interior of the trailer is dark and full of novel smells and footing, and thus will be avoided by livestock. Animals also resist being confined because they lose the ability to escape from danger.

To load stock into a trailer, without a chute, open the entire back trailer door to form a barrier on one side. Open the back door at a 90° angle to the trailer to form a corner. Allow the stock to take a moment to look into the trailer once they approach it. If you can, place some bedding that is similar to what is in the trailer on the ground at the back of the trailer. Stock may balk if the trailer is bedded with a material that they are not familiar with.

If you can place some gates to funnel the stock into the trailer, do so, but remember to keep the trailer gate configured such that it can be quickly closed once the animals are on the trailer.

Once the stock goes into a trailer and walks as far forward as they can, they will immediately turn around and attempt to get off of it. Have the trailer back door ready to swing closed as soon as all of the animals have been loaded.

If your trailer has compartments (usually trailers have 2 or 3 compartments separated by swinging gates) only attempt to load the number of animals that will fit into each compartment at one time. Fill a compartment, close the gate, and then bring up the next group of animals to fill the next compartment. Often once there are animals in the front compartment, the next group will load easier if they can see the animals that are already on the trailer.

When using your dog to load livestock into a trailer, aim the livestock for the hinge of the rear door or trailer gate. Depending on the tameness of the stock, you will either stand at the end of the rear door or back a distance from it.

Working multiple dogs

If you have more than one dog, you certainly can work them together on your livestock.

*Working two dogs together is called a **brace**.*

Advanced handlers sometimes trial with two dogs at once in a brace class. They often put opposite flank cues on each dog so that *come bye* means flank clockwise to one dog and flank counter-clockwise to the other. Fortunately, you don't have to be that sophisticated to work two dogs at the same time.

An easy way to work two or more dogs at once is to precede each cue with the name of the dog that is to take the cue. You will need to practice with each dog individually to get them used to the addition of their name before their cues. So if I were working Mattie and Lex, I might cue *Mattie come bye* and then *Lex walk in*. If you work with several dogs, they will quickly learn that they are only to take the cues that follow their name.

When I start working two dogs together I begin by sending them at the same time, one from each side of me. I want to see if they will honor each other. Honor *means to work with and complement each other. One dog should not work as if the other does not exist, but instead, they should work together as a team to fetch the flock.*

Another easy way to work multiple dogs is to take into account how your dogs respond to cues. For example, you are working Mattie and Lex. Mattie flanks fast and Lex flanks much more slowly. You need the dogs to flank around a group. If both dogs are next to you when you give them the same flank cue, Mattie will flank faster than Lex, such that the dogs will naturally space themselves around the livestock. Keep in mind how each dog will respond to a certain cue and adjust when you give that cue. This sounds more complicated than it is!

I have worked three dogs at one time on 200 head of ewes without any problem. Just experiment before you need to get a job done, and you will be amazed at how easy it is to work multiple dogs at one time – if you know the dogs well!

When two dogs work together they usually learn to honor the other dog. If you send both dogs on a fetch from your feet, they need to work together to bring the flock and not work exactly as they would if they were alone. **Honoring** *the other dog means working with it, instead of working as if it did not exist.*

After working together for a while, dogs will usually learn to honor each other. Some dogs will be more dominant and work as if the other dog doesn't exist. Since it is easier for two dogs to handle a large herd or flock if they share responsibilities, they usually learn to work together fairly quickly. If they don't, you can help them figure it out by giving their name before their cues to help them to learn to work together efficiently.

Working multiple dogs is essential if you have a large flock or herd to gather or move. One dog can only do so much and cover so much ground.

Working mothers with young

Livestock with newborn or very young calves, lambs, or kids at their sides are potentially dangerous and should be worked with care. If the mother perceives your dog as a threat, she may turn and fight to protect her offspring.

If the stock has been worked by dogs before they lambed or calved, they are more likely to move away from your dog, *if* your dog allows them enough time and space to gather their young and take them along.

Often your dog can move mothers with young by stopping, applying pressure with their eyes, allowing the pairs to move away from them, and then walking forward.

Some dogs instinctively have a better feel for moving stock with newborns. Once the young animals get some age on them, so that they can easily keep up with their mothers, there is usually less concern that the mothers will feel the need to fight your dog. Every animal is different, so be alert when handling any stock with very young animals as part of the group.

Having a dog around your farm or ranch can provide not only a great helper but also a wonderful friend and companion. When the cows break out of the dry lot and get into spring pasture, it is amazing how much easier it is to move them back to where they belong with a good dog. When it is time to vaccinate, worm, or shear the flock there is no better help to have on hand than a good dog or two.

You will become so dependent on your dog for help around your farm or ranch that you will quickly realize that you need to have two or three, in case one gets injured or too old to complete the work you need to do. It is truly eye-opening to do a job, that you previously did with a dog, without one. Once you get used to having good dogs as helpers, you will never want to be without them!

Section 5
Final Thoughts

Chapter 22 Crossover dogs and handlers 309
Averse to aversives 311
Crossover dogs 311
The lone ranger 312
Sculptor or potter? 313
Having faith 314
Regrets 314
Keeping the faith 315
You and your dog are in this together 315
Old habits and livestock 316
I commend you 317

Chapter 23 Positive trainers new to herding 319
Going positive 321
Frustrations 322
Regrets, I have a few … 323
My next dog 324
Positive benefits 324

Chapter 24 Where to from here? 327
It's all about the dogs! 327
The learning never ends 328
Finding a coach 328
Happy trails, happy trials 339

CHAPTER 22

Crossover dogs and handlers

Violence begins where knowledge ends. – Abraham Lincoln

I am a crossover trainer and intimately know the frustration and confusion encountered when changing from traditional to positive dog training methods. I wish I could tell you that it was a quick and easy transition, but it was not. I found starting over and learning a new way to train my dogs extremely difficult. Fortunately, I found positive training intriguing, logical, and inherently reinforcing.

What kept me motivated to learn this new method was my conviction that my dogs deserved to be taught with praise and reinforcement, rather than with corrections. How I looked at my dog's behavior was to change 180° and my eyes were opened to a whole new world of animal training.

So what is the main difference between traditional and positive training? In my mind, it is what the trainer is looking for as they watch and interact with their dog. Traditional trainers look for behavior they do *not* want and use punishment to eliminate it, while positive trainers look for behavior they *do* want and use reinforcement to build it.

Using punishment can be highly reinforcing to the trainer and thus become a habit that is extremely difficult to change. A major reason that crossover trainers struggle to leave their punishment-based training behind is that they are very familiar with how to effectively employ corrections, but become stymied when faced with building wanted behaviors that don't respond readily to their efforts to use positive training methods.

Punishment makes the punisher feel powerful! If using punishment were not reinforcing to the punisher, it would be easier to cross over to using positive training methods.

Learning positive training takes time and effort. The concept seems so simple, but as Bob Bailey says, "Positive training is simple but it is not easy." There is a lot to learn and implement, and each animal offers new possibilities and unique problems. Where you once felt proficient and confident in your training, you may now feel clumsy and insecure. It is not easy to go from being a proficient trainer to almost a complete novice! Your identity and self-esteem may be tied to your self-image as a competent trainer. You may also find that your friends don't understand why you even want to train differently.

Two problems with punishment are that it only tells the animal what not to do, without teaching them what to do, and it only generates minimal effort. The animal will only do the least it has to do to avoid being punished.

Because you may have quickly achieved good results using punishment in the past, there is always the lure to return to that method. Old habits die hard when you are frustrated or angry and the urge to return to familiar correction-based solutions can be almost overwhelming. I still find that if I am getting angry or frustrated, I catch myself automatically thinking of using punishment-based methods.

Old habits die very hard! Keeping my training fun is easy in my training room, but something I still struggle when outside working livestock.

It is amazing how subtly punishment can creep back into your training. Be on the lookout for tugs on a leash or long line as indicators that you are drifting backward. Remember that a leash or long line is an emergency brake and not a steering wheel. They are only to be used to prevent the rehearsal of unwanted behavior in the short term until self-control and skills are built. Be aware of your voice becoming harsh, as no reward markers can easily become verbal punishers.

Averse to aversives

An **aversive** is anything an animal will work to escape or avoid and can be primary or conditioned. In other words, your dog may find walking on hot blacktop aversive the first time they experience it (primary), but they may not find going near a busy road aversive until punishment has been paired with approaching it (secondary).

By punishing your dog, you may become a conditioned aversive to them. Many traditional trainers force their dogs off of stock and then wonder why their dog will not come to them when they want to shed or recall their dog.

So how do you keep from falling back into old habits? First, check your ego at the gate and commit to having fun before you worry about your dog being correct. Stay on guard for anger or frustration creeping into your training session, especially training that you initially learned using traditional methods which usually includes livestock. Remember that you, as a dog trainer, have a huge advantage over most positive trainers who work with animals that do not engage with tugs or toys. Not only can you reinforce with food but you also have tugs and flirt poles at your disposal.

Because you have a very positive relationship with your dog, you can add praise, petting, verbals cues, and even laughter to your arsenal of reinforcers. Tugs and flirt poles can also be used to increase the arousal of your dog without livestock present. Conversely, food can be used to lower your dog's arousal near livestock. Using reinforcers wisely and managing unwanted behavior with a leash or long line makes most punishment unnecessary.

Crossover dogs

As you cross over to positive training, so does your dog. Some of your dogs may have had substantial traditional training before you crossed over. This situation can leave both you and your dog in a quandary as to how to proceed. Most traditionally trained dogs have learned *not* to offer behavior, as it is safer to wait for instruction or direction. A good resource to address this situation is the book *The Thinking Dog* by Gail T. Fisher. This is a very readable and instructive book.

Dogs trained using traditional punishment-based methods are much less likely to offer behavior since they have been taught that waiting for instruction is much safer than offering behavior. These dogs can be super frustrating to train until they learn that it is safe to offer behavior, but that realization may take a long time!

Pure Gold, my heart dog and first crossover dog. I wish I knew then what I know now about positive herding training.

Since you probably have thought about crossing over for quite a while, you may have a dog or puppy that has little traditional training and is more of a clean slate. The better a positive trainer you are, the less punishment you will need to use. Eventually, you will become such a good positive trainer that you will need to use almost no punishment, but until that time just do the best that you can and keep learning.

Positive is not permissive! The problem is that although you want to train positively you may not immediately have all of the necessary skills. It can be embarrassing to have a dog that is not as obedient as your other dogs have always been. Learning positive training is a process for both you and your dog.

If you need a short, simple book to get jump-started on learning positive training, try *Clicker Basics for Dogs and Puppies* by Carolyn Barney. There are many books available to help you learn positive training. If you can find a peer or mentor to work with, all the better!

The lone ranger

Chances are you will be the odd duck if you are training herding using positive methods. Although many traditional trainers have caught on to the idea that people want kinder, more compassionate training, very few are truly positive trainers. They will say they use positive methods and limit corrections, but almost all of them start dogs on stock with very little pre-herding foundational training.

The first test of a positive trainer, in my opinion, is if they train foundation behaviors away from livestock.

An analogy for starting a dog directly on stock with limited foundation work would be teaching someone to drive a car using the following method: In the driveway as they sit behind the wheel you show your student the controls for the vehicle; the brake, accelerator, steering wheel, turn signals, etc. Then they start the car, pull out of the drive, and shortly thereafter you direct them to enter a six-lane highway at rush hour.

How successful would your novice driver be with all of the overwhelming distractions that they would immediately encounter? Do you think yelling at them to switch lanes or use their blinker would be helpful?

Saying "good dog" when a dog does the desired behavior does not make a traditional trainer a positive trainer. Positive herding training starts months before your dog has access to loose livestock!

Sculptor or potter?
The main difference between traditional force-based training and positive reinforcement training is that traditional trainers are like sculptors chipping away behaviors they do not want until they have revealed the animal inside a block of stone. Positive reinforcement trainers are like clay potters molding and building behaviors to form an animal with the behaviors that they desire.

A dog that is trained by chipping away unwanted behaviors may look exactly like a dog trained by building wanted behaviors, but they definitely are not equal and will not act exactly alike.

The problem with being a sculptor is that if you make an error and remove a piece of behavior from a dog, you may never be able to replace it, but if you are a potter and make an error you can always retrain, and move forward with little harm done.

Having faith

You can read a lot of books, attend a lot of seminars, and take a lot of online classes and become convinced that positive training is right for you, but until you have some real success using positive training, you will find doubt creeping in over time. You know it can work, but can it work for you?

My epiphany came when I returned from my first week of Chicken Workshops with Bob Bailey and Parvene Farhoody a couple of years into my transition from a traditional to a positive trainer. I had worked with my dogs on their downs and they would down okay, but they did not have the quick, crisp behavior I craved. Upon my return, I worked with my older border collie using the positive training techniques I had just learned and within 5 minutes his down was better than it had been with several months of previous positive training. I was totally hooked!

Like any other skill, positive training takes time and effort to master. It truly is simple but not easy. When I first picked up a clicker I thought, "How hard can this be?" I was about to find out! Learning positive training is similar to learning herding. You watch a dog/handler team working in sync and it looks effortless. The dog is always where they need to be and the stock seems to flow smoothly and calmly around the course or field. Everything is easy when you know how to do it, but acquiring true expertise is neither quick nor easy.

Hang in there and training positively will become easier, quicker, and lots more fun!

Regrets

Many people who cross over to positive training, myself included, feel regret for how they trained their previous dogs. Although you may have tried to be as kind as possible to your dog, you probably now realize there are much more compassionate and positive ways to train. You can only work with the knowledge you have. As you grow and learn, your knowledge expands, and your training changes. You do the best you can with the knowledge you now have. You may not be able to go back, but you can move forward with the determination not to repeat the past.

We all want our dogs to have the best lives possible and positive training can definitely be a big part of that picture. Unfortunately, correction-based training often gets a firm foothold before reinforcement training is discovered. Most people who have trained for many years were introduced to force-based training as the status quo and had few other options. Now we have more options available to us. If you can forge your regret into a strong determination to use positive training methods, then it will serve a worthy purpose.

Keeping the faith

Remaining committed to reinforcement-based training is not always easy. There are always new things to learn, new skills to master, and new situations to deal with. It is a difficult path to travel alone. Try to find support on your journey. Positive training is not a skill you learn overnight. Building your skills can take months or years and there will always be more to learn!

Online is a good place to find fellow travelers. A good positive training community bolsters your faith that you will get there and that all your time and effort is worth it. Plus, you may find a teacher or mentor to guide you along the way. The Internet has opened up the world to you, so use it! Please join my email list of fellow travelers on their positive herding journey by going to my Facebook group: Positive Herding Dog or the bottom of the page found at *https://www.positiveherdingdog.com*.

Another great tool is a training journal. Keeping a journal not only helps you remember what and how you trained a behavior but gives you a written account of how far you have come! It is easy to get down when you struggle with a problem and forget how far you have progressed.

You and your dog are in this together

Remember that your dog may be just as confused and uncertain as you are as you both learn new positive training skills. Whenever you or your dog struggle, stop and break things down so that it is easier to achieve success. You will be amazed at the number of steps a behavior can be broken down into. As you and your dog gain expertise, you will be able to take bigger steps or lump behaviors a bit, but always be ready to break things down if need be.

If you and your dog are not having fun, you are doing something wrong! If you get angry – quit training, take a break, and regroup!

Most importantly, don't be afraid to move away from training on stock and go back to working with cone circles and a flirt pole, or move back into your smallest paddock. This advice is easy to give but difficult to follow. Once you have your dog working stock, it is almost impossible to convince yourself to move away from livestock. Who wants to go back to working with cones when you can work real stock?

Livestock work is the sexy, addictive stuff, and I have yet to meet the person who finds working with cone circles sexy or addictive.

Frustration is your friend! If you find yourself being continually frustrated at some point in your training, it is a sure sign that you need to break a skill down into smaller pieces. If need be, go back to cone circles and flirt poles, using a pen, or your small paddock.

If you do decide to go back to cone circles and flirt poles, take a week or two break from training so that your dog is psyched to train again, even if stock is not involved. Going from stock directly back to cones is often not a good plan.

Also, don't be afraid to take a break and give your training a rest. Sometimes a few days or weeks away from training can refresh you and your dog. Although it is good to train consistently, a break will not do your dog any harm and may do you both a lot of good.

Old habits and livestock

Unfortunately, old habits are often just below the surface and ready to burst onto the scene in the blink of an eye. Because you probably have a long history of training traditionally with livestock, your default behavior may be to train with corrections around stock. You may have little trouble staying positive when you are training in your house, in your back yard, or even in a paddock when no livestock is present, but when you add stock to the equation your old habits tend to rear their heads.

You may have 10 or 20 years of training herding traditionally. That history is going to make those old punishment-based training habits rock solid.

You will have to be on your guard, especially when you are working stock, to prevent your old habits from resurfacing. I struggle with this at times even years down the positive training road. Because I had 20+ years of traditional training experience before I crossed over, it should not be a surprise to me that I still sometimes struggle, but it is. The most helpful question I have found to ask myself during training is: *Am I having fun?*

Be on guard for this problem and know that you are not alone in fighting it. It gets easier over time, but I am not sure it ever goes away completely. Keep fighting the good fight!

I commend you

It's not easy to break away from old habits, friends, or communities and forge new habits and relationships. If it were easy, everyone would be doing it! Instead, you will have to be convinced that you are doing the right thing for you and your dog. Stay committed to what you believe.

Fight the good fight, your dog will thank you!

CHAPTER 23

Positive trainers new to herding

Since Sally is eminently more qualified to address questions and concerns of reinforcement-based trainers who are new to herding, I will step aside and give her center stage in this chapter. But first, let me give you some insight into my introduction to handling and training a stockdog.

Barb's story

I remember when I started learning traditionally taught herding, many years ago, as if it were yesterday. It was the most unsettling and confusing experience I have ever had! I was supposed to be functioning and learning while I stumbled around with my dog and the sheep whirling before my eyes. I understood what I was supposed to be doing, from working with an advanced handler, reading books, and watching DVDs, but I had no idea where to position myself, when to move, or where to move to. The first teacher I found had the philosophy that the handler moves, the dog moves, and the sheep move. It was overwhelming as I had no previous experience handling a herding dog, my dog had no previous herding training, and the sheep took full advantage of our combined lack of experience.

After a month or two, I was at an open handler's home and she graciously allowed me to work her sheep as she watched. Her only comment when I finished was, "You always move in the wrong direction." Probably precise criticism, but not particularly helpful.

I persevered and drove many miles from our dairy in upstate New York, where we lived at the time, for day-long lessons with a trainer in Pennsylvania as often as possible, which usually meant once or twice a month. At this time my young dog was still just learning the ropes. One day we were working about seven sheep, in a good-sized rectangular pen, when the sheep got stuck in a corner. I cued a flank but my dog was hesitant to go into the corner. My teacher gave me the sage advice, "Help your dog get the sheep out of the corner." I stopped and just stared because I was clueless as to how to help my dog. Was I supposed to go into the corner with my dog or back out of the way and open up a bigger escape route for the sheep? Again, it was probably good advice, but not very helpful.

When I started herding I received a lot of advice and instruction, but I was so overwhelmed that it was not helpful. Fortunately, I found herding so addictive that I kept at it. Eventually, I found a trainer who made things substantially easier by insisting that I initially stand still. What a relief! With fewer decisions to make and consistent instruction, I slowly sorted things out.

I hope your herding journey will be less frustrating and more fun than mine was. I am reasonably sure Sally's experience was, although I know she faced her share of frustration and confusion. And she had to put up with me!

Renn practicing one of her behaviors taught with positive reinforcement training.

Renn was the fifth dog Sally taught obedience, tricks, and agility using primarily positive reinforcement but the first dog that she ever taught herding.

I had a similar experience to Barb when I went for a couple of horse-riding lessons a few years ago. The instructor was experienced and well-meaning, but her feedback was very seldom positive and usually rather critical. It would go from "your hands are in the wrong place" to "put your heels down", "sit upright" then back to "your hands are in the wrong place again". As soon as I was doing one thing correctly, she would find something else to pick on, instead of telling me what I was doing right and giving me a chance to practice that position for a while. I so wished that she had a clicker in her hand, marking when my body was in the correct shape. As the student, I found it demoralizing, frustrating, and unhelpful, but it did reinforce for me that a positive method of teaching is an infinitely better experience for the learner.

Going positive

I stumbled across clicker training in 1996 and became an instant devotee and advocate, introducing the idea to our South African dog club. Once they saw the potential, most of my agility students switched to training positively, with brilliant results.

After we moved to our small farm and acquired some sheep, I decided I needed a sheepdog to help out. I had long been fascinated by sheepdog work and I was keen to train my own dog from scratch, positively. However, it seemed to me that there were not a great deal of complicated tasks to do on the farm and that I should aim a little higher – could I get to competition level? Perhaps even attain certification?

Friends who had switched from obedience and agility competitions to herding assured me that all other disciplines paled into insignificance next to sheepdog trialling. I thought they were being dramatic. They were not. If you get the chance to work your sheepdog on stock, go for it. You'll see a side of your dog that may not have been apparent before. And the level of control you eventually have on your dog will astonish you: it still amazes me that I can drop my dog from hundreds of metres away – not something any of my previous dogs could ever do. That said, don't expect it to be easy to train a sheepdog. If I'd known how difficult it would be to train on my own, using new, untested methods with just Internet support, I might not have tried.

In the days when I was a mere trial spectator, I wondered why the handlers needed to do quite so much yelling and why they always sounded so darn *grumpy*. I felt that if only they had trained using positive reinforcement, dogs would respond instantly to quiet cues, the handler would be calm because the dog was highly responsive, and the sheep would, well, they would do what they were told. Oh, how naive I was ...

Yes, it helps to teach the dog the cues away from sheep. Yes, it helps to use positive reinforcement to keep everything calmer than it might otherwise be. But never underestimate just how different your dog will be in the vicinity of sheep and how hard you are going to have to work to keep your dog focused on you and to keep yourself in a less agitated state (that is, not shouting your head off).

Frustrations

It was indeed frustrating working with Barb, but only in the sense that we live 14 000 km (8 700 miles) and several time zones apart! I would get feedback only after I'd finished a session, uploaded the video, and waited for Barb to wake up. It was slow going and a bit lonely at times. If possible, find someone close by that you can train with and bounce ideas off.

The most frustrating thing about training a herding dog is trying to get the sheep to cooperate so that you can work on your training plan for the day. Up till now you have carefully planned your lessons and cunningly manipulated the environment to allow the dog to succeed. Having taught, say, a nice clockwise flank to the dog using a ring of cones in the garden, you confidently take the dog out to your training flock, imagining that you would be able to recreate the identical scenario but with sheep in the picture. You would be wrong.

Sheep frequently have other ideas. They might refuse to move. They might bunch up in a corner, or dash towards you as soon as the dog leaves your feet, or try their best to break out through the fence (this is where you will be pleased that you put so much effort into getting a good "stop!" on your dog). Frequently a lesson does not go to plan, and that's the way it is and you might as well get used to it. Be grateful when your sheep work goes smoothly because it can so quickly go to pieces, as any stockman will tell you.

For a beginner, keen to get on to actual herding, it was frustrating to spend time trying to do other behaviours near the sheep.

"But Renn can't concentrate near the sheep", I'd whine, regularly.
"Well exactly", Barb would reply unsympathetically. *"And how do you expect her to respond to herding cues if she can't even do a trick near sheep in a pen?"*

But it's such an important part of the process – **perhaps even the most important** – that one simply has to grit one's teeth and know that the dog will eventually start to tune in to you.

Regrets, I have a few ...

What would I have done differently? One of my big issues with Renn is that she is sticky – on a fetch, she will creep up to the sheep and eyeball all of them instead of getting a move on, and it's almost impossible to get her to speed up or to continue flanking past the point from where she has decided to creep. I simply never grasped the idea that a flank should mean "run in that direction around the sheep and keep going until told otherwise" and was just happy because my dog knew where to stop at balance. I should have sorted this out before we ever left the small paddock, but I couldn't figure out a way to do it positively. Having seen how carefully and consistently Barb has worked through such problems has taught me that everything is possible with positive work. You just need to break down the behaviour and be consistent in what you expect from the dog.

Once one starts work on real livestock, it is so thrilling that it is easy to let one's standards (criteria) slip. In the excitement of watching one's dog fetch the sheep for the first time, one might overlook that sliced flank, that missed stop. I think this is particularly true if the dog does real work on the farm and not just trialling. Sometimes one just wants to get the job done and on a freezing wet evening, it's not at all tempting to call the dog back to do a re-run because they sliced into the sheep at the top of the paddock. You can't allow one behaviour at home but expect another one at the trials. Still, I could have been more consistent about certain cues.

It is so hard to admit to yourself that your basic training might be a little shaky, and it is not appealing to go back to working cones in the garden, but bite the bullet! Like learning multiplication tables, it's painful at the time but without that foundation, it's hard to improve your math.

Sally and Renn worked together on some challenging terrain of rolling fields and multiple pastures.

My next dog

It's an interesting exercise to consider how I would change things the second time around. Of course, my next dog would likely be the polar opposite of Renn, and I'd have to revise my plans entirely. I would at least have the confidence of knowing that this is do-able, that a sheepdog's instincts and drives can be tempered and moulded and brought under our control without resorting to physical punishment. I would take the time it takes to perfect each cue and not rush to sheep or to working in a larger area. I would video every single session, review it critically, and not be tempted to delete footage of the bad days, as these will be more instructive and will also encourage me down the line, once an improvement is obvious. And there is no doubt I would be consulting this set of books on a daily basis – Barb has done a phenomenal job of setting out a structured training plan, breaking down every exercise into understandable chunks, explaining the way forward, anticipating possible pitfalls, and suggesting fixes.

Positive benefits

One of the greatest benefits of training without punishment is that the dog is never worried that there will be harsh consequences to whatever she does and is freer to use her instincts. In situations where I am out of sight, Renn is confident to think through and act on problems herself. I saw an example of this early on.

Renn had progressed to the stage where she could be trusted to collect the sheep in a large field and herd them into their overnight enclosure. One evening she disappeared over the top of the rise: the flock then appeared, running towards me back over the hill, but there was no sign of Renn. There was no response to my recall whistle, so I assumed she was sticking somewhere and grumpily set off to find her. Blow me down if she wasn't lying next to a tiny newborn lamb forgotten in the grass, and intelligently refusing to respond to my calls. As fun as trialling is, I get immense satisfaction from sending Renn to "go find the sheep" and getting on with other tasks while she finds the flock, winkles them out of the bushes, and brings them in without any further instructions from me.

Whatever your intentions and goals for your sheepdog, a trial run or a homestead chore, I wish you similar moments of delight.

CHAPTER 24

Where to from here?

I hope you have an enlightening and enjoyable journey as you train positive herding along with Sally and me. It is not easy to become a successful dog and handler herding team. There are many skills you and your dog must learn, both away from and around livestock. As you build these skills, your dog's self-control and confidence will develop and your relationship with your dog will blossom. Positive training has a way of bringing out the best in us and our dogs. I sincerely hope you reach a new level of teamwork and communication with your dog as a result of training herding using positive methods.

Once you and your dog have the skills and self-control to add livestock to the mix, a whole new world opens up to you. Granted at times it can be dazzling and overwhelming, but hopefully it is also challenging and achievable. Both you and your dog will do a lot of growing and maturing as you work your way through the exercises in this set of books. I hope both you and your dog have fun training positive herding every step along the way!

It's all about the dogs!

I came to reinforcement-based training because I wanted to train herding with more compassion and fewer corrections. Amazingly, I found positive training to be more fun and much clearer for my dogs. My dogs no longer sulked or blew me off and I learned they never really had. Dogs do what works for them. We do what works for us. The trick is to get your dog to want to do what you want them to do. When you are both working toward the same goals, instead of at cross purposes, it is a win-win situation.

If through these books I have been able to inspire one person to change one dog's life, from a life filled with suppression to a life filled with reinforcement and joy through positive training, then I have accomplished my mission.

It breaks my heart to see young dogs act as if they are ancient because they have learned that being invisible is the safest way to avoid punishment.

By using positive methods to train herding, you give your dog the chance to show you just how brilliant and joyful they can be!

The learning never ends

The good thing, or the bad thing depending on how you look at it, is that there is always more to learn about handling, herding, stockmanship, and positive reinforcement training. Every dog has lessons to teach you and you can learn something from every handler, no matter if they are a big hat or a novice. I have had some of my best insights when working with novice handlers. Because of their lack of experience, they did not carry the herding baggage that I do and could see things more clearly than I could.

Teaching herding to Sally and Renn made me re-examine *everything* I had learned about herding and positive training. Why, when, how, and what, were constant questions that, if I did not ask them, then Sally did. I probably learned as much from working with Sally as she learned from me. Working with someone who can guide you, as well as learn with and from you, is an ideal situation. If the relationship grows into a friendship, even better!

Finding a coach

If at all possible, find someone who can support you on your positive herding journey. If you can find an experienced handler who is willing to work with you, take advantage of what they can teach you. Hopefully, the explanations and pictures in this book have given you plenty to move forward with, but it is impossible to cover every scenario in herding because every handler, dog, and set of livestock are different.

Good instruction is like having a set of training wheels. You may make minor mistakes as you go along, but hopefully, you never crash and burn.

Finding a herding coach who really understands positive training is nearly impossible. Beware of traditional trainers who say they train positively. Do they start dogs away from livestock and eschew punishment for reinforcement? Are they balanced trainers? Do they use a marker but also rely on endless corrections? Is their idea of a reward saying "good dog" when your dog is correct?

Happy trails, happy trials

I wish you and your dog the absolute best positive herding experience! I hope this series of books has met your expectations and that together we can work toward a brighter future using positive reinforcement to train herding. I especially hope this book benefits the amazing dogs that work their hearts out for us.

It truly is all about the dogs!

Acknowledgments

Writing and developing the training in this book has been a challenging yet satisfying endeavor. It has also been a lonely and frustrating one at times. I have been fortunate to share this journey with some great friends, both two- and four-legged.

Sally Adam has been a brilliant, taciturn training partner, contributor, and editor. She is a great positive herding trainer and handler who is not shy about expressing her views. Sally always cuts straight to the heart of the matter, wasting no words along the way. When she talks, I listen.

I have been extremely fortunate to have had Jane Roznovsky as a friend, mentor, and editor extraordinaire! Jane encourages me when I am down and is always up for a hike and an update on the progress of the book. She is one of the few people I know who is more technologically challenged than I am. We both long for a computer that lets us into password-protected programs with the concessionary response, "close enough".

Of course, I have to give extra special credit to my husband Kerry. He hears everything that I can't say to anyone else. He puts up with my moods, migraines, and midnight herding epiphanies. He is beyond understanding and encouraging and I would not have written or published a word without his undying belief in me. He also gets bonus points for living with my brilliantly psycho border collies, not a mean feat!

Lastly, I would like to pay tribute to all of the animals I have been privileged to know, train, and love along the way. They have done an amazing job of training me, much better and more thoroughly than I have done training them. Other than the chickens that I have trained, they have all granted me infinite patience and unconditional love. Certainly, my dogs have given me their all, without reservation.
I have been truly blessed.

BB
Purdin
August 2022

Glossary

Arousal: The state of being alert, awake and attentive. Performance will be affected if a dog is under- or over-aroused.

Aversive: Anything an animal will work to escape or avoid. Can be primary or conditioned.

Back chaining: Teaching the last behavior of a chain first, then the next to last, etc. until you have trained the first behavior of the chain.

Balance: The point where a dog controls the stock and if they turn into and apply pressure to the stock at this point, the livestock will move straight toward the handler.

Behavioral momentum: Consists of the mass and velocity of behavior, and is a theory developed by John A Nevin to explain why behaviors differ in strength.

Bite: A grip of an animal usually on the nose or lower rear leg. A desired bite is a grip with a quick release.

Blind gather: A fetch of stock that is out of sight of the dog, usually over a hill or behind other geographical obstructions.

Bridge: A marker that "bridges" the time between the marking of the correct behavior and the reinforcement that is to follow.

Bump flank: A mini-flank that ranges from a dog taking a step or two sideways while continuing to face the stock, to just shifting their weight from one front foot to the other.

Chain: A series of behaviors that always occur in the same order. The chain starts with one cue and the following behaviors are cued by the behavior that came directly before them.

Cheap shot: A dog bite on the side of the body of an animal rather than on the nose or heel. The dog may bite and release or run along with the animal while continuing to grip the animal's wool or hair.

Clapper: A dog which often lies down quickly and is reluctant to get up and move when working stock.

Classical conditioning: Also known as Pavlovian conditioning. Determines involuntary responses – an animal responds automatically and has no control over the response, eg. the sound of a bell causes a dog to salivate.

Conditioned emotional response: A learned emotional reaction or response to a certain conditioned stimulus.

Contact (with stock): The mutual attention between the dog and stock or predator and prey. If a dog works too far away from their stock the livestock will no longer pay attention to them and the dog is said to have "lost contact" with their stock, which is highly undesirable.

Cover: The desire to control stock by instinctively flanking around them to prevent their escape.

Criteria/Criterion: The parameters that define a behavior. Almost every behavior is composed of many criteria. Criterion is singular, criteria is plural.

Cross driving: Driving stock perpendicular to the direction the handler is facing.

Crossing over: Any time on an outrun that the dog goes over an imaginary line between the handler and the stock, the dog has "crossed over". This is highly penalized at trials.

Crossover dog: A dog that was initially trained using primarily positive punishment but has been switched to being trained with primarily positive reinforcement.

Cue: A discriminative stimulus: a stimulus, an event, or thing that elicits a certain reaction, that when present the behavior will be reinforced.
Distraction training: The dog is trained to be responsive to the trainer while ignoring competing environmental stimuli.
Engagement training: The dog is trained to be responsive to the trainer while simultaneously being responsive to competing environmental stimuli.
Extinction: The gradual lessening of a behavior due to lack of reinforcement.
Extinction burst: The tendency of a dying behavior to return in full force for a short period, often right before it finally extinguishes.
Fading (a cue): Making a physical cue, such as a hand motion or a target, smaller and smaller until it is eliminated.
Fence runner: A dog that, instead of doing an outrun just wide enough to get behind the stock without disturbing them, falls out and attempts to find and then run along a nearby fence.
Fetch: The drive from the lift to the handler's feet.
Flank: The curved or circular path that the dog takes to move around livestock, either clockwise or counterclockwise. The flank can be split into two parts; flank, going to balance, and off-balance flank, flanking away from balance. (See "Off-balance flanks".)
Flight zone: The stock's comfort or safety zone. The size of this zone varies depending on the dog or person involved and the livestock's perception of the threat they embody.
Flirt pole (FP): Light flexible pole or lunge whip with a toy on the end of an attached line.
Foot target:: A target on the floor that the dog touches with their foot or feet.
Forward chaining: Teaching the first behavior of a chain first, then the second, and so on until the end of the chain is reached.
Generalization: A process in which an animal takes a learned behavior and performs that behavior to criteria in new environments and situations.
Gripping: The dog biting the stock. (See also "bite".)
Hold: The dog freely flanks, without cues, to keep stock in front of them while not allowing the livestock to get away from or past them.
Hook up: The instinctive behavior of herding dogs to look at and immediately lock onto their prey with laser focus.
Instincts: Innate behaviors an animal is born with, which they have not had to learn. Instinctual behaviors generally override learned behavior. (See "Modal action patterns".)
Jackpot: Giving a large quantity of treats for exceptional performance, a form of differential reinforcement.
Jug: A small enclosure where a ewe and her newborn lambs are kept for a few days to ensure that the lambs and ewe bond and that the lambs get off to a good start.
Kick out: When a dog, feeling the pressure from the livestock, automatically opens up or flanks farther from the stock to prevent disturbing it.
Knee-knocker sheep: Sheep that run to and stay tightly gathered around the handler. (Also known as Velcro sheep.)
Latent learning: Learning that is not immediately expressed and occurs without any obvious reinforcement of the behavior. Latent learning may take place between training sessions when an animal processes the training.
Lift: The point at which the stock begin to move under the influence of the dog
Line dog: A dog which naturally holds a line on the fetch or drive, once it is established.
Mechanical dog: A dog that always waits to be cued and never moves unless cued.

Modal action patterns: A set of instinctive behavioral sequences that usually run to completion. For herding breeds this would be: orient > eye > stalk > chase > (grab bite).

Modifier cue: A cue that labels a concept rather than a behavior, eg. "hurry up".

No reward marker (NRM): A verbal cue that tells the dog they are no longer heading towards reinforcement, in other words they are incorrect. A form of negative punishment.

Off-balance flank: The part of the circle where the dog has moved off of balance and is heading away from the point where they have control of the livestock.

OIL behavior: Override Instinctual with Learned behavior

Operant conditioning: Also known as Skinnerian conditioning. Determines voluntary behaviors. The animal has a choice over its response, which will be influenced by the consequence to its past behavior. (See also "Reinforcement" and "Punishment".)

Outrun: Flanking from the handler's feet out and around stock before lifting and fetching them.

Power: The confidence a dog has in their ability to deal with truculent stock. The dog will stand up to and bite, if necessary, stock that challenges them.

Presence: The ability of a dog to project self-assurance to the livestock, be readily noticed by them, and thus be less likely to be challenged.

Pressure: Pressure is the opposite of pull – it is the desire of the stock to move away from perceived threats. (See "pull".)

Proprioception : The ability to sense the position, location, orientation, and movement of the body and its parts in space.

Protective contact: The use of a barrier between animals, or between trainer and animals, to prevent an animal from harming other animals or the trainer.

Pull (or "draw"): The desire of the stock to move towards perceived safety and comfort.

Punishment: Anything that weakens a behavior and decreases the probability of recurrence.

Ram: Intact (uncastrated) male sheep.

Rate of reinforcement: The number of reinforcers earned and delivered in a set amount of time.

Recall: The behavior of the dog coming back to the handler immediately when cued.

Reinforcement/Reinforcer: Anything that strengthens a behavior and increases the probability of a behavior occurring.

Release word: Word which tells the dog the behavior has ended.

Response cost: Removing the handler's attention from the dog for 10 seconds to decrease the behavior they just performed by withholding reinforcement. Response cost is by definition a negative punisher.

Reward: Something given in return for wanted behavior, but a reward is not necessarily reinforcing. A reward is not another word for a reinforcer. (See "reinforcer".)

Sequence: A series of behaviors that follow each other in no particular order. The most common example of sequences are found in agility. An agility run consists of many numbered obstacles but each run is unique in terms of the order of the obstacles.

Shaping: A training procedure that uses the reinforcement of successive approximations to build a desired behavior. Almost all training is shaping.

Shedding: Separating one or more animals from a group and maintaining control of those animals.

Silent gather: An outrun, lift, and fetch to the handler with only one cue given, the fetch cue.

Sliced flank: A flank that the dog begins by shifting their weight forward and moving towards the stock.

Square flank: The desired movement of a dog when flanking, so as not to put added pressure on the stock. The dog shifts their weight backward and turns to start their flank at a 90° angle to the stock.

Stimulus: A thing or event that sets the stage to elicit or initiate a behavior.

Stimulus control: Four requirements for control of a behavior to be complete; animal responds to the cue each time, animal does not perform the behavior without the cue, animal responds with the correct behavior, animal doesn't offer this behavior for another cue.

Stockmanship: The knowledgeable and skillful handling of livestock.

Time-out: A form of negative punishment. Removing the dog from a situation the dog likes such as working sheep for several minutes, to reduce unwanted behavior such as lunging at sheep.

TRaC skills: Timing, Rate of reinforcement, and Criteria.

Tucking the corners: To keep a larger group of livestock bunched together while driving them a dog will flank out to a corner to push the animals fanning out back into the group.

Turning the post: Part of a trial run in which the stock is fetched close to and then around the handler and the post before the stock is driven off toward the drive gates.

Velcro sheep: Sheep that run to and stay tightly gathered around the handler. (Also known as knee-knocker sheep.)

Wearing: The lateral movement of the dog behind stock to move a large group or the dog holding stock to the handler.

Wether: Castrated male sheep.

Resources

Behavior and Learning
Burch, Mary & Jon Bailey. 1999. *How Dogs Learn.*
Chance, Paul. 2006. *Learning & Behavior.*
Clothier, Suzanne. 2002. *Bones Would Rain from the Sky: Deepening Our Relationships with Dogs.*
Coppinger, Raymond & Lorna. 2001. *Dogs: A New Understanding of Canine Origin, Behavior, and Evolution.*
Donaldson, Jean. 2005. *The Culture Clash.*
Garrett, Susan. 2005. *Shaping Success: The Education of an Unlikely Champion.*
Pryor, Karen. 1999. *Don't Shoot the Dog: The New Art of Teaching and Training.*
Pryor, Karen. 2009. *Reaching the Animal Mind: Clicker Training and What It Teaches Us about All Animals.*
Reid, Pamela. 1996. *Excel-erated Learning: Explaining How Dogs Learn and How Best to Teach Them.*

Marker training
Barney, Carolyn. 2007.*Clicker Basics for Dogs and Puppies.*
Bartlett, Katherine. 2018. *Teaching Horses with Positive Reinforcement: A Guide to Achieving Success with Clicker Training.*
Book, Mandy & Cheryl Smith. 2001. *Quick Clicks: 40 Fast and Fun Behaviors to Train with a Clicker.*
Book, Mandy & Cheryl Smith. 2006. *Right on Target: Taking Dog Training to a New Level.*
Fisher, Gail T. 2009. *The Thinking Dog: Crossover to Clicker Training.*
Laurence, Kay. 2009. *Teaching with Reinforcement: For Every Day and in Every Way.*
Laurence, Kay. 2008. *Clicker Training: The Perfect Foundation* combines *Clicker Foundation Training* by Kay Laurence (2003) & *Clicker Novice Training* by Kay Laurence (2003)
Laurence, Kay. 2008. "Whippits – Teaching: self-control & play skills" (DVD).
Laurence, Kay. 2004. *Clicker Intermediate Training*
Theby, Viviane. 2009. *Dog University.*

Herding
Hartnagle-Taylor, Jeanne Joy & Ty Taylor. 2010. *Stockdog Savvy.*
Holland, Virgit. 1994. *Herding Dogs: Progressive Training.*

Training aids
Just Be Ewe Bungee Tug with Hol-ee Cow Ball from Clean run
Outward Hound tail teaser wand/flirt pole

Companion website
www.positiveherdingdog.com/blog
Positive herding dog Youtube channel and Facebook group

About the author

No one knows Barb Buchmayer as well as I do. Since she has spent innumerable hours with me, her border collie Sir, I feel eminently qualified to tell you her history, qualifications for writing books on positive herding, and her foibles. Trust me, although I am featured in hundreds of photos in her Positive Herding Dog book series, I am more than just a pretty face.

Barb's journey with dogs started long before I came into her life. She grew up in Ohio on a few acres. Over the years her family had several dogs that were all named Smokey and several cats named Twinkles. Not very creative, but what can I say? Her first animal of choice was the horse, another bit of poor judgment, IMO.

After her infatuation with horses ran its course, she eventually saw the light and became focused on dogs. Now she was getting somewhere! She became intrigued with guide dogs and raised a black lab named Clay for Guiding Eyes for the Blind. That was her first foray into traditional dog training. Clay went on to be a well-loved and successful guide dog. Next, she moved on to golden retrievers and trained general pet obedience with Altair and Raini.

Still a bit slow on the uptake, Barb did not get into herding for several more years and then only by chance. Her sister-in-law had an Australian shepherd puppy that she had won at a horse show but didn't want. About this time, Barb was thinking that having a dog around to help bring in the dairy cows on their farm would be useful, not to mention, very cool.

So Raffles came to live on Barb and Kerry's NY dairy farm and began his very, very short career as a herding dog. Unfortunately, Raffles was afraid of cows, sheep, and lambs and so became the resident guard dog. Once Raffles abdicated the herding dog position, Barb brought border collie puppy Brooke in to fill the void. Barb soon became hooked on herding and would remain so for the next 30 years and counting.

Brooke grew into a serviceable herding dog, nowhere near as good as me of course, but both she and Barb learned a lot. After moving to Missouri, Barb started taking traditional herding lessons on a regular basis. By training many dogs she grew into an Open handler, which means she competes at the highest level of herding trials. My grandma Mattie was probably her most celebrated dog, although I am partial to my great aunt Lex because of her calm coolness. Nothing ever rattled Lex!

Things were good, except Barb kept thinking that there must be a better way to teach her dogs what she wanted rather than always telling them what she didn't want them to do. Enter positive dog training!

Many DVDs, books, and online courses later, as well as years, things were still somewhat fuzzy for her. The breakthrough came while training chickens at Bob Bailey and Parvene Farhoody's Chicken Workshops. Who would have thought chickens were good for anything but eating? Finally, positive dog training started to make sense.

Now that she had a grasp of science-based dog training, how was she ever going to parley that knowledge into herding training? It was a formidable task and one that she would wrestle with for years.

It was about this time that my border collie dad, Pure Gold, entered the picture or should I say was born in her kitchen. He was all fire, heart, and love. A year later my uncle Qwest was born and he was the polar opposite of Gold, a quiet almost tentative soul. They were the first lucky dogs to learn herding using a positive approach. Their journey consisted of tons of fun for them and equal amounts of frustration for Barb as she struggled to construct a framework for teaching positive herding.

Sally Adam of South Africa and her BC Renn entered Barb's world a few years later and, with Barb's help, became an amazing herding team. The rest is history, as they say. I came along after Barb had hammered out her basic positive herding training protocol so I was able to hit the ground running. Of course, all of my natural herding ability and amazing brilliance allowed me to excel, even if I say so myself.

I would be happy to tell you that is where the story ends, but Barb continues to learn, experiment, and refine her understanding of positive herding. I am thrilled to be a part of whatever the future holds for my herding dog mates and the folks who partner with and love them.

If I could ask one favor, it would be that you give this book and *Positive Herding 101* honest reviews. As Barb tells me, reviews are key to helping others find our books and … spread the herd!

www.ingramcontent.com/pod-product-compliance
Lightning Source LLC
Chambersburg PA
CBHW081614100526
44590CB00021B/3431